LEADERSHIP
BEHAVIOR

Edited by

Joseph P. Cangemi
Casimir J. Kowalski
K. Habib Khan

University Press of America,® Inc.
Lanham • New York • Oxford

Copyright © 1998 by
University Press of America,® Inc.
4720 Boston Way
Lanham, Maryland 20706

12 Hid's Copse Rd.
Cummor Hill, Oxford OX2 9JJ

Library of Congress Cataloging-in-Publication Data

Leadership behavior / edited by Joseph P. Cangemi, Casimir J.
Kowalski, K. Habib Khan.
p. cm.
Includes bibliographical references.
l. Leadership. I. Cangemi, Joseph P. II. Kowalski, Cash. III.
Khan, K. Habib.
HM141.L3925   1997   303.3'4—dc21   97—40212 CIP

ISBN 0-7618-0940-6 (cloth: alk. ppr.)
ISBN 0-7618-0941-4 (pbk: alk. ppr.)

"We are what we repeatedly do. Excellence then is not an act, but a habit."

Aristotle

This book is dedicated to two exemplary medical professionals of Vanderbilt University, School of Medicine, Nashville,Tennessee whose high standards of excellence undoubtedly are what Aristotle had in mind when he authored the above quote. They are a model for the rest of us:

Michael Koch, M.D.
Vice-Chairman
Department of Urology

And

Michael Christie, M.D.
Director
Vanderbilt Joint and Replacement Center
Department of Orthopedics and Rehabilitation

Both have had a profound effect on my life.

This book also is dedicated to my wonderful wife, Amelia Elena Santalo Cangemi, who never left my side.

Joseph P. Cangemi

GANDHI'S SEVEN SINS

√ *Wealth without work*

√ *Pleasure without conscience*

√ *Knowledge without character*

√ *Commerce without morality*

√ *Science without humanity*

√ *Worship without sacrifice*

√ *Politics without principle*

CONTENTS

Contents

PREFACE

This book is a compilation of readings about leadership and its many dimensions. More than half of the articles in the book were either authored or co-authored by its editors. The rest were written at the specific invitation of the editors.

The three editors of this book have over 100 years of national and international experience among them, including significant leadership responsibilities (college and university presidencies, business and industrial leadership positions, department of state directorships overseas, US-AID responsibilities, Fortune 500 consulting worldwide, etc.). The array and scope of the articles included in this manuscript are quite diverse and should prove interesting and helpful to many participants in the field–*those actually doing the work*–from department managers to supervisors, to vice-presidents and presidents. *The intent is to provide an essentially pragmatic perspective to the responsibility of leadership.*

Leadership has been one of the most frequently written about subjects over the years. This book is not meant to provide answers to the myriad of problems confronting leaders, nor to be any sort of definitive work on the subject. Rather, the book was developed as an expression of some perspectives, ideas, and issues considered important to the editors. The selection of materials chosen, for whatever benefit they might be to the reader, was theirs alone, and they take full responsibility for their inclusion.

Throughout the manuscript, on occasion, some of our authors utilized the word "management" with the intent to communicate the concept of "leadership." Also, some overlap of ideas was necessary due to the focus of the articles selected for this book.

Joseph P. Cangemi
Bowling Green, Kentucky

Casimir J. Kowalski
Pretoria, South Africa

K. Habib Khan
Washington, D.C.

ACKNOWLEDGMENT

We would like to acknowledge the kindness and encouragement we received from the fine people at University Press of America. They were always interested in this project and worked diligently with us until its completion.

The senior editor, Joseph Cangemi, is indebted to the administration of Western Kentucky University for the sabbatical leave they awarded him, during which time this project was initiated.

Tom Cole deserves a special thanks for the work he did in getting this book ready for press. The task was much greater than he had ever imagined, but he never complained. He stayed with the project over its tedious course with a great attitude. Jennifer Reece, Dr. Cangemi's graduate assistant, contributed to the completion of this book and deserves a well earned "thanks." Another well earned thanks goes to Eddie Fuqua for his valued assistance with the work that went into this book.

The editors wish to extend their gratitude to the various authors who agreed to write specifically for this book. A special note of appreciation likewise is extended to the journals and their editors listed below for their permission to republish these articles:

"Why TQM Fails" by R. Miller and J. Cangemi originally was published in 1993 in *Journal of Management Development,* Vol. 12, pp. 40-50.

"The *Other* Side of Japanese Leadership" by S. Chaffins, J. Baali, S. Crabtree, E. Fuqua, J. Cangemi, & C. Kowalski was published in *Organization Development Journal* in the Summer issue, 1997.

"Groupthink: A Hinderance to Effective Decision Making in Originations" by E. Fuqua, S. Chaffins, J. Cangemi, & C. Kowalski originally was published in *National Forum of Education Administration and Supervision Journal,* Vol. 13, No. 1, pp. 47-59.

"Some Observations of Successful Leaders and Their Use of Power and Authority" by J. Cangemi was originally published in the journal *Education,* Vol. 12, No. 4, pp. 499-502, in 1992.

"The Glass Ceiling:—Are Women Where They Should Be?" by S. Chaffins, E. Forbes, & J. Cangemi originally appeared in the journal *Education,* Vol. 15, No. 41, pp. 380-386.

"Leadership and The Psychological Contract" by H. Fuqua, J. Cangemi, and K. Payne was published in the *Journal of Individual Employment Rights* in 1997.

INTRODUCTION

We live in uncertain times. The society, the economy and the organizations where we work are in a continual state of change. The markets in which we operate are more accessible, competitive, and complex than at any time in our history. There is every reason to believe these changes will continue to be rapid and dramatic in the future.

Companies have responded to this new environment with a broad range of initiatives which have been disruptive to individuals. They have included corporate restructurings, mergers, acquisitions, divestitures, process re-engineering, increased mechanization, etc. Organizations have become flatter, with more localized decision-making. Emphasis has been placed on external performance measures, such as customer satisfaction, product lead-time, delivery performance, etc., in addition to the traditional financial measures.

Employees frequently react to these changes with increased skepticism. The transitions are viewed negatively and considered threatening to individuals, their economic security, and their future. Employees openly assess their leaders on their technical abilities and their success in promoting order and stability.

Nonetheless, the roles and performance measurement of senior executives remain unchanged. Leaders must successfully transform companies under difficult conditions and at the same time continue to meet shareholder, employee, and customer expectations. We look to leaders for solutions. When leaders are unable to deliver or lack simple, direct and compelling answers to complex issues, we tend to experience frustration and distrust their leadership abilities.

We do them a disservice. We may be placing unrealistic demands and expectations on our leaders. This generates a lack of confidence when leaders fail to meet their constituents' needs and expectations.

Today's leaders have to balance the demands of the external environment with the need to introduce change into organizations. They have to develop skills well beyond the traditional skills of managers in authority-driven, hierarchical organizations. Leaders must have a special combination of qualities and skills with which to exercise good judgment, make wise decisions, and get along well with others. Some of the skills are readily taught—such as knowledge of sales, production and accounting, for example. Others are acquired by background and observation.

Exercising leadership has come to mean providing a vision and influencing others to realize it through non- coercive means. Leaders must possess four main skills: envisioning the future, gaining the cooperation of others, altering the way others think about things, and possessing an ability to introduce positive change.

This book discusses the various aspects of leadership–what it is and how it operates to bring value to employees, customers, and shareholders in today's environment. It addresses a broad range of issues involved with effective management in this new environment, and provides important insights into the educational, psychological, personality, and perspectives of effective leaders. Also discussed is the importance of changing the organizational culture by developing leaders throughout the organization. Valuable insights are provided on how to avoid group think, which often occurs when organizations lack decisive leadership and attempt to become more democratic and decentralized in their decision making processes.

This book provides clear prescriptions for any individual who needs to take a leadership role under most organizational situations, whether in business, government, or nonprofit endeavors. These perspectives apply not only to people at the top of organizations, but also to those who must lead, even without full authority, including managers, supervisors, and line workers. It is likewise helpful for those individuals who will be entering the workforce, as well as for a broad range of new and experienced salaried employees, who wish to gain a better understanding of how organizations work and develop ways of becoming a more integral part of the enterprise. Middle managers also may benefit from re-examining their managerial and leadership style and senior managers may refresh their perspectives as they lead their organizations through structural, technological, and/or competitive transitions.

Robert M.Linton
President and CEO
Redman Industries, Inc.
Dallas, Texas

EDUCATION FOR LEADERSHIP AT THE TOP

By

Sven B. Lundstedt

In 1979 an unusual and successful seminar was held at The Aspen Institute for Humanistic Studies in Aspen, Colorado. It was unusual not only for its timeliness and concern for the issue of corporate leadership, particularly the modern chief executive officer, but also for its involvement of leading chief executives in the discussions. This was done so that we could benefit from the knowledge of successful leaders and chief executives (Lundstedt, 1979). A Conference Board study described how the chief executive's job was generally viewed by the business community at the time of the seminar (Stieglitz, 1969).

Chester I. Barnard was one of the first American chief executives to view leadership from a new perspective in his *Functions of the Executive* (Barnard, 1938). The seminar recognized advances in the conceptualization of the functions of the corporation and the executive identified earlier by Barnard and others, as well as the innovations in management and organization theory that were to come, particularly from the applications and uses of the social and behavioral sciences (March, 1979; Leeds & Smith, 1963).

Leadership skills have steadily improved in this century. Yet our perspective about leadership is widened by knowing that there have been earlier examples of progress in managerial human relations and in organizational and administrative innovations and discoveries. Recent managerial innovations have distant roots in human history. Some can be traced to the fourth century B.C. in China and perhaps even earlier (Creel, 1964). Modern leadership practices that have been developed in the twentieth century to increase efficiency and effectiveness in management in modern corporations may only *seem* to follow a linear development historically from less civilized to more civilized.

My hypothesis is that barbaric and civilized management trends may have appeared and receded as dominant values at different times in history, waxing and waning as various cultures throughout history reflected the ascendancy of each point of view of how people should be treated. Some human societies seem to be identified with the use of harsh, often cruel, infliction of pain and suffering to motivate workers. But even in this case there are probably exceptions.

Now, once again, in the latter part of the twentieth century, in the West especially, we can observe a resurgence of the principle that pain and suffering are not the most effective motivators and that basic human needs have to be met before workers can be productive in modern organizations. Important questions can be raised as to the particular origins of effective leadership behavior. Cultural influences during socialization, as well as suffering and adversity, both physical and psychological, play a key role in influencing the formation of a leader's personal values, character and personality.

Situational factors also play a key role. To this day, we remain uncertain as to whether leaders are predominately born or made, their characteristics being due to nature or nurture, or some combination of the two.

Environment is critically important, however. Social psychological research has shown that people often respond with compliance, obedience and conformity under social pressure. Yet great leaders are often expected to demonstrate an ability to remain uninfluenced by such pressures and situational factors, in general; in other words, to respond from within their own personal framework of values. Reviewing the modern application of the social and behavioral sciences to our understanding of leadership in modern organizations, Dorwin Cartwright summarizes progress at mid-century in our social psychological understanding of influence, leadership and control (Cartwright, 1994). These are important principles of behavior that form some of the central characteristics of leadership behavior from a social psychological perspective.

The view that companies are more effective when they are managed in a democratic fashion, in contrast to an undemocratic or despotic manner, is widely held today (*The Economist*, 1994). Faced with the challenges of global competition, corporations, and less often, governments, have been forced to adopt democratic forms of leadership and management in order to reach modern levels of efficiency and effectiveness in their productivity. Times have indeed changed dramatically, due in no small part to global competition, global communication and cross-functional and cross-national learning. Yet, as I have suggested, it may not be the first time a switch to democratic leadership styles has been required of, or chosen by, top leaders. In its own way, is this a hopeful sign that the cycles of democratic management may be returning more quickly?

It is interesting to note that among the great American presidents who faced enormous adversity, Abraham Lincoln continues to stand out as an example of humane and effective leadership strongly determined, I would presume, by his particularly unique character and personality (Phillips, 1992). Some of the same personal characteristics of leadership that led to Lincoln's way of behaving as a chief executive are described by Likert as "System 4" (or democratic) leadership behavior (Likert, 1962, 1967), as well as by McGregor as "Theory Y" leadership behavior (McGregor, 1960), also democratic. Furthermore, in major forms of government business transactions in the implementation of regulation, democratic management appears to be related to increased cost efficiency and effectiveness (Lundstedt, Likert et al., 1982).

KNOWLEDGE OF THE HUMAN CONDITION, NATURE AND LEARNING

From the enormous demands of the CEO's job today we may surmise that the education of chief executives would require much more than courses on managing human relations on the job. A fundamental concern for improving the general human spiritual condition is also necessary for that higher quality of personal effectiveness that would seem to be part of modern high level leadership. Spirituality in this sense refers to the presence of a wider and deeper personal vision, and a higher level personality integration. This vision of what life may become may have nothing to do with organized religion, but may simply reflect an effective philosophy of life. In any case, self-knowledge and understanding of one's own personality and values is an essential part of the development of the chief executive officer (Maslow, 1954; Bray, Campbell, & Grant, 1974).

This awareness would also include Herzberg's finding that what motivates and sustains human productivity on the job is the enrichment of the individual personality or arises from satisfaction from work itself and not only better human relations, though we know them to be important (Herzberg, Mausner, & Snyderman, 1959; Herzberg, 1966). Gordon Allport, in the tradition of William James, drew attention to the importance of spiritual development for personality development (Allport, 1961).

Allport would also have agreed that individual people are the real basis of organizations in society and that social and cultural processes as we describe them in the social sciences are mere epiphenomena of the concrete reality embodied in the individual. Consequently, the study of individual differences is important (Tyler, 1965) not only as a determination of the strengths of diversity among people, but to chart the outer limit of the human personality.

A constant challenge for the CEO remains to continue to search for a proper balance between individual needs and the needs of the corporation. One could say that an important part of the top leader's daily stewardship is to seek a proper balance in this sense, as Lincoln's behavior during his presidency demonstrated.

Individual differences in one's style of thinking are now an important consideration, as we now realize more than in the past that several kinds of thinking, or "cognitive styles," may exist. Variety in intellectual, cognitive behavior is not only developmentally possible, but even at times necessary for human survival. Is there more than one intellectual style associated with successful high-level leadership behavior? If so, which is the best form to use at any one given time for successful leadership in high places? And, how is this intellectual ability learned by the individual, under what environmental conditions, and when? At one time in the history of thought, deductive thinking seemed to predominate. At others, inductive thinking seemed to take over. Combinations of these may exist. Such epistemologies are common. What is the role of intuitive thinking and intuition supposedly found among artists, yet common also in chief executives?

If all this is indeed true, then the distinction between what is now loosely called formal rational (logical inductive or deductive thought) thinking, in contrast to earlier forms of animistic, pre-scientific thought, or even the pathological thinking disorders, may need to be reconsidered.

New ideas about the functional aspects of human thinking encourage us to recognize the unusual forms of thought and, in most cases, not to condemn out of hand those who choose to exhibit them. The challenge is to understand them better.

Even so, we see another, darker, side to this story. The history of tyranny has always forewarned us that there are forms of homicidal thinking in humans that are inherently dangerous and may ultimately be destructive to the human race and other living creatures. They can be found in political leaders at the highest level, as the history of the twentieth, and earlier centuries amply demonstrates (Lundstedt,1994; Arendt, 1968).

Chief executives are also required to be generalists in their thinking rather than only specialists in the usual sense. Writing about specialists and generalists, Alfred North Whitehead pointed out important differences in the intellectual styles of each. In his 1925 Lowell lectures at Harvard University he warned that, ". . .the progressiveness in detail only adds to the danger produced by the feebleness of coordination." Coordination (an integrative intellectual ability), whereby different kinds of knowledge are brought to bear on strategic problems, is often a salient mental characteristic of the successful leader. Whitehead elaborates in this passage from *Science and the Modern World:*

Another great fact confronting the modern world is the discovery of the method of training professionals, who specialize in particular regions of thought and thereby progressively add to the sum of knowledge with their respective limitations of subject. In consequence of the success of this professionalizing of knowledge, there are two points to be kept in mind, which differentiate our present age from the past. In the first place, the rate of progress is such that an individual human being, of ordinary length of life, will be called upon to face novel situations which find no parallel in his past. The fixed person for the fixed duties, who in older societies was such a godsend, in the future will be a public danger. In the second place, the modern professionalism in knowledge works in the opposite direction as far as the intellectual sphere is concerned.

The dangers arising from this aspect of professionalism are great, particularly in our democratic societies. The *directive force* of reason is weakened (italics mine). The leading intellects lack balance. They see this set of circumstances, or that set; but not both sets together. The task of coordination is left to those who lack either the force or the character to succeed in some definite career. In short, the specialized functions of the community are performed better and more progressively, but the generalized direction lacks vision .... (Whitehead, 1925).

Whitehead would probably have cautioned that placing the reins of highest power in the corporation in the hands of narrow specialists from any one of the disciplines from accounting to finance, marketing, human resources, engineering or the sciences or humanities, would, by itself, be problematic unless the abilities to be a strong generalist are present as well. This vexing problem of achieving adequate overall intellectual preparation for top leadership that avoids a critical imbalance in thinking styles deserves our closest attention.

We again have to ask if the generalist way of thinking is an inherent factor and tendency, or a result of personal experience and education, or both. A number of mid-career executive programs like the one at The Aspen Institute for Humanistic Studies and at Dartmouth College, and many other excellent ones in other places, seem to assume that a broadening, integrative education is possible throughout life even though one may have started out as a specialist.

The subject of intellectual style is, however, far more complex than my brief comments would indicate, especially the manner in which such a style must be applied and used in high-level leadership and strategic thinking in a global corporation. Probably the most critical of all abilities for those who occupy the highest and most responsible levels of the corporation is the ability and desire to learn constantly, both implicitly and explicitly, reflected in a constantly enlivened curiosity about the world around them. Unfortunately, just such a curiosity and openness to further learning is often destroyed in early schooling and the family, and as such becomes a hidden intellectual cost to society. Thus, loss of greater overall competence to individuals, and eventually society, remains high. The preservation of an initial ability and desire to learn, not only in school, but from one's own experience, is essential for successful personal development throughout life, as is the restoration of this ability later in life.

Yet we learn from the technical literature on human learning that the state of the art in both learning research and its applications is still discouragingly far behind the pressure of those human problems requiring advanced learning abilities for their solution. Ernest Hilgard and Gordon Bower's noted book on learning theories illustrates some of the difficulties arising from the existence of many schools of thought and separation of them into warring theoretical camps (Hilgard & Bower, 1966). Many practical educational and technical research issues reach beyond these major families of approaches, and transcend them in some combinatorial higher level form or other. The evolution of cross functional sciences such as biophysics, mathematical biology, astrophysics and bioengineering are examples. All of this makes the improved design of new implicit and explicit integrative learning experiences necessary.

ACHIEVING WHOLENESS

Should a chief executive officer become an integrative and integrated person? One example of many has been chosen as an answer to this question. It is provided by Abraham Maslow and is about the virtuousness and importance for any human personality of seeking through self-knowledge and experience a holistic integration of his or her personality, where the tendency to develop toward such a goal of higher personal integration is the embodiment of self–actualization, as Maslow suggests. Maslow said that self-actualizing (integrative) people seem to have the following characteristics. They are realistic. They accept themselves and the world as it stands. They possess spontaneity. They are problem-centered, not self-centered. They are autonomous and independent. They are able to be original in their appreciation of people and things rather than stereotyped. They do not confuse means with ends. They are creative. Most of them have had profound spiritual experiences although not necessarily religious. They identify with mankind. Their values are democratic. They seem to resist conformity to the culture. And, their intimate relationships with a few specially loved people tend to be profound and deeply emotional (Maslow, 1954).

We may note two additional integrative values that may be associated with the belief system of the modern chief executive: One is the obvious and ancient value of self-awareness and commitment to continuing personal growth throughout life. Another is the chief executive's concept of the locus of his or her personal control. As applied to anyone, locus of control may be viewed as either *external or internal* to an individual. Modern democratic management increasingly seems to favor self–management and self-control, or an internal locus of control, in contrast to having that locus appear as coming from other people or technology, as in an autocracy (Rotter, 1966; Spector, 1982). In other words, the chief executive of today is more often characterized as a democratizing, empowering, trusting, leader, and not an authoritarian personality (Adorno et al.,1950; Christie et al.,1993).

PREPARATION FOR LEADERSHIP

Following Whitehead's warning about overly narrow specialization, a strong, yet undoctrinaire, liberal education would seem to be one of the best early undergraduate educational preparations for those who eventually may show the talent and ability to assume higher leadership in later life. A deeper, more thoroughgoing exposure to the physical and natural sciences, social and behavioral sciences and the humanities would seem to be essential in helping the mind to be integrative. Exposure to the very best in Western and Eastern scientific, historical, philosophical and artistic thought and culture should help immeasurably to form that greater breadth of human perspective and sense of taste and value so important in a cultured person. The ability to sustain a higher quality of decision making in any organization of the future seems to require it.

Robert M. Hutchins, a champion of integrative, cross–functional, undergraduate education at The University of Chicago during his tenure there as chancellor, would have agreed with this statement: that pernicious vocationalism, marching only to the drum beat of an all consuming, narrow economic ethic, would appear to undermine the ability of chief executives to do their job of making wise decisions in society (Hutchins, 1953; The University of Chicago Faculty, 1950).

Thorton Bradshaw, former CEO of the RCA corporation, speaking at the original Aspen seminar in 1979, laid stress on the growing internationalization of business and the increasing challenge of world markets. All of his predictions of 1979 have come true. We no longer need to be reminded that the constant updating of knowledge of this rapidly increasing trend is obviously essential for economic survival. It requires not only knowledge of international economics, but of geography, geopolitics and knowledge about other languages and comparative cultures as well. It remains a challenge for the CEO of the future to become more broadly and deeply educated.

A narrowly educated leader would be a person at risk in the world of the twenty-first century.

A critical, darker, underside of the overall challenge of corporate leadership is the growth in the deleterious side effects of human economic activities on the biosphere and the world's environment. The integrative intellectual and moral challenge to corporate leadership and leaders in government is enormous. An example of integrative, systems-oriented ecological thinking is illustrated in the work of Howard Odum (Odum, 1971). Top leaders now may have to be able to understand the logic of complex modeling procedures, and to be able to work with scientists, so that necessary connections between the knowledge community and the policy communities throughout business and government organizations can be deepened and increased by a broader vision and improved tools for political, organizational and public policy decision making. The recent extension of ecological systems-oriented thinking creating the idea of "industrial ecology" is an example (National Academy of Sciences,1992; GATT, 1994, 1994; Committee for IIASA,1992).

FINAL OBSERVATIONS ON THE EDUCATION OF CHIEF EXECUTIVES

The larger educational community, and social and behavioral science community, would seem to have no other choice than to rise to the educational challenges of 21st century modernization and renewal in providing a new generation of leaders educated in the ways described. The content and form of learning has to become more suitable to enable leaders and others to respond to the growing challenges of the 21st century. High-level executive education has to become more integrative and cross-functional, thus recognizing the challenges presented by the growing need to understand complex systems and how they work.

Such changes will necessitate that life-long learning at all career stages has to become not only more integrative and systems-oriented to enhance the proper comprehension of critical problems, but to enable a civilized, cultured, quality of life to be sustained and shared throughout society wherever it is possible to do so. Combinations of

scientific disciplines and the humanities, eventually evolving into new
disciplines, will be needed for those combinatorial solutions required by
today's problems and environments.

REFERENCES

Adorno, T. W., Frenkel-Brunswik, E., Levinson, D. J., & Sanford, R. N.
    (1950). *The authoritarian personality.* New York: Harper.

Allport, G. W. (1961). *Pattern and growth in personality.* New York: Holt,
    Rinehart & Winston

Arendt, H.(1968). *Totalitarianism.* New York: Harcourt, Brace,
    Jovanovich.

Barnard, C. I. (1938). *Functions of the executive.* Cambridge: Harvard
    University Press.

Bray, D. W., Campbell, R. J., & Grant, D. L. (1974). *Formative years in
    business: A long term study of managerial lives.* New York:
    JohnWiley

Cartwright, D. (1965). Influence, leadership and control. In J.G.
    March (Ed.), *Handbook of organizations.* Chicago: Rand
    McNally & Company, 1-47.

Christie,R.,Stone.W.F., &, Lederer, G. (1993). *Strength and weakness:
    The authoritarian personality today.* New York: Springer-Verlag.

Creel, H. G. (1964). The beginnings of bureaucracy in China: The origins
    of the Hsien. *Journal of Asian Studies, XXIII,* 155-184.

Committee for IIASA. (1992). *Science and sustainability.* Laxenburg,
    Austria: International Institute for Applied Systems Analysis,
    1992.

GATT. (1994). *Report on the GATT symposium on trade, environment
    and sustainable development.* Geneva, Swizerland: General
    Agreement on Tariffs and Trade, July, (TE 009).

Herzberg, F., Mausner, B., & Snyderman, B. (1959). *The motivation to
    to work* (2nd edition). New York: Wiley.

Herzberg, F., (1966). *Work and the nature of man.* New York: World
    PublishingCompany.

Hilgard, E. R.,& Bower, G. H. (1966). *Theories of learning.* New York:
    Appleton, Century, Crofts.

Hutchins, R. M. (1953). *The university of utopia.* Chicago: The Univer-
    sity of Chicago Press.

Leeds, R., &., Smith,T. (1963). *Using social science knowledge in busi-ness and industry: Report of a seminar.* Homewood, Illinois: Richard D. Irwin.

Likert, R. (1961). *New patterns of mangement.* New York: McGraw Hill Publishing Co.

Likert, R. (1967). *The human organization: Its management and value.* New York: McGraw Hill Publishing Company.

Lundstedt, S. B. (1979). *The education of the chief executive officer.* Aspen, Colorado: The Aspen Institute for Humanistic Studies. (Report in monograph form to the Charles F. Kettering Foundation).

Lundstedt, S. B. (1994, June). Pathogenic cybernetics. *Working paper series.* Max F. Fisher College of Business, The Ohio State University, WPS 94-26.

Lundstedt, S. B., Likert, R., Drtina, R. I., & Likert, J. G. (1982, Spring). A strategy for reducing the social and monetary costs of environmental regulation. *Environmental Economics Journal, 1,* pp. 85-112.

March, J. G. (1979). *Handbook of organizations.* Chicago: Rand McNally & Company.

Maslow, A. H. (1954). *Motivation and personality.* New York: Harper, 199-260.

McGregor, D. (1960). *The human side of enterprise.* New York: McGraw Hill.

National Academy of Sciences. (1992). *Proceedings of the National Academy of Sciences, 89,* 3.

Odum, H. T. (1971). *Environment, power, and society,* New York: JohnWiley.

Phillips, D. T. (1992). *Lincoln on leadership.* New York: Warner Books.

The Economist (1984, August 27). Democracy and growth. In the *Econo-mist, 332,* 7878, pp. 15-17.

Tyler, L. T. (1965). *The psychology of human differences* (3rd edition). New York: Meredeth Publishing Company.

Rotter, J. B. (1966). Generalized expectancies for internal and external control of reinforcement. *Psychological Monographs, 80,* pp. 183-188.

Spector, P. E. (1982, May). Behavior in organizations as a function of
  employees' locus of control. *Psychological Bulletin,* pp. 487-489.
Stieglitz, H. (1969). *The chief executive and his job.* New York: The
  Conference Board.
The University of Chicago Faculty. (1950). *The idea and practice of
  general education.* Chicago: The University of Chicago Press.
Whitehead, A. N. (1925). *Science and the modern world.* New York:
  Macmillan.

CAPABILITIES, CAPACITY, COMPETENCE AND CULTURE —MORE THAN JUST MANAGEMENT: LEADERSHIP

By
Thomas Hollopeter

When we look at leadership, let's start by making a distinction. We might say management is part of leadership or being a good leader is part of being a good manager. I'd rather consider them two different tasks. This has been characterized as: If we're in the jungle and trying to make our way through, I'd want a good manager in charge to efficiently use the labor, materials, water, food, etc., that would insure our survival. The leadership task would be to make sure we were in the right jungle. Peter Drucker talked eloquently about efficiency and effectiveness. Efficiency is "doing things right" while effectiveness is "doing the right things." A manager can delegate efficiency, but a leader must deal with effectiveness personally. We can generalize by saying that managing is doing things right while leadership is doing the right things.

To illustrate, let's say we were hired to be a manager of a Wendy's hamburger store. We could consider this a leadership position, while in truth, most of the leadership would have been done by Dave Thomas and his staff. The equipment, the menu, the infrastructure, the systems—even the purpose and core values that differentiate Wendy's from McDonald's, would have been provided. Our job would be to do things right, to efficiently operate the store. This stewardship, a vital and noble task, is managing *not* leadership.

Our job as manager would be, in general, as follows: First, we need to be a good example of working as hard as we expect our crew to work. We must have *high expectations,* to be a positive Pygmalion, to *believe* we can get the best from people and believe they have the ability to meet our expectations. It is imperative to *show them how,* that is to train and coach and provide feedback so they become experts at their tasks. Finally, we must fulfill their psychological contact, to *meet their needs.* Luckily, people's needs are easy to remember. The needs begin with "A's": appreciation, acceptance, affection, accomplishment, and attention. Dr. Clark Wilson developed a model of managing he called a *task cycle.* It starts with establishing goals *(high expectations).* Then we must gain commitment to the goals by encouraging upward communication *(accepting and believing in others).* Next, we engage in problem solving and facilitating *(showing them how),* guiding and coaching with regular feedback and applying goal pressure to ensure that the task is completed on time. When the job is finished the job is to provide reward and recognition (meeting people's needs).

Hopefully, I've illustrated, particularly in the area of people management, that we can describe the job of managing quite clearly. I believe we can begin to see managing is separate and different from the task of leadership.

EFFICIENCY IS NOT ENOUGH

If we look at the automobile industry, faced with global over-capacity, we can see a good example where efficiency is not enough and where leadership is required. Most experts agree the Japanese auto industry has led in efficiency while they have been largely bereft of strategy. Their retirees now consult and help others to become efficient. However, this no longer gives them competitive advantage because others have caught up in the efficiency race, and have largely caught up in the quality imperative. Ford Motor recently had to take controlling interest in Mazda (a niche marketer), so that they could redirect the strategy of that company and protect their investment. Since efficiency is not leadership, one of the key jobs of leadership is developing a strategy that differentiates the product and service and provides competitive advantage.

If we look at Saturn we must applaud General Motors. They took a good but not great product, focused on the "buying experience," and made that brand wildly successful and profitable, which many experts felt would never happen. By eliminating, or at worst greatly reducing, the anxiety most people feel when they purchase a car, they have established a strong brand identity and customer loyalty. This success has spawned imitators. Circuit City with their "Car-Max" used car centers is applying this strategy, generically, so far with mixed results. I think it is important to say that once a winning strategy has been established through leadership, it must be implemented skillfully and managed so that it is manifested in reality.

The process of leadership within an organization is to ensure that an external strategy is matched with the capabilities, capacity, competence and culture of the organization. For example, if we want to compete on the basis of *low cost* in the manufacturing area, we need highly automated equipment with a minimum of low cost, low skilled, probably temporary labor *(capabilities).* We need an infrastructure that deals effectively with sophisticated computer controlled equipment. That will require highly skilled technicians and *engineers (competence)*. We'll need long run standardized production with few change-overs. We'll have to implement innovative preventive maintenance programs to keep the equipment running because we need to size our *capacity* to operate around the clock, seven days a week. Our distribution needs to be directly to the customer so that we avoid warehousing costs. From this thumb nail sketch we can see that the leadership job is *focusing* the organization.

CULTURE IS IMPORTANT

It also requires instilling a low cost *culture*. Culture is not the strategy and the focus, it is the measure of its sociability and its solidarity. How well do its members interact with one another and in what manner. Then how solidly are they aligned to core values and principles. Sociability largely is dependent on management and solidarity largely dependent on leadership. So in developing a coherent culture the key leadership job is instilling core values and principles aligned with the strategy and focus. We owe credit to Dr. Edgar Schein for the following model.

UNCOVERING THE LEVELS OF CULTURE

Levels of Culture:

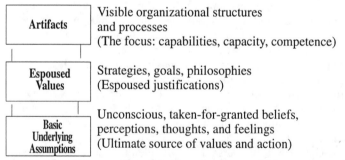

Artifacts	Visible organizational structures and processes (The focus: capabilities, capacity, competence)
Espoused Values	Strategies, goals, philosophies (Espoused justifications)
Basic Underlying Assumptions	Unconscious, taken-for-granted beliefs, perceptions, thoughts, and feelings (Ultimate source of values and action)

    In our example of low cost, we would have at our basic assumptions level the belief that this strategy would give us competitive advantage. At the espoused values level, we might have key missions and principles that were understood and widely distributed in handbooks, letterheads, etc., that embrace the principles of eliminating all waste in materials, methods, machinery and manpower. There would surely be goals, objectives, bonuses tied to reduced cost. At the artifacts level we would see the physical reality of this exposed value in the focus we have described above.

CASE: AN UNFOCUSED ORGANIZATION

Sadly, in my work as consultant, I usually found gross misalignment. Most organizations I attempted to improve were without succinct strategy and were often quite mixed in focus. This made the management job nearly impossible. I have in mind a particular plant which was part of a large management organization. In this company, upper management (fulfilling their leadership responsibilities) had adopted the core value of empowerment and self-management. Their mission, handbooks and reward structure were testimonies to the core value. With best intentions and benign neglect, they instilled this method of operation in pilot locations throughout the manufacturing sector, leaving implementation to plant personnel and hired consultants. The particular plant I wish to describe was unionized with an adversarial relationship. This plant was originally low tech with a simple to manufacture "cash cow" core product. It was produced using non-automated equipment. This plant and process had been traditionally managed for over 30 years. Being modern times and embracing the new core values, a new high tech process with a complex product was installed at the other end of the plant with high automation and was operated by a crew of autonomous workers chosen from the original work force. The original consultant who aided in implementing the self management believed in the "struggle" as the best method for workers to learn. So showing them how, meeting their needs, and being positive, Pygmalion was replaced with "fend for yourself." Through investigation it became clear the unionized work force had a core value of stretching each day to maximize overtime. This lack of strategy, complete lack of focus and adversarial culture left the young modern managers, who were in charge, faced with an impossible task. They had no infrastructure or plant competence to deal with modern high tech equipment. How could these managers make their plant successful based on such ill conceived leadership?

The answer, of course, is they couldn't. Instead they did what we all do, they followed the path of least resistance and avoided the pain. They either spent inordinate amounts of time on conference calls, paperwork and meetings, or they immersed themselves in intense activity. They frantically changed schedules, orders, and expedited materials or fought the inevitable emergency situations that constantly arose. These activities are *not* management work as I have described above.

When asked to intervene as a consultant the plant culture had evolved to a point where it balanced on the edge of chaos; all aspects of time were lost and only the present mattered. This makes change ever more difficult, since learning from past experiences means little as does planning for the future. I wish I could tell the reader all matters were resolved by my intervention, but that wasn't the case. We focused on enhancing plant competency and did work with both management and union members on core values. While good progress was made in restoring plant performance and defusing the adversarial relations, the inevitable occurred. The upper management people responsible for the perverse leadership were given golden handshakes and the non-managers at the plant level were replaced with more experienced and traditional managers.

Not a pretty picture to be sure, but clearly we see that our employees deserve more than management—they are owed leadership!

CORE VALUES ARE A COMPANY'S ESSENTIAL TENETS
Some examples of core values and principles:

Merck
√ Corporate social responsibility
√ Unequivocal excellence in all aspects of company
√ Science-based innovation
√ Honesty and integrity
√ Profit, but profit from work that benefits humanity

Norstrom
√ Service to the customer above all else
√ Hard work and individual productivity
√ Never being satisfied
√ Excellence in reputation; being part of something else

Philip Morris
√ The right to freedom of choice
√ Winning - beating others in a good fight
√ Encouraging individual initiative
√ Opportunity based on merit, no one is entitled to anything
√ Hard work and continuous self-improvement

Sony
√ Elevation of the Japanese culture and nation status
√ Being a pioneer—not following others; doing the impossible
√ Encouraging individual ability and creativity

Walt Disney
√ No cynicism
√ Nurturing and promulgation of "wholesome American values"
√ Creativity, dreams and imagination
√ Fanatical attention to consistency and detail
√ Preservation and control of the Disney magic

CORE PURPOSE IS A COMPANY'S REASON FOR BEING —SOME EXAMPLES

3M To solve unsolved problems innovatively

Cargil   To improve the standard of living around the world

Fannie May To strengthen the social fabric by continually democratizing home ownership

Hewlett-Packard To make technical contributions for the advancement and welfare of humanity

Lost Arrow Corporation To be a role model and tool for social change

Pacific Theaters To provide a place for people to flourish and to enhance the community

Mary Kay Cosmetics To give unlimited opportunity to women

McKinsey & Company To help leading companies and governments be more successful

Merck To preserve and enhance human life

Nike To experience the emotion of competition, winning, and crushing competitors

Sony To experience the joy of advancing and applying technology for the benefit of the public

Telecare Corporation To help people with mental impairments realize their full potential

Wal-Mart To give ordinary folk the chance to buy the same as rich people

Walt Disney To make people happy

REFERENCES

Collins, J.C., & Porras, J.I. (1996, September/October). Building your company's vision. *Harvard Buisness Review.*

Du Pree, M. (1969). *Leadership is an art.* N.Y.: Doubleday.

Drucker, P.F. (1973) *Management: Tasks, responsibility, practices.* N.Y.: Harper and Row.

Gaffee, R., & Jones, J. (1996, November/December). What holds the modern company together? *Harvard Buisness Review.*

Killian, R.A. (1979). *Managers must lead.* N.Y.: Anacom

Porter, M.E. (1996, November/December). What is strategy? *Harvard Buisness Review.*

Schein, E.H. (1992). *Organizational culture and leadership.* San Francisco: Jossey-Ross.

Seman, D. (1979, July/August). Management by motivation. *Associates Magazine.*

GLOBAL LEADERSHIP FOR THE 21ST CENTURY

By
R. Wilburn Clouse

The world has changed drastically and unexpectedly through-out the course of history. However, in the last decade, the rate of change has accelerated. Technology has made our world much smaller. Slightly more than three years ago, communists ruled Eastern Europe. In recent years, elections held in Poland, Romania, and Hungary have changed their nations. Russia has changed from a communist country to a quasi–free enterprise system. In China, students continue to call for democratic reforms. East and West Germans have been united into one free Germany. For the first time in history, Israel and other nations of the Persian Gulf have met and hammered out peaceful solutions to very difficult situations (Clouse, 1993).

In the past, the world has been filled with international crises. Many of us remember the construction of the Berlin Wall, the Cuban Missile Crisis, the Afghanistan War and the United States and Panama's disagreement over the canal. We have witnessed the conflict between Argentina and Great Britain over the Faulklands, the Iranian hostage ordeal, the unrest in Nicaragua and other central and south American countries, the Persian Gulf conflict, and the uneasy relationship between the Philippines and the United States.

These world events have affected every life in this world. Some of these situations have been resolved by the use of power and negotiations, while others have been resolved through military action. Most of us have observed the unfolding of many of these world events through the technology of television. We have seen the Berlin Wall fall. We have witnessed both Eastern and Western Germans hammering away at the obstacles that divided their city for many years. We have read in the newspaper about the Russian downing of the Korean Airline flight 007. We have heard the rhetoric between Saddam Hussein and former

President Bush, and we have witnessed the major conflict in the Middle East which involved the Persian Gulf countries, as well as the major world powers such as the United States, Russia, Great Britain and France (Clouse, 1992).

All of these world events had and will continue to have a major impact on the globalization process. Through the use of satellites, microwave transmission, fiber optics, video conferencing, and virtual reality simulations, we can see and live the major events of the world taking place in real time analysis.

CHALLENGE FOR THE 21ST CENTURY

Our society is facing a monumental challenge in the closing years of the 20th century. The leadership of the 21st century needs a vision of the future unlike the past. Leadership for the 21st century must be global and must encompass both the "haves" and "have nots" of the world. We have witnessed great changes in some of the largest business organizations of the 20th century. The major computer corporations, such as IBM, Digital Equipment, Apple Computer, have been involved in the most exciting technology development of our time, yet have needed to make major changes in organizational structure, value systems and organizational loyalty.

Through a phrase that has become known as "downsizing" or "rightsizing," many middle level creative employees have been displaced. Similarly, the airlines, such as American Airlines and Delta Airlines, at one time two of the most profitable airlines in the world, have been forced to undergo major downsizing activities. The list of corporate changes can go on and on.

The leaders of the 21st century will find it necessary to change their viewpoints concerning organizational structure, people within organizations, market share, and the marketplace. To some extent, they will have to ask the questions raised in the 1950's by Peter Drucker:

1) *What is our business?*
2) *Who is our customer?*
3) *What does the customer buy?*
4) *What will our business be?*
5) *What should our business be?*

In many cases, we have forgotten some of the basic principles outlined by Peter Drucker. However, these principles must be extended to be global in nature and to empower individuals, at all levels, to make effective decisions about their own work life.

FUTURE CORPORATE STRUCTURE

It is clear that organizational structures needed for corporations to flourish in the future must be different. Corporate structures of the second wave (Toffler, 1980), which are currently in use today and are characterized by hierarchical and an authoritarian form of management, will not be very effective in the global economy. These structures are inflexible and are unable to respond quickly to change. The 21st century will be a century of rapid and major changes. Technology will continue to make the world much smaller, and face-to-face communications through Internet will be a worldwide possibility (Clouse,1993). The current structure of many organizations disempowers people and fosters diverseness, double agendas and destructive conflicts (Maynard & Mehrtens, 1994).

The so-called baby boomers of the 1960's in the United States are now beginning to take positions of power in organizations. It has been said by the current generation, "I am very cynical about the 60's: peace, love, groovy, let's get high—and look what happened." These people turned out to be worse than the people they rebelled against. They are materialistic hypocrites (*Business Week,* December 14, 1992). The current generation will be demanding changes brought about by the "baby boomers." To a great extent, the "baby boomers" have, in fact, been very destructive to concepts related to trust, value systems and organizational loyalty. They have moved into positions they once demonstrated against.

There is little incentive in current corporations for a manager to abandon the traditional role—which insists he or she is in charge. More recently, the Matrix model in business has emerged. The Matrix organization affords the benefits of economy, ununified loyalties and single focus with some degree of flexibility. Organizations such as General   Electric have shifted towards this type of flexible organization.

The new leader of the 21st century must be a part of the team value model which is driven by the desire to create value. The team value model must be collaboratively developed with co-workers and customers. It will take on the perspective of everyone on the team being equal. For the 21st century, this model will take on a structure as a community model. Values will shift from being a bottom-line organization to an organization interested in global consciousness, with a democratic focus on the customer as a participant, somewhat along the same lines as suggested by Drucker in the 1950's.

CORPORATIONS AS COMMUNITIES

The long term health of an organization in the 21st century will depend on its response to globalization and its ability to be flexible. Corporations will be called upon to respond more to community needs, both at local and international levels. Companies may be called upon to be more effective in issues such as education and the environment, much like the Xerox Corporation's and the DuPont Company's involvement in these issues. Maynard and Mehrtens (1994) have indicated 21st century organizations must support the following:

1) Diversity embraced —the development of a truly diverse workplace in racial, ethnic and sexual terms that will produce a profound shift in values and a richer and more diverse set of perspectives for   corporations.

2) Truth and openness promoted —a climate where individuals are free and encouraged to state concerns and suggest changes for the growth and development of the organization.

3) Structural violence ended —employees must be free to be creative in their thinking and in their work development. A climate of truth and openness must exist. Employees must not live in fear of being punished, but encouraged to be creative.

4) Employee health and well-being supported —an awareness of the value of the "wellness place" will be an important part of new organizations. Changes in the way medicine is practiced will be manifest in the 21st century.

A leader in the 21st century must find tomorrow's opportunity today. Tomorrow will be too late in a global society. For example, in 1968 the watchmakers of Switzerland were so good they owned 65% of the market for all types of timepieces manufactured. By 1980, some twelve years later, the Swiss share of the market had dropped below 10%. What happened? Did the Swiss forget how to make quality timepieces? No. *They could not see the future.* They scoffed when entrepreneurs suggested quartz movement would replace the main spring. The Japanese listened, and the Seiko Company seized the market. The rest of the story is history. Failure of vision in the 21st century will be an unpardonable sin (Clouse, 1994).

The 21st century leader does not plan for tomorrow by study-ing what happened yesterday. As technology continues to change, the rules of the game will continue to change. One day it may be spring-driven watches, the next day it is CDs. It is not enough to keep up with the change. The leader of the 21st century must predict it. He/she must anticipate change and identify new opportunities.

How do we develop leaders for the 21st century? *Most of our current training programs in the world today will not develop the person who will be successful as a leader in the 21st century.* Perhaps the key may be to develop the ability to make intuitive judgements and the courage to act on them (Clouse, 1994).

The decision-making process in organizations is already a complex and difficult task and will become more difficult and more complex in the future. At one time in our history, a few executives held in their minds the information and data needed to operate organizations. This is not the case in a global economy (Clouse, 1988). Today, organi-zations are more multidimensional, complex structures that use sophisticated computer systems to collect and store vital organizational information. Leaders in the 21st century who have the ability to act fast, manipulate and use information in a "just-in-time" mode, will have a better chance of being successful than those who do not. Data bases of the future must look at who is the customer from a global perspective and leaders must be able to synthesize from this data the particular niche their organization can secure.

In 1985, Clouse reported American business crossed a technological rubicon in that year (Clouse, 1985). For the first time in history, capital investments for office workers exceeded the investments for factory workers in the United States. Information had surpassed material goods as the country's basic resource. Information has become a major source of power in organizations. Information is a new form of capital, perhaps more critical to the future of the world economy than money capital (Clouse,1987).

SUMMARY

We have just begun to see change in organizations. To be inventors and entrepreneurs in the twenty-first century, we need the courage to let go of the old world, relinquish some of what we have cherished, and abandon some of our interpretations about what does and does not work. As Einstein is quoted as saying "no problem can be solved from the same consciousness that created it" (Wheatley, 1994). We must see the world anew through a different lens.

Technology has made the world smaller for everyone. We must develop new paradigms, especially for the global entrepreneur, whose technical universe must expand to encompass cultural, legislative, geographic and value concerns. With these concerns, along with international networks, we have a major task for the future, a job that is fit for a Titan.

REFERENCES

Business Week. (1992, December 14). Move over boomers, the busters are here—and they're angry.

Clouse, R. W. (1992). *Entrepreneurship education for a global economy in the 21st century.* Paper presented at the 10th Annual International Entrepreneurship Education Forum, Lake Tahoe, Nevada.

Clouse, R. W. (1993). *Technology based distance learning.* Paper presented at the 18th Annual Conference of the Association of Private Enterprise Education, Washington, D.C.

Clouse, R. W. (1985, Fall). The next corporate crisis. *Corporate Learning Instute Newsletter.* Nashville, TN: Vanderbilt.

Clouse, R. W. (1993). *Entrepreneurship in education: Views from educators and business executives.* Paper presented at the 18th Annual Conference of the Association of Private Enterprise Education, Washington, D.C.

Drucker, P. (1950). *The practice of management.* New York: Harper & Row

Garrett, L., Garrett, J.A., & Clouse, R. (1987). Beyond evalution: Planned organizantional response to change. *Organization Development Journal, 4,* 3.

Maynard, H. B., & Mehrtens, S. E. (1994). *The fourth wave: Business in the 21st century.* San Francisco: Barrett-Koehler Publishers.

Toffler, A. (1980). *The third wave.* New York: Morrow.

Wheatly, M. (1994). *Leadership and the new science.* San Francisco: Barrett-Koehler Publishers.

LEADERSHIP AND THE PSYCHOLOGICAL CONTRACT

By
Harold Fuqua, Jr.
Joseph P. Cangemi
Kay Payne

Leaders develop both written and unwritten expectations of their subordinates in organizations. Likewise, employees join organizations with many unwritten expectations and perceived obligations of the organization toward them. These mutual, unwritten expectations and perceived obligations of each party toward the other operate as *a psychological contract.*

As competition increases, as organizations grow more complex, and as employees become more difficult to understand, it becomes increasingly difficult for leaders to directly satisfy the needs of individual employees. Moreover, employee expectations of their employers grow higher and higher, in terms of psychic as well as material rewards, as cultures become more highly educated. Consequently, the leadership and overall climate of an organization must fulfill the needs of its individual employees in order to provide a supportive culture. The essential element of this new supportive culture involves the development of mutual trust. A people business, leadership must involve itself in the business of developing a vision and providing hope for employees. Employees must believe in the organization's leaders, and the organization's leaders must behave in ways which promote and develop trust and belief in them. The breakdown of trust in leadership initiates the downward slide of an organization and, generally, leads to morale problems, turnover, negative attitudes, decreased profits, and ultimately, in some cases, the complete deterioration of an organization and its demise (Cole, 1996).

Understanding the leader's responsibility in keeping up the *psychological contract* and fulfilling its obligations ensures the development and maintenance of a healthy and effective organization.

THE PSYCHOLOGICAL CONTRACT

What is the psychological contract? Rousseau (1989) argued "The term psychological contract refers to an individual's beliefs regarding the terms and conditions of a reciprocal exchange agreement between that focal person and another party" (p.122). Levinson (1962) stated: "The psychological or unwritten contract is a product of mutual expectations. These have two characteristics: (a) they are largely implicit and unspoken, and (b) they frequently antedate the relationship of person and company" (p.22). *Nothing about the psychological contract is written or spoken.* "Many Japanese scholars writing in English have tried to explain to bewildered Americans the ethics of a culture in which greater value is placed on silence than on speech, and ideas are believed to be best communicated without being explicitly stated" (Tanner, 1994, p. 96). Kahn et al., (1964) refers to a psychological contract as unwritten expectations which operate continuously at all times between all the various members of an organization and its leaders. The organizational viewpoint of the contract implies every role has a set of behavioral expectations. Schein (1980) claimed each subordinate in an organization has expectations about salary, working hours, benefits, and privileges which go with a position---such as a belief no employee will be terminated unexpectedly. The many unwritten expectations in the psychological contract involve a persons' self-worth and value as an individual in the organization. Employees expect organizations to treat them fairly, to provide opportunities for upward mobility, and to give them feedback (Schein, 1980). Employees want to be involved in making decisions about their own behavior in organizations, using their abilities to think, reason, and anticipate future events.

RECIPROCAL OBLIGATIONS

A psychological contract includes elements or reciprocal obligation. Rousseau (1989) noted:

"When an individual perceives that contributions he or she makes obligate the organization to reciprocity (or vice versa) a psychological contract emerges. Belief that reciprocity will occur can be a precursor to the development of a psychological contract. However, it is the individual's belief in an obligation of reciprocity that constitutes this contract. This belief is unilateral, held by a particular individual and does not constrain those of any other parties to the relationship" (p.124).

Robinson and Rousseau (1994) inferred the phycological contract involves a belief in the mind of an employee of what the organization obligates itself to provide, based on perceived promises of reciprocal exchange between the employee and employer. "The psychological contract is an implicit contract between an individual and his (or her) organization which specifies what each expects to give and receive from each other in their relationship" (Kotter 1973 p. 92). Kotter further argued mutual reciprocal expectations exist between an individual and the organization. The individual expects to receive from the organization advancement opportunities, a decent salary, and challenging work, as well as expectations to give to the organization time and technical skills. The organization also has expectations from the subordinate, such as loyalty and competent work skills (Kotter, 1973). "Psychological contracts are an individual's beliefs regarding reciprocal obligations" (Rousseau, 1990, p. 390). Rousseau further regarded psychological contracts as beliefs which when entered into cause an individual to believe he or she owes an employer contributions such as hard work and loyalty. When employees recognize the importance of behaving and performing their jobs in a certain manner they expect the organization to reciprocate by fulfilling its obligations towards them, such as providing fair compensation and job security. When both parties recognize these obligations Rousseau (1990) claims a true psychological contract exists.

The advantage of fulfilling these reciprocal obligations increases trust both ways; the obligations invigorate high trust which tends to stimulate high performance. For example, when a leader demonstrates high trust in an employee he or she tries to justify his or her bosses' good estimation of them. Axiomatically, high performance reinforces high trust. For example, when one trusts and respects a person who meets or exceeds his or her expectations and that person reciprocates with recognition of some kind, more trust develops. On-the-other-hand, low performance from employees also reinforces low trust from supervisors, which produces a kind of self-fulfilling prophecy.

The trust-performance cycle suggests an interesting communication parallel—the mutual interdependence of a trusting relationship and effective communication. When the organizational culture functions as supportive and trusting, communication usually revolves around open discussions focused on task accomplishment. The aura of open communication makes it possible to candidly express feelings and ideas without fear of reprisal. Individuals support and assist one another when mistakes occur, carrying one another and compensating for each other's errors. The forgiving and nurturing atmosphere functions as an opportunity to learn from mistakes rather than as an occasion for punishment. Effective communication contributes to reinforce and enhance an existing trusting climate.

When the organizational culture functions as unsupportive and nontrusting, communication often arouses backbiting and focuses on deep, long-lasting feelings of betrayal which creates destructive relationships (DeMeuse & Tornow, 1990). As the culture becomes increasingly hostile and threatening, communication suffers; people suppress their true feelings, fearful of revealing them lest they be punished. In normal behavior, individuals tend to want to protect themselves rather than expose themselves to negative reprisals. Unfortunately, in hostile organizational cultures, people who want to misunderstand or be misunderstood look for such opportunities even when perfect communication exists.

THE NEW PSYCHOLOGICAL CONTRACT

A new psychological contract must be created between employees and organizations. "The agreement must become, in some respects, less emotional. There can still be loyalty, security, and commitment, but these must be achieved in different ways than in the past" (Tornow & DeMeuse, 1994,p.169). Finding a new way to reestablish the mutual benefit from the agreement, for both parties, must be found. The responsibility for finding this new way of reestablishing mutual benefit falls on leadership. The idea of a shared vision, which benefits the organization and the employee, should provide job security, corporate loyalty, and increased productivity. The primary key involves an interdependent relationship between the employee and the organization, with information available to both parties, and shared, rather than one-sided decision making power. Both power and risk must be shared (Tornow & DeMeuse, 1994).

VIOLATION OF THE PSYCHOLOGICAL CONTACT.

Argyris (1964) believed organizations create conditions which cause employees to experience "psychological failure." This internal conflict increases as one moves down the hierarchy, as jobs become more specialized and mechanized, as leadership becomes more directive, as the formal structure becomes tighter, and as people become more able (task mature), and more educated. When organizations begin to operate within this kind of culture, Johnson and Induik (1994) advocate the psychological contract will become violated and tremendous morale problems and power problems will arise. *When companies ignore human feelings and provide no mechanisms of support for their employees, frustration may take the form of some creative forms of revenge.* For example, employees might quit, or psychologically withdraw from the organization through frequent absenteeism, indifference, apathy or passiveness. They might resist the organization by restricting output, deception, featherbedding, or sabotage. They might attempt to rise higher in the organization to better jobs, or create organizational subcultures, such as unions, to redress the power imbalance (Bolman & Deal, 1991). Disgruntled employees might come to work merely to do enough work to collect their paychecks. Their minds, far too often distracted by their unhappiness, become fertile ground for injuries, accidents, poor quality products, and high turnover. Did the Peruvian airliner crash in November, 1996 happen because of psychological withdrawal from the organization? Post crash investigation found duct tape, placed over the airplane's sensors during cleaning, *still there* after cleaning and takeoff. The mistakenly marked gas canisters on the Valu Jet crash in the Florida Everglades of 1996–could they also have resulted from distracted employees? Poor attitudes developed on the job often can be linked to broken psychological contracts. These conditions create situations where behaviors, such as those mentioned above, could certainly occur.

Robinson, Kraatz, and Rousseau (1994) believe violation of the psychological contract erodes the relationship and the belief system of the reciprocal obligations in organizations when one party perceives the other has violated their agreement. Violation of the psychological contract by the employer may not only affect what the employee believes the organization owes him or her, but it also may affect what the employee believes he or she owes the organization. When an organization violates the psychological contract, the employee views the organization as no longer sharing (or maybe never did share) a common set of values and mutual expectations. When this happens, communication breaks down, understanding fails, and frustration increases (Sims, 1992). This unwritten psychological contract binds the employee and employer in a guarantee of reciprocal benefits. *Violations weaken the bond,* and the violated party feels abused and loses faith in the benefits of staying in the relationship (Rousseau, 1989). The costs of securing and retraining replacement employees, or the insecurity of searching for a new job and then retraining oneself to fit in, far outweigh whatever it costs to maintain the interdependent relationship implied in the psychological contract.

SUMMARY

This article defines and describes the psychological contract. It explains the reciprocal obligations of employees and employers who psychologically agree to fulfill unwritten reciprocal obligations. It describes opportunities for change from old notions of psychological contracts to new ones. Violations and the consequences of those violations increase the likelihood of psychological withdrawal and sabotage in organizations, and those were described. The importance of trust in maintaining the psychological contract cannot be over emphasized as the key to making the contractual agreement work.

REFERENCES

Argyris, C. (1964). Integrating the individual and the organization. New York: Wiley

Bolman, L., & Deal, T. (1991) *Reframing organizations.* San Francisco: Jossey Bass.

Cole, T. (1996). *Road scholars.* Bowling Green, KY: Unpublished Manuscript.

Demeuse, K.P., & Tornow, W. W. (1990). The tie that binds has become very, very frayed! *Human Resource Planning, 13,* (3),203-213.

Kahn, R.L., Wolfe, D.M., Quinn, R.P., Snoek, J.D., & Rosenthal, R.A. (1964). *Organizational stress: Studies in role conflicts and ambiguity.* New York: Wiley

Kotter, J.P. (1973). The psychological contract. *California Management Review, 15,* 9199.

Johnson, P.R., & Induik, J. (1994). Workplace violence: An issue of the nineties. *Public Personnel Management, 223,* 515-23.

Levinson, H. (1962). *Men, management, and mental health.* Cambridge, MA: Harvard UP.

Robinson, S. L., Kraatz, M.S., & Rosseau, D.M. (1994). Changing obligations and the psychological contract: A longitudinal study. *Academy of Management Journal, 37,* 137-52.

Robinson, S.L., & Rosseau, D.M. (1994). Violating the psychological contract; Not the exception but the norm. *Journal of Organizational Behavior, 15,* 249-59.

Rousseau, D.M. (1989). Psychological and implied contracts in organizations. *Employees Responsibilities and Rights Journal, 2,* 121-129.

Rousseau, D.M. (1990). New hire perceptions of their own and their employer's obligations: A study of psychological contracts. *Journal of Organizational Behavior, 11,* 389-400.

Schein, E.J. (1980). *Organizational psychology.* Englewood Cliffs, NJ: Prentice-Hall.

Sims, R.R. (1992). Developing the learning climate in public sector training programs. *Public Personnel Management, 21,* 335-46.

Tannen, D. (1994). *Talking from 9 to 5.* New York: William Morrow.

Tornow, W. W., & DeMeuse, K.P. (1994). New paradigm approaches in strategic human resource management. *Group and Organizational Management, 19,* 165-170.**INTUITIVE**

INUTITIVE HUMOR: A LEADERSHIP STYLE

By
R. Wilburn Clouse

For years I have been interacting with others by using humor. I do not mean by telling stories or ethnic jokes; what I do mean is to play off of the moment and the circumstance. I have used this intuitive style in grocery stores at checkout counters, in banks with tellers, in airports with ticket agents, in graduate classes, in management seminars, in management groups, and in board rooms. Almost, without exception, people like to laugh.

In these situations from the ticket counter to the board room, I have left feeling either satisfied as a customer, or pleased with the joint decision of a board. My counterparts with whom I have interacted also have seemed to be pleased and, in most cases, smiles were on their faces. What is this thing called humor and how can it help us move organizations into the 21st Century?

I have seen intuitive humor operate effectively in most cases, here in the United States, and in international situations. Recently, while in a meeting with one of the sheiks from the United Arab Emirates, there was a pause in our discussions and the arabic people all began to laugh. I thought I had done something wrong, but my arabic friends said, 'Oh no, it is just a bit of local humor." Likewise, I used intuitive humor in Luxembourg, Paris, and Frankfurt recently very successfully. People of all cultures like to laugh.

On some occasions the intuitive humor has not worked. On one occasion, while sitting in the office of a school superintendent, I made the statement that learning should be fun. I was quickly corrected by the superintendent when he said, "Boy, learning is not fun but hard work, and the sooner you realize that, the better off you will be." I quickly thought about my work in public schools around the world and realized that here is an organization that is essentially dysfunctional. When fun leaves the classroom, so does the student.

Fun, laughter, and humor make the work environment a pleasant place to be, or the classroom a wonderful place to learn. Many fads have come and gone in management. I remember zero defects, management by objectives, quality circles, theory x y, situational management, and many others. Whatever happened to the simple concept of treating people as you would like to be treated, and to make work and learning fun activities.

DEFINITION OF HUMOR

The history of humor research separates into three distinctly different divisions according to Goldstein (1978). The first stage, the theoretical stage, focuses on observational studies of laughter and smiling. The psychoanalytic stage, or second stage, focuses almost entirely on the view of Freud's interpretation of wit and humor. Third, and current stage research, focuses on the cognitive element of humor (p. 104). Goldstein reported that current research advances theories into one of the following areas: the development of a child's sense of humor through cognitive maturation or socialization and the cognitive processes that allow the interpretation of jokes as jokes, the use and effect of humor in various settings, and field studies related to joking (p. 105).

While most of the research on organizational humor has been qualitative, some examples of combined qualitative–empirical exist. Qualitative humor studies tend to focus on the social patterns found in organizations. Handelman and Kapferer (1992) proposed that humorous behavior was not random, but rather occurred in regular patterns. Supported by frequency tables, the empirical data revealed that certain men joke more than others, were joked with more than others, and were the more frequent targets of jokes. In a more recent study, Duncan and Feifal studied the social organizational aspects of humor in the sociological frame to determine the relationship between humor and friendship, leadership, and perceived employee performance (Feifal,1989). Because humor is becoming a more recognized element in the environment of an organization, the need for formal programs is on the upswing. Williams and Clouse have identified five categories in which research indicates humor is used in the workplace, (Williams,1994; Clouse, 1993). These categories include:

1)   the organizational environment
2)   as a socializing agent
3)   as a reliever of stress
4)   as a management tool
5)   as a function of communications

William Fry (1963) has conducted studies on laughter and humor for more than three decades. He has identified humor as a form of play. He has also identified humor as a play-frame in which humor can be demonstrated openly, or through force intonation and body language. Hall (1959) identified ten different categories of human activity that assists in the understanding of cultural social phenomena."Play" is described as the primary message system through which man comprehends culture. Hall suggests that "if you can learn the humor of a population and really control it, you know that you are in control of nearly everything else."

Researchers believe that humor has managerial applications. (Philbrick, 1989; Clouse & Williams, 1993; Williams, 1994). Although humor is often considered a random "fun" activity, attorney turned humor consultant Malcomb Kushner (1990) proposes that it is also a form of communication that builds morale, manages conflict, motivates people, influences corporate culture, and improves productivity. Cornett (1986)considers additional uses for humor that include: changing perceptions and perspectives, problem solving, reinforcing desired behavior, transmitting culture, values, energizing, and developing a positive self image.

Humor is a cultural phenomenon found in every society. What we do and repeat suggests that humor has a far-reaching organizational significance. Some of the most profound thinkers in history have examined humor and have proposed separate theories as to its purpose and function. Men like Aristotle, Charles Darwin, Sigmund Freud, author Koestler, all respected scholars have proposed various theories on the origin and value of humor to society. Men have struggled to explain the function of humor. Although there is some disagreement in that the theories reflect only the roles of humor rather than function, there is general agreement in the models proposed in Burger's research (1987). Aristotle, Hobbes, Kant, Freud, Jung, and Piaget are but a few of the contributors of the four persistent classifications of humor theory (Berger, 1987). These models are superiority, incongruent, psychoanalytic, and cognitive. In order to better understand the use of humor in organizations, these four models will briefly be discussed.

SUPERIORITY THEORY

The predominant superiority theories such as Aristotle and Robbes' interpreted humor through its social perspective. This theory supports the notion that we perceive a situation as humorous when we feel superior to either our former sense of self or others. Application of these phenomena is noted when an action or activity becomes funny in hindsight (falling down stairs, slip of the tongue, etc.). Additionally, humor may be interpreted through the theory of superiority as it is expressed in ethnic "jokes" that relay the jokers belief in the inferiority of an individual group. This humor serves to emphasize culture differences, and in most cases, prohibits social, political and economic advancement (Clouse, 1993).

INCONGRUENT THEORY

Theorists, Kant and Bergson, maintain humor is expressed when an incongruity exists between what an individual expects and what one gets. The response to incongruous behavior is a "manifestation of the highest cerebral process encompassing the ability to jump across gaps in logic and find delight in the process" (Williams, 1993). In fact, much of our intuitive humor is based on incongruous situations. If one is unable to assess the degree of incongruity, one cannot appreciate the humor. For this reason, the inability to recognize the humor in a situation implies insufficient appreciation or understanding of its various elements (Clouse, 1993). The unexpected and intuitive humor is potentially the most useful humor in developing organizational culture.

PSYCHOANALYTICAL THEORY

Freud theorized that humor camouflages aggression. In this context, humor is viewed as a coping mechanism that enables the initiator to release expressed feelings. It is similar and analogous to Prigogine's (1989) theory of chaos, where a lack of equilibrium within the psychic energy channels permits an overload of entering psychic energy. Humor then becomes the junction at which point aggression is released into a state of entropy. All permitting, *some interaction with the other classifications of humor,* this theory predominantly invokes social and cultural behavior norms. As individuals, we may regress to the use of humor rather than confront social exile (Spurgeon & Clouse, 1995).

COGNITIVE THEORY

Another significant humor theory suggests that humor is also a cognitive process as indicated when an individual is confronted with oppositional information or the paradoxical nature of humor. Cognitive theory is focused on the way the brain processes oppositional or paradoxical information when required, Piaget states that the existence of symbolic humor is a developmental process appearing at different stages for dependence on each child by a logical and maturational timetable. Clouse has also found that humor can be used in organizations based on a relationship timetable and composition of the group.

THE SOCIAL FUNCTION OF HUMOR

Bateson (1972) suggests that humor is a subset of the idea play. Coser (1959) suggests that humor is a social activity that is regulated by society. Bolman and Deal (1988) state that "play is what people do when they're not working" thereby implying that work activities are not play activities. Clouse (1993) states that one may assume the social context in which humor is initiated may therefore influence its function.

These are some of the reasons that organizational humor is seldom seen in the literature. Humor is generally considered a social experience, rather than an organizational one.

HUMOR APPLICATIONS

People find their stability and security in the culture and direction of organizations (Kanter, 1983). In companies that are in need of a complete management and employee overhaul, these companies often look to the success of other companies and try to replicate the process. Hewlett-Packard managers are evaluated on their ability to create enthusiasm. Pepsico managers must insure an exciting place to work. The leaders of successful companies are concerned about clarifying the corporate value system and breathing life into the organization. However, each corporation must possess its own peculiar and unique culture system.

Several corporations have successfully used humor as a management strategy. The foremost company in this area could very well be Southwest Airlines. The colorful and eccentric Herb Kelleher is a distinct and humorous leader of Southwest. Kelleher believes in a "back to basics" approach where the airline provides service, cheap fares, and fun on each flight. Kelleher believes in making work fun. He considers himself more a company clown than corporate chief. He encourages flight attendants to wear tennis shoes during the summer, and allows pilots to improvise flight announcements. Ann Rhoades, whose title is Vice President of People, says "what we look for in employees is a sense of humor. We don't take ourselves too seriously. We find that when people are very relaxed, they are very productive" (Englere, 1990).

Patagonia, Inc., of the fastest growing makers of outdoor clothing, believes in ecology for the individual. Yvon Chouinard, the company master-mind, spends six to seven months each year away from the office. His MBA philosophy believes in "management by absence." Susan Green, Director of Human Resources, says "we never wanted to create a company we wouldn't want to work for."

Wayne Rosing, Vice President of Sun Micro Systems Laboratories, Inc., found a life-size replica of his office constructed at the bottom of a shark tank in San Francisco aquarium. He was the target of the annual April Fool's Day prank, planned and carried out by the company engineers. Other pranks have included turning the CEO's office into a one-hole, par four miniature golf course, complete with two sand traps and a bird bath (Caudron, 1992).

Many other examples of humor in organizations can be cited. Companies are realizing that humor is one of the most effective ways to deal with workplace challenges and the stress they cause.

SUMMARY

Clouse (1993, 1994) reports that humor has been found to minimize differences between employee status, alleviate tension, facilitate work, improve socialization, bond employees together, improve communication, break down barriers, relax everyone, create rapport, and boost morale.

In working in the corporate environment, I have found that humor is a wonderful way to get attention, either in a meeting or while conducting a speech. It is a very effective way to make a point and to stimulate new ideas. In group meetings, it reduces anxiety, relaxes the audience and the speaker; in classrooms, it makes learning fun and reduces stress.

The organizational humor that I refer to is not the telling of jokes or making fun of other people, nor putting people down. It is the intuitive humor that rises out of the culture of the organization and the individual is empowered to be himself/herself in their work environment. It is an environment that takes our work seriously, but not ourselves. Humor is the element that makes work enjoyable and fun. Laughter is the expression of a happy person.

REFERENCES

Bateson, G. (1972). Steps to an ecology of mind. New York: Ballantine.

Berger, A. A. (Ed.). (1987). Anatomy of a joke. *Journal of Communication, 23* (3), 113-115.

Bolman, L. G., & Deal, T. E. (1991). *Reframing organizations.* Jossey Bass Publishers: San Francisco.

Caudron, S. (1992). Humor is healthy in the workplace. *Personnel Journal, 71,* 63-68.

Clouse, R. W., & Williams, R. A. (1993). *Administrative styles and humor.* Paper presented at the 11th Annual International Conference of Humor and Laughter, The International Society for Humor Studies, Dulibois European Center, Miami University, Centre Universitaire De Luxembourg, Lyeu De Garcons De Luxembourg.

Clouse, R. W. (1993). *Humor: It's impact on school culture.* Paper presented at the 11th Annual International Conference on Humor and Laughter, The International Society for Humor Studies, Dulibois European Center, Miami University, Centre Universitaire De Luxembourg, Lyeu De Garcons De Luxembourg.

Clouse, R. W. (1994). *Using humor to enhance teaching.* Paper presented at the 12th Annual International Conference on Humor, The International Society for Humor Studies, Ithaca College, Ithaca, N.Y.

Cornett, C. E., (1986). *Learning through laughter: Humor in the classroom.* Phi Delta Kappa Educational Foundation, 241, n.p.

Coser, R. L. (1959). Some social functions of humor: A study of humor in a hospital setting. *Human Relations, 12,* 171-182.

Emgeler, A. (1990). A busy boss can never fly solo. *CEO's Journal, 136,* 22-23.

Fry, W. F. (1963). *Sweet madness: A study of humor.* Palo Alto, CA:Stanford University.

Goldstein, J. H. (1978, Summer). Theoretical notes on humor. *Journal of Communications, 20* (3), 104-112.

Hall, E. T. (1959). *The silent language.* Garden City, New York: Doubleday.

Handelman, D., & Kapferer, B. (1972). Forms of joking activity: A comparative approach. *American Anthropologist, 74,* 485-517.

Kanter, R. (1983). *The change masters: Innovations for productivity in the American corporation.* New York: Simon & Schuster.

Philbrick, K. D. (1989). The use of humor and effective leadership. *Dissertation Abstracts International, 51.*

Spurgeon, K., & Clouse, R. W. (1995). *An analysis of humor and its management applications.* Research paper, Vanderbilt University, Nashville, TN.

Williams, R. A. (1994). The perceived value of administration humor to school climate. *Dissertation Abstracts International, 55.*
New York: Wiley

BENEATH THE VEIL OF LEADERSHIP: OUT–SOURCING AS AN EXPRESSION OF THE POWER MOTIVE

by
Susan E. Heinbuch

Out–sourcing, the market derived provision of services to and through an organization, is an increasingly selected business alternative by today's leaders. Today's new out–sourcing differs from that of the past. Traditionally, organizations out–sourced for basic materials and supplies to make possible their own creation and performance of downstream services at the core of their business. Today, however, in addition to past practices, organizations are increasingly contracting for services closer to the core of their business (Cowan,1989; DeHoog,1984: Donahue, 1989; Osborne 1989; DeHoog, 1984; Donahue, 1989; Drucker, 1968, 1989; Handy, 1990; Heinbuch, 1993,1994; Osborne & Gaebler, 1992; Prager, 1992; Quinn, Doorley & Paquette, 1991). For example, organizations contract for the management of functional or staff departments such as payroll, collections, or accounting. Some use out–sourcing as a way to expand their service offerings as when hospitals out–source the "setup" and operation of nursing homes to shorten hospital stays when revenues per stay are fixed (Heinbuch, 1993).

At the extreme, the entire management of some organizations is out-sourced. This latter practice, particularly observed in the high tech industry, gave rise to the terms "virtual corporation" (Byrne, 1993) and "virtual leadership" (Huey, 1994). The new organizational realities embodied in these concepts have caused some to question how the organization of tomorrow should be defined. They create images of leaders as broker-dealers of out–sourced services toward some mission (Handy, 1990; Heinbuch, 1994; Huey, 1994).

There are many practical benefits that can accrue to the organization for out-sourcing. Broadly, it provides organizational and governmental leaders with opportunities to control costs, while gaining access to greater capacity and expertise than is employed directly (Kanter, 1989; Quinn, Doorley & Paquette, 1991). As a result, organizational efficiency and effectiveness may be enhanced.

[1] The author thanks Hrach Bedrosian, Professor of Management and Organizational Behavior, Stern School of Business, New York University, for his comments on an earlier draft of this article and Irina Benfeld for her research assistance.

OUT–SOURCING POWER PARADOX

Many practical issues confront the rational leader in making an out-sourcing decision. For example, what are the short and long run costs in human, fiscal, and service quality terms if out-sourcing fails? What are the human concerns of displacing hundreds or thousands of workers? What may be the union issues? How does one rebuild an entire organization, or one of its departments, or re-establish a major governmental program that may have taken many months or years and involve millions, occasionally billions, of dollars in its out–sourcing?

Opportunities presented by either out-sourcing or in-sourcing services also offer unique and practical organizational power dilemmas. Specifically, concerns with power and control issues present an organizational out-sourcing paradox for achieving performance and ensuring survival (Heinbuch, 1994). On one hand, an organization can be viewed as having more control when it delivers a service itself. However, the inevitable employee obligations or lack of up-to-date expertise may mean that less can be accomplished. On the other hand, out-sourcing may mean less direct control by the organization over how tasks get done. But absent organizational encumbrances, such as those imposed by providing fringe benefits or collective bargaining agreements, more may be accomplished.

One potential out-sourcing benefit, then, is that an organization can pay for the work performed, rather than the job that exists to do such work. It can terminate at will (for nonperformance) rather than be saddled with under-performing marginal employees who are able to demonstrate sufficient employable effort to task without achieving results. The extent to which leaders exercise the termination option, in reality, may be very revealing of their intent and ability to avail and utilize the potential derived from out-sourcing.

THE PROBLEM

Unfortunately, some leaders have been resistant to out-source even when evidence strongly suggests it was a prudent organizational decision. Others have aggressively pursued it even when it was clearly demonstrated that its pursuit may bring about serious negative organizational consequences. How can we understand these seemingly irrational out-sourcing decisions? Exactly, what motivates leaders' out-sourcing decisions? Why do some leaders choose to out-source and others do not?

Extant understandings about out-sourcing decisions are largely found in the organizational theory literature. They range from the economic, the firm as proactive profit maximizer (David, 1988; Donahue, 1989; Downs & Larkey, 1986; Eisenhardt, 1985,1989; Rehfuss, 1989; Savas, 1987; Scott, 1987; Williamson, 1975,1981), to the institutional, the firm as reactive structural by–product of larger societal forces (Covaleski & Dirsmith, 1988; DiMaggio & Powell, 1991; Mick & Conrad, 1988; Meyer & Rowen, 1991; Meyer and Scott, 1983; Oliver, 1991; Scott, 1987; Tolbert & Zucker, 1983; Zucker, 1991). Implicit in the former is an assumption of organizational leaders making rational decisions, the latter, a metaphor for chaos-- helpless cads at the mercy of uncontrollable external forces. These explanations largely mitigate the human and psychological dimen- sions of out-sourcing decisions.

At present, literature focussed on underlying human and psychological aspects of out-sourcing decisions is virtually nonex- istent. This article brings attention to this issue by exploring how some out-sourcing decisions might also be understood as manifesta- tions of a leader's conscious and unconscious concerns with retain- ing or acquiring power. Of specific concern to this discussion are those psychologically addictive aspects of power that may dominate leaders decisions to the detriment of their organization, its employ- ees and ultimately society.

POWER–ADDICTION AND LEADERS' OUT–SOURCING DECISIONS

Kets de Vries (1991) suggested that leaders' often become addicted to power for both conscious and unconscious reasons. As a result, their susceptibility to this addiction manifests itself in patho- logical behaviors. Building on his ideas, it is postulated that con- scious and unconscious forces underlay leaders out-sourcing deci- sions, and that many can be understood as leaders aversion to relin- quishing power or their desire for its acquisition. Briefly reviewed below are psychological concepts, with supporting examples, that provide insight into how leaders' become addicted to power, how it is revealed in their out-sourcing decisions, and how colleagues may contribute to the leader's addiction.

NARCISSISM

"If there is one personality constellation to which leaders tend to gravitate, it is the narcissistic one" (Kets de Vries, 1991, p. 341).

The concept of narcissism has evolved in the psychological literature from Freud's drive-theory perspective (Freud, 1914) to that of self-psychology (Kohut, 1971,1977). For this discussion, narcissism is conceived of as all forms of psychological self-interest (refer also to Kets de Vries, 1991; Meissner, 1981).

There are two basic manifestations of narcissism, constructive and destructive, that may be discussed with respect to leaders and their out-sourcing decisions. Few will deny the appropriate, if not, essential importance of many narcissistic qualities to effective and successful leadership (Levinson, 1992). These may be characterized as constructive narcissism. For example, successful leaders have been shown to be ambitious, risk takers, self-starters, desirous of public recognition, yet easily able to overcome rejection, and are comfortable with controlling and managing others (Bennis & Nanus, 1985; Kotter, 1988,1990; Levinson, 1992; Pfeffer, 1992). All of these facets of leadership are consistent with current psychological conceptions of narcissism. These qualities, coupled with rational analyses of an out-sourcing opportunity, allow leaders to constructively decide, implement and manage out-sourcing toward the benefit of the organization.

Of concern, however, is the transition from constructive narcissism to its destructive, "addictive forms, as symptomized by tenacious holding onto power" (Kets de Vries, 1991), or ill-informed decisions toward its acquisition. Unwillingness to out-source when rational logical analysis suggests it is the best organizational choice signifies the former. Out-sourcing to oust internal organizational competitors, such as closing a department, or for obtaining trust and loyalty, the latter.

Anecdotal evidence provided to the author, by contractors, during a study examining managers' decision making processes when out-sourcing, provide clues to the narcissistic tendencies underlying some leaders out–sourcing decisions. One contractor suggested that he perceived a key factor in closing the "deal" was the hospital-manager's excitement at being regularly featured in the contractor's quarterly newsletter. Another noted the appeal of "vanity press" in an out-sourcing decision when it was indicated to the leader that the contractor had a journal publisher who would feature an article about the hospital's adoption and provision of a new service through contract. Of themselves, these examples would reveal little had they not been coupled with evidence that these two out-sourcing decisions were made based on few other organizationally-sound considerations.

AGGRESSION

Leaders' abilities to cope "with the hazards and uncertainties of working life while fulfilling [their] aspirations, place high demands on the most essential defense needed for [their] self preservation" (Kets de Vries, 1980). Aggression, best known as the 'fight or flight'impulse, refers to the attacking aspect of the personality (Levinson, 1986) emergent in self-preservation and power enhancing activities (Kets de Vries, 1980). It is the outward manifestation of an emotionally derived hostility state. Some leaders out-sourcing decisions may be understood in these terms.

Consider the case of the newly hired individual into a senior leadership position, such as a new Chief Executive Officer or President or Executive Vice President. This person typically arrives in the new   organizational environment sans an existing power base from which to operate, and thus, must create one. How might they do this? Assuming rational leadership behavior, it may be expected that the leader will take time to observe their new environment, 'get the lay of the land.' He or she will identify those organizational players, individuals and functional departments, that can advance or threaten their opportunities to engage in and demonstrate effective organizational leadership. This process generally requires a reasonable amount of time, at least a few months. As a result, the rational leader may be expected to actively develop those relationships and situations providing the best opportunities to successfully lead the organization.

However, some leaders' power-addiction may cause them to exhibit aggressive tendencies as they actively out-source services as a way to quickly and conveniently re-configure power relationships and relational loyalties within the organization sans a reasoned consideration of the alternatives. Preliminary evidence for this inference was found by Heinbuch (1994). Her multiple-case comparative examination of managerial contracting (out-sourcing) processes conducted by nonprofit hospitals managers found that "a change in senior management was a predominant event (an associated factor) immediately preceding the initiation of the majority of observed contracting processes" (p. 103).

Moreover, she found that with respect to out-sourcing legal services, senior managers, upon arrival, actively sought to acquire personal trust and loyalty by replacing existing senior legal advisors (those with institutional memory) with those with whom they had known prior to accepting their current positions at the hospital. These legal service out-sourcing decisions were made by processes that were typically "1) noncompetitive; 2) costs not specified in advance; and 3) interpersonal in their orientation" (Heinbuch, 1994, p.192).

Clearly, a leader's arrival in a new organization is fraught with uncertainty and ambiguity. It is a legitimate pursuit of the successful leader to seek to acquire and retain power. The self-preserving act of turfprocurement and protection is a requirement of leadership. At issue, is the extent to which these activities, particularly exemplified by aggressive and ill-considered from an organizational perspective, are manifest in leaders out-sourcing decisions. In short, while necessary to effective leadership, it is a matter of which turf is protected or acquired, how and why.

In summary, neither helpful nor harmful in and of itself, aggression is an underlying force that should be recognized and carefully managed if it is to serve leaders in their organizational activities and decisions. And, like narcissism, it plays an important role in leadership. For example, when mastered, it can be productively used to provide guidance and direction to others, and toward leaders' management of their organizational environment and experience. Leaders should engage in aggressive actions designed to make the organization more efficient and effective.

POWER BLINDNESS AND ADAPTIVE DENIAL

Most leaders speak of their out-sourcing decisions as if they were purely guided by organizational interests, offering practical and economic rationales, even when colleagues suggest these were not the case. The previous discussion explored how some out-sourcing decisions may be understood with respect to leaders' psychological power issues. Accepting that leaders generally do not make decisions in a vacuum, then others must participate. How do seemingly unwise, a-rationally justified major out-sourcing decisions come to be made?

It is suggested, here, that in concert with leaders conscious and unconscious power issues are followers and colleagues supporting the leaders existing power drives and belief systems. By failing to question the bases of a leader's decision, they inactively participate or unwittingly assist the leader in developing *power blindness,* the inability of a leader to access the underlying reasons for their decisions, and engaging in adaptive denial. In effect, they create a self-feeding power-addiction that reduces leaders' decisions to those absent informed input from knowledgeable others.

Denial is often viewed as a problem—"an unproductive way of coping with unpleasant realities" (Levinson, 1986, p. 39).

However, denial is a neutral term, its correctness or incorrectness is situationally dependent. Adaptive denial can be a constructive and essential defense mechanism when one is faced with a decision for which there exists no other alternative (Levinson, 1986). For example, when one has been diagnosed with a incurable illness However, by failing to question leaders' out-sourcing decisions, others allow the leader to be consumed by their power needs, ones driven by narcissism and displayed through aggression. As a result, leaders take part in seemingly valid adaptive denial, as in the a-rational out-sourcing decision, because, from their power-blind perspective, there is no other choice.

CONCLUSION

The underlying premise of this article is that current understandings and decisions about out-sourcing can be enhanced and refined if the topic were also considered and localized at the human level. This is accomplished by integrating ideas and theories that recognize the psychological dimension of leaders' decisions.

Leader-corrupting influences of conscious and unconscious psychological forces related to power have historically been the domain of philosophy (Kets de Vries, 1991). Plato long ago offered a depiction of an ideal society, one lead by the philosopher-king, a wise, self-reflective, counsel-seeking and heeding leader (Plato, 1955). And, most recognize the insight and warning provided by Lord Acton's phrase, "power corrupts and absolute power corrupts absolutely" (Kets de Vries, 1991).

In more recent times, the field of psychology has developed rich extensions of the philosophical allusions with examinations of unconscious power as a driver in human behavior and decision-making. Yet, this important aspect of humanity as we seek to understand leaders' out-sourcing decisions, is neglected.

Power is not the "last dirty word" (Kanter, 1989; Pfeffer, 1992). Few dispute the requisite need of the ability to acquire and retain power and influence as crucial to becoming and maintaining an organizational leadership position, that is the power to access vital resources and influence others to do the work of the organization (Pfeffer, 1992). Nor do they disavow many of the theoretical premises advanced in the organizational literature that contribute to understandings of leader's out–sourcing decisions. However, to advance our understanding of out-sourcing, leadership behavior, with respect to underlying psychological power issues, should be investigated.

REFERENCES

Bennis, W., & Nanus, B. (1985). *Leaders*. New York: Harper and Row.

Byrne, J. A. (1993, February 8). The virtual corporation. *Business Week*, 98-103.

Covaleski, M. A., & Dirsmith, M. W. (1988, December). An institutional perspective on the rise, social transformation, and fall of a university budget category. *American Science Quarterly, 33*, 562-587.

Cowan, G. L. (1989). A global overview of privatization. J. Sherrod (Ed.), *Privatization: A sourcebook* (pp. 129-138). Detroit, MI: Omnigraphics, Inc.

David, I. T. (1988). Privatization in America. *The municipal yearbook*, (pp. 43-55). Washington D.C.: International City–County Management Association.

DeHoog, R. H. (1984). *Contracting out for human services: Economic, political and organizational perspectives.* Albany: State University of New York Press.

DiMaggio, P. J., & Powell, W. W. (1991). The iron cage revisited: Institutional isomorphism and collective rationality. In W.W. Powell & P. J. DiMaggio (Eds.), *The new institutionalism in organizational analysis* (pp. 63-82). Chicago: University of Chicago Press.

Donahue, J. D. (1989). *The privatization decision: Public ends, private means.* New York: Basic Books.

Downs, G. W., & Larkey, P. D. (1986). *The search for government efficiency: From hubris to helplessness.* New York: Random House.

Drucker, P. F. (1968). *The age of discontinuity: Guidelines for our changing society.* New York: Harper & Row.

Drucker, P. F. (1989). *The new realities: In government and politics/in economics and business/in society and world view.* New York: Harper & Row.

Eisenhardt, K. M. (1985, February). Control: Organizational and economic approaches. *Management Science*, 134-149.

Eisenhardt, K. M. (1989). Agency theory: An assessment and review. *Academy of Management Review, 14,* 57-74.

Freud, S. (1914). On Narcissism. In J. Strachey (translator and editor), *The standard edition of the complete psychological works of Siqmund Freud,* vol. XII. London: Hogarth Press and Institute of Psychoanalysis, 1957.

Handy, C. B. (1990). *The age of unreason.* Boston: Harvard Business
     School Press.
Heinbuch, S. E. (1993). *Contractors' perceptions of bases for managers'
     positive decisions to contract.* Unpublished raw data.
Heinbuch, S. E. (1993). Walk the talk: Applying TQ principles to an
     element of management development-contracting.
     Journal of Management Development, 12 (7), 60-70.
Heinbuch, S. E. (1994). *Contracting processes in nonprofit hospitals:
     Issues and implications.* Doctoral dissertation, New York
     University, New York.
Huey, J. (1994, February 21). The new post–heroic leadership.
     Fortune, 42-50.
Kanter, R. M. (1989). *When giants learn to dance: Mastering the
     challenge, strategy, management and careers in the 1990's.*
     New York: Simon & Schuster.
Kets de Vries, M. F. R. (1980). *Organizational paradoxes:
     Clinical approaches to management.* New York:
     Tavistock.
Kets de Vries, M. F. R. (1991, July). Whatever happened to the
     philosopher-king?: The Leader's addiction to Power.
     Journal of Management Studies, 28 (4), 339-351.
Kohut, H. (1971). *The analysis of the self.* New York: International
     Universities Press.
Kohut, H. (1977). *The restoration of the self.* New York: International
     Universities Press.
Kotter, J. P. (1988). *The leadership factor.* New York: Free Press.
Kotter, J. P. (1990, May, June). What leaders really do. *Harvard Busi-
     ness Review, 68,* 103-111.
Levinson, H. (1986) . *Ready, fire, aim: Avoiding management by im-
     pulse.* Cambridge: Levinson Institute.
Levinson, H. (1992). *Career mastery: Keys to taking charge of your
     career throughout your work life.* San Francisco: Berret
     Koehler.
Meissner, W. W. (1981) . A note on narcissism. *The Psychoanalytic
     Quarterly, L (1),* 77-89.
Meyer, J. W., & Rowan, B. (1991). Institutionalized organizations:
     Formal structure as myth and ceremony. Chapter in
     W. W. Powell, & P. J. DiMaggio (Eds.), *The new institutionalism
     in organizational analysis* (pp. 41-62). Chicago:University
     of Chicago Press.
Meyer, J. W., & Scott, W. R. (1983) . *Organizational environments,
     ritual and rationality.* Beverly Hills: Sage.

Mick, S. S., & Conrad, D. A. (1988, September). The decision to vertically integrate in health care organizations. *Hospital & Health Services Administration, 33* (3), 345-360.

Oliver, C. (1991, January). Strategic responses to institutional processes. *Academy of Management Review, 16,* 145-179.

Osborne, D., & Gaebler, T. (1992). *Reinventing government: How the entrepreneurial spirit is transforming the public sector.* Reading, MA: Addison-Wesley.

Pfeffer, J. (1992, December). Understanding power in organizations. *California Management Review,* 29-50.

Plato (1955). *The Republic.* Translated by H.D.P. Lee.Harmondsworth: Penguin.

Prager, J. (1992, October 15). Contracting out: Theory and practice. *Economic Research Reports: RR92-50.* C.V. Starr Center for Applied Economics: New York University Faculty of Arts and Science, Department of Economics.

Quinn, J. B., Doorley, T. L., & Paquette, P. C. (1991). The intellectual holding company: Structuring around core activities. In J.B. Quinn & H. Mintzberg (Eds.), *The strategy process: Concepts, contexts, cases* (2nd), (pp. 324-330). Englewood Cliffs, N.J.: Prentice Hall.

Rehfuss, J. A. (1989). *Contracting out in government: Guide to working with outside contractors to supply public services.* San Francisco: Jossey-Bass.

Savas, E. S. (1987). *Privatization: The key to better government.* Chatham, N.J.: Chatham House Publishers, Inc.

Scott,W.R .(1987). *Organizations: Rational, natural, and open* (2nd). Englewood Cliffs, N.J.: Prentice Hall.

Tolbert, P. S., & Zucker, L. C. (1983) Institutional sources of change in the formal structure of organizations: The diffusion of civil service reform, 1880-1935. *American Science Quarterly, 28,*22-39.

Williamson, O. E. (1981). The economics of organization: The transaction cost approach. *American Journal of Sociology, 87,* 548-577.

Williamson, O. E. (1975). *Markets and hierarchies: Analysis and antitrust implications.* New York: Free Press.

Zucker, L. G. (1991). The role of institutionalism in cultural persistence. In W. W. Powell, & P. J. DiMaggio (Eds.), *The New institutionalism in organizational analysis* (pp. 83-107). Chicago: University of Chicago Press.

WHAT IS LEADERSHIP? RISK TAKING IN A MARKET ECONOMY

By
Charles Udell

This past summer, in addition to my full-time occupation, I had the pleasure of being an assistant coach for my eleven year old son's little league baseball team. At the end of the season, the parents of the team members gave each coach a little token of appreciation for our efforts. My gift was a picture of a baseball player sliding into second base with the inscription: *Opportunity always involves some risk. You can't steal second base and keep your foot safe on first.* I believe this quote states very well what leadership is all about and what it takes for businesses world-wide to be successful. That is, to have a thriving business, the leadership of a company must be able to take advantage of opportunity. And when the decision must be made to be able to take advantage of opportunity, not all of the facts are known. This means the corporate leader must take a chance. Decisions must be made even though there is unknown information. There is risk because while there is a chance the decision may be a good one, there is also the chance it may be a bad one.

So, in a market economy, what can a business leader do to insure that when risk is taken, the chances the decision to do so is the right one is greater than the it being a wrong one? I believe the leader must focus on the following to minimize risk is taken at the wrong time:
- education and training of the leader himself/herself and support staff,
- understanding other people and building rapport,
- developing a vision & mission for the business,
- being adaptable to change, able to make decisions that are not popular, and
- establishing measurement criteria to create a learning vehicle.

THE NEED FOR EDUCATION

Business education is one important component in risk taking.

The leader has to know when it is appropriate to take risk, when it is not, and what are the degrees of risk. As the song writer Kenny Rogers has said, "You got to know when to deal and know when to hold." A leader does not only have to grow personally, but he/she has to be able to grow the organization's people as well.

There are many examples of respected leaders who do not stop educating themselves and their people. An example is the president of a 17 distribution center automotive parts warehouse and parts store company in the eastern and middle United States. His business is extremely successful. Yet, he never hesitates to take advantage of a new seminar where he and his people can learn an additional skill or idea. He and his staff have used new information from these seminars to create several innovative marketing opportunities. It is so easy for managers to say: "I do not have time for education. It is a luxury. We are so busy meeting customer requirements, paying suppliers, manufacturing products." But this is the short-sighted view. True leadership means taking the long-term view and in this case making time to improve himself and his staff. If he or his people do not understand the forces that drive a market economy, understand how to determine what his customers want, or understand how to determine customer demand and what to do to meet that demand, then how will he be able to analyze when to make a risky decision, or when not to. Education is a cornerstone and starting point on which the skills of a leader are built. It will help the leader determine if an idea makes sense or if it does not.

UNDERSTANDING OTHER PEOPLE & BUILDING RAPPORT

Another important element to help a leader understand risk is that of understanding other people and building rapport with them– especially with those people who work with him. This includes the basic leadership skills of being honest and building trust. A leader must tell the truth – even when it can hurt him or others around him. This is such a basic point to rapport building that without honor, the rest of these issues are meaningless. And along with integrity, the leader must act in a consistent and predictable manner. So what does this have to do with risk taking? Everything – education will provide the leader with basic skills. But, he will have to rely on others who work with him to provide information that can help in his decisions. A leader must have people working with him who are not "yes" people. That is, they will give the leader the bad as well as the good news. They will challenge the leader and make him think. They will tell the leader the truth and not be fearful of losing their positions or that the leader will think ill of them.

For example, as the president of a trade association educational arm, the Automotive Warehouse Distributors Association (AWDA) University, I am very dependent on what the association members feel they need in the way of managerial education. Many of our warehouse distributor members have purchased automotive parts stores. They have told me they need seminars on how to operate these stores. At a recent association committee meeting, I presented several ideas regarding store operations training. Some were well received, but others were not. The members attending told me why some ideas would not work and proceeded to voice their thoughts on ideas they believed would work. After this meeting, I felt very good that we had developed a rapport and atmosphere in which these members felt comfortable challenging me. The end result of this meeting is a change of direction on store operations training. Setting an atmosphere that allowed people to speak their mind greatly reduced the risk that our direction would be a bad one. A leader must develop and maintain a culture within his business so that his people will give the input that is needed – not just the good news – but the bad as well. And, without the building of rapport, this will not happen. Along with the leader creating an atmosphere to encourage his group to challenge him and make him think, the leader also must set an atmosphere to encourage his people to take risks, to fail, and to learn from their mistakes. In many companies in the United States and other market economy countries this is not happening. The leader in many of these businesses has allowed an atmosphere of fear to develop. In such an enveroment people will not offer ideas or take reasonable chances because they believe if they are wrong and if they make a mistake, they will lose their jobs. The result of this atmosphere is stagnation, loss of market leadership, and loss of profit.

In the mid-western United States, there is a mid- size pharmaceutical company that, during the early and mid 1980's, was one of the most profitable in their industry. In one major market, they were the market leader. They licensed a drug from a Japanese pharmaceutical company that had a questionable chance of success. Four major drug companies had turned down this opportunity. However, our midwestern company's leaders felt comfortable in their environment and they took the risk. The result – market leadership and record profit.

But in the late 1980's a change of management and atmosphere occurred. People working for this company grew fearful. They saw that risk takers would be punished if they were wrong. They saw back-stabbing started to occur. Today, this company is not a nice place in which to work. People no longer make suggestions. They no longer tell their management anything about an idea but "yes" – no matter what the merits of a proposal are. The people are fearful for their jobs and the company's profits have decreased. A leader must create an atmosphere where it is safe to make a mistake and learn from it. This will encourage people to take reasonable risks and seek opportunity.

DEVELOPING A VISION AND A MISSION

Now, before the reader will think that a successful leader in a company in a market driven economy should permit any risk taking to occur, I should emphasize this is not the case. Risk taking, while it must be encouraged, must occur within a framework. And what is this framework–this set of limits? It is a business's vision and mission. There are many seminars and books written on how to develop these state-ments. That's where education is a must. All we will state here about these statements is that *a company's vision tells what the company wants to be*. A company's *mission tells how this vision will be achieved*. And the leader must encourage – not demand, the participation of key employees in the development of both of these statements. These give the leader and his management team a set of limits to help in the risk taking decision.

The vision of the AWDA University is to provide managerial education for the members of AWDA. The mission states this education will be provided through in-class seminars and self-study programs that are affordable to our members. So when a proposal a year ago was made to the University leadership to develop technical education for garage technicians, this was rejected. Technician training was outside the vision of managerial education. On the other hand, when the proposal was made to develop senior executive level business education for our member companies, this was a very easy decision to make. It is a new area and a new market for us – the senior executive level. This proposal is consistent with our vision and mission, and we believe the chances of it being successful were much greater than if it were outside the vision and mission scope.

BEING ADAPTABLE TO CHANGE AND MAKING THE UNPOPULAR DECISION

Another leadership quality we must look at is leaders must be adaptable to change and possibly make decisions that are not popular. These may be very risky decisions to make, but at times the viability of a business can be significantly effected by this decision. A leader, having some of the qualities we discussed earlier, will help decrease the riskiness of this decision. I know of the president of an automotive parts warehouse distribution company in the south-central United States who was faced with this type of a decision. This leader had just started in his new position. The prior president was asked to leave. The new leader looked at his company's sales and profits and decided that in the many markets they served, prices would have to be raised. Distributing automotive parts in many areas is a commodity type of business where price is important. If a customer does not like the price of a part from one distributor, he can very easily shop around until he finds the part he needs at the lower price he wants. So, the decision this new president had to make was not without risk. It was not a popular one with not only his customers, but also his sales force. Raising prices will make it more difficult to maintain current business. But, this leader remembered an important concept from his education and experience, which was, "the only reason to make a sale is to make a profit." An unprofitable customer is worse than no customer. The decision was made. The sales force had to adapt to changes in the environment. This decision was made over two years ago. It was a good one and helped to return this distribution company to profitability.

ESTABLISHING MEASUREMENT CRITERIA

One other area concerning leadership and risk we should discuss is that of measurement. If the leader has developed rapport with his people that encourages risk taking, he must be prepared for and no doubt realizes mistakes will be made. And while the rapport building leader will not punish any subordinate because of his taking a reasonable risk and making a mistake, he will definitely want to know what went wrong and why the mistake was made. Education is, as discussed, a critical element for the leader and his staff – and this is one way to learn what went wrong. Another method is that of measurement. Without measurement one does not have a base point from which to learn. For instance, if a manager makes a decision to enter a new market, he does so on the strength of proposed market size, sales, profit, as well as what it would take to promote and advertise his new products. He would then want to track these variables to see how the actual sales, expenses, and profits compare with the estimates. The manager would then be able to determine what went right and what did not. Armed with this information, the risk to the leader could be reduced the next time a market entry decision needs to be made. Other measurement examples are measuring factory productivity before and after making a decision to expand a plant.

CONCLUSIONS

In a market economy one definition of leadership is how comfortable and willing is a leader in making risky and possibly uncomfortable decisions. If these decisions are not made and risk is not taken, then opportunity can be missed. How can a leader reduce risk levels so that opportunity can be taken advantage of? The leader can continue to educate himself and his managers; build rapport among himself and his managers so he can receive information regarding both sides of an issue; establish a vision and a mission statement to build a framework for decision making; be adaptable to change and be able to make the unpopular decision; and be able to measure what happens so he knows what happens successfully and what does not. By reducing risk levels, better decisions can be made with the result: more opportunity and more profit.

AMERICAN LEADERSHIP AND TEAMWORK
—FOR APPLICATION IN RUSSIAN ORGANIZATIONS

By
Harold Lazarus
Jame Shanahan

One does not have to be an ornithologist to conclude that the behavior of geese may provide useful lessons for leaders and subordinates in Russian organizations. For example, as each goose flaps its wings, it creates an "Uplift" for the following bird. By flying in a "V" formation, the whole flock adds more flying range than if each bird flew alone. In human terms, people who share a common direction can get where they are going more quickly and more easily because they are using the momentum of the group. When a goose falls out of formation, it suddenly feels the drag and resistance of trying to fly alone, and quickly gets back into formation to take advantage of the "lifting power" of the bird immediately in front. Teams of humans might, similarly, choose to stay in formation with those who are headed where we want to go.

When the lead goose gets tired, it rotates back in formation and another goose flies at the lead position. Russian executives might also take turns doing the hard tasks and sharing leadership with others. Geese in formation honk from behind to encourage those up front to maintain their speed. Similarly, communication from behind in Russian organizations needs to encourage, not discourage those ahead of us. When a goose gets sick or wounded or shot, two geese drop out of formation and follow it down to help and protect the disabled goose. They stay with the goose until it is either able to fly again or it dies. Then they launch out on their own with another formation or catch up with the flock. Russians can learn from geese to help teammates who are having trouble.

WHY APPLY TEAMWORK IN RUSSIAN ORGANIZATIONS?
American experiences suggest that benefits accrue from teamwork; for example, decline in employee turnover, increase in productivity, in customer satisfaction and in corporate profits. The General Electric plant in Shelby, North Carolina, uses a *team system* to change product models a dozen times daily to produce lighting panel boards. Productivity increased by 250 percent compared with General Electric plants that produced the same products on an *individual basis*. While productivity skyrocketed, employee turnover fell from 15 percent in the first year of the new team system's operation to 6 percent four years later" (Serpa, 1991).

A recent survey on teamwork, administered by the American Society for Training and Development, found that: (1) productivity improved in 77 percent of the respondents' companies (2) quality improvements due to teamwork were reported in 72 percent of the companies (3) waste was reduced in 55 percent of the firms (4) job satisfaction improved in 65 percent of the respondents' firms and (5) customer satisfaction improved in 57 percent of the companies. Additional benefits cited by the respondents included more efficient production scheduling, improved production goal setting and increased ability of team members to resolve their own disputes (Montebello & Buzzotta, 1993). Organizations, however, should approach teamwork realistically, since results of teamwork are not instantaneously achieved. Teamwork results are achieved over time through the *cooperation* of team members. How can team members in Russian organizations be encouraged to cooperate?

One approach is the use of games. These are based on the performance of team players and the principles of team sports; for example, cooperation and teamwork. Why do we say this? Because many employees in Russia are probably interested in and motivated by team sports and games: the competition, challenge, and winning .

The sports team, like the business team, could consist of a group of individuals working together in a cooperative environment to achieve predetermined goals. These goals may be winning the basketball game for the basketball team or meeting the sales quotas for the sales team. In either case, incentives can work because they are that "something extra" employees may not strive for on a daily basis. Employees not only gain something extra, but they have a little fun and excitement in aiming for high performance and corporate goals. However, as the great American baseball manager, Casey Stengel, once said "It's easy to get the players. Gettin' 'em to play *together,* that's the hard part." Team members need to develop into a cohesive unit in order to achieve high performance and organizational goals.

WHO DEVELOPS AND LEADS THE COHESIVE TEAM?

The effective team leader does. A common metaphor for the leader is the symphony conductor. The manager of a team can be seen as the conductor, while the employees are the musicians. Together they can play harmoniously. In order to do so, the leader of an effective team should demonstrate a wide array of skills required for attaining organizational objectives.

According to Resnick (1992) there are 5 tools team leaders can utilize in order to attain organizational objectives:

1.   Effective leaders need to encourage their people to create

      cooperative environments that spark excitement, enthusiasm and synergy.

2.   Excellent leaders set and communicate clear visions. Team

      members understand these visions and accept them.

3.   Excellent leaders translate these visions into clearly-defined,

      measurable goals. These goals are challenging, yet attainable. Employees know what is expected and the criteria for success.

4.   Effective leaders provide clear feedback. Everyone knows where they stand. Feedback is the most powerful form of communication provided to employees by leaders.

5.   Excellent leaders give recognition. They notice not only the individual performances of employees, but more importantly the overall performances of the team and organization. If the team and organization is successful, everyone is a winner.

      If Russian employees feel their team leader has created a solid team environment, those employees will take the initiative and strive for the teams' goals.

HOW CAN GAMES BE TIED TO DAILY JOBS?

The following three examples attract the attention of employees and can be used as motivational vehicles in Russian organizations.

Example # 1

An American client, who owns a firm that sells and repairs photocopiers, presented the following series of problems. He said that he was not training and motivating salespeople, and his labor turnover was much higher than he would have liked, since many potentially good sales people quit for lack of training and effective supervision. The client admitted also that he was not training sales managers. What was he doing? He promoted his best sales representatives to sales management positions. However, without proper training, those sales managers were ineffective, inefficient supervisors. Consequently, they either quit or were fired. What did this mean? It meant that he lost his potentially effective sales managers, just as he lost his effective salespeople and that his employees were unmotivated. "Tell us something about your sales force," we asked our client. "They love sports, they really love sports," the client replied. "How can you make use of that information?" we asked."One thing I could do," the American client said, is to use different sports in different seasons as competition for several teams of salespeople and sales managers in order to motivate them. In the baseball season, I could have several teams of baseball players. A salesperson who sells one of our small photocopiers would hit a 'single.' A salesperson who sells a larger photocopier would be credited with having hit a 'double.' Similarly, a salesperson who sells an entire copier system would get credit for a 'home run.' "How would this work?" we asked. As consultants, we did not give this client the answers. Instead, *we drew the answers from this creative executive by asking questions.* It was obvious this client understood his subordinates far better than we did. Our function, therefore, was to help him prepare and use rational solutions to his problems. That is exactly what our client did. "How would baseball games solve your problems?" we asked again. "Don't you see? If we put a 'heavy hitter' in as leader (captain) of each of the teams, that 'heavy hitter,' that effective salesperson, would be required to train less effective sales people in order to win the baseball game," the client explained. "What would be the incentive for winning this simu-lated baseball competition?" we asked. "That's easy, I would give all the members of the winning team major league baseball tickets for them and their families. The cost to me would be small, while this incentive for sports enthusiasts could boost sales tremendously. They would not lose their bonuses, and, in addition to their bonuses, they would also get baseball tickets in the baseball season, and hockey tickets in the hockey season, and basketball tickets in the basketball season," the client explained with great enthusiasm. This client and other American executives realized they can profitably increase their sales by supplementing their regular salary plans with sports incentives.

Example # 2

A similar motivational vehicle used for American employ-ees is the creation of a "football game." As predetermined offensive yardage, they can move towards "touchdowns" which are worth 7 points. Team penalties (incorrectly filled out orders, incomplete sales presentations) give the opposing team a "field goal" (three points). The highest scoring team at the end of the sales campaign is the win-ner. In the United States, this type of contest is most effective when affiliated with very important games, such as the World Cup games, the Super Bowl, etc. (Worman, 1991).

Example # 3

"Most salespeople are sports addicts, since selling is a challenge; hence, create teams and run a sports pool. Contestants are salespeople. Post scores of teams weekly or semi-weekly. The goal here is to encourage a more intense interchange of account information among team members to increase sales. Co-incidentally, to establish new territory quotas, establish a ground zero level and, at the end of the fiscal or calendar year, a run off champion team based on units sold" (Brookman, 1993). In the United States, the champion team is awarded football tickets, or tennis tickets, depending on the timing of the game.

Whatever type of creative game is chosen, a leader should reward every team, so that a negative atmosphere is not developed. For example, if there are three teams then have 3 different sports incentives. The **#1** ranking team might get an expense-paid weekend trip to the French Open tennis tournament each year, the **#2** ranking team might get basketball playoff tickets and the **#3** ranking team might get baseball tickets. Thus, the average and below average teams can win something, while the top performing team is even more richly rewarded for its superior results. All three teams are rewarded and, thus, team morale and motivation is maintained since each team has received *some* recognition.

Leaders should consider rewarding all members of a team equally. "One group of researchers found that distributing 80 percent of the available rewards on a group basis and assigning the remaining 20 percent to the most productive worker in the group resulted in significantly lower productivity than distributing all the rewards on a group basis" (Herrick, 1990). Unequal distribution of team rewards can inhibit team morale and stir up conflict among team members, thus reducing their cohesiveness and devotion to the common goal.

BEWARE OF POST-GAME LETDOWN

After games have been completed, your organization should be aware of the potential adverse effects of diminishing performance levels of employees. "One of management's biggest concerns regarding contests is post-contest letdown. The fear that performance levels of your employees will diminish after a contest is a genuine concern" (Worman, 1991). In order to maintain high performance in a Russian work force, a series of short-term and long-term games should be implemented, so that team games overlap. This will help maintain employee excitement and enthusiasm for team games. Likewise, Russian team members will realize that a new game will begin shortly and there is a new chance for winning that top reward. There will always be a new excitement and a new sports incentive to strive towards.

WHAT IS THE COST OF *NOT* HAVING TEAMWORK IN AN ORGANIZATION?

In the United States, one cost is labor turnover. Organizations are consistently faced with many direct and indirect costs related to employee turnover. Sailors and Sylvestre (1994) divided employee turnover costs into two categories: visible and invisible (hidden) costs.

Visible costs are those directly associated with the cost of employee turnover and account for about 20 percent of the total costs of employee turnover. Visible costs include the costs of recruiting and selecting new employees, advertising expenses, interviewing costs, and on-the-job training costs for the new employees. Invisible costs account for 80 percent or more of the total costs of employee turnover. These costs are not identified directly as costs of employee turnover. They are usually classified instead as inefficiency associated with the incoming employee, inefficiency of the co-workers of the incoming employee, inefficiency of the departing employee, inefficiency of the co-workers of the departing employee, and inefficiency of the position being temporarily filled.

Consider the following case study by Kazemek and Shomaker (1990) which shows some of the costs of employee turnover. A 350 bed urban American hospital, experiencing annualized turnover of 20 to 25 percent, incurred the following turnover costs in one year:

- Recruitment and advertising for replacement staff:$400,000;
- Agency or contract personnel to fill staff vacancies: $2.3 million;
- Non-productive staff time of newly hired employees during orientation, training, and assimilation: $300,000;
- Cost of human resource and inservice staff to recruit, train, and orient new employees: $350,000.

These sample expenses total $3.35 million, and while this specific American case may not apply to every Russian organization, it does demonstrate that costs related to turnover can be significant to an organization's financial results.

CONCLUSION

If organizations in Russia have employees who are sports enthusiasts, we suggest the leaders consider applying games of the type mentioned earlier in order to enhance team performance.

Why do we say this? Because, at least in the United States, the use of games can be an effective way to motivate and train employees and leaders, reduce labor turnover, increase sales and share of the market, and profits.

Appropriate games can do a great deal for a Russian leader's organization. But just as Russian organizations evolve and change, so too must their incentive programs. A successful program today may not be useful five years down the road. Therefore, games should be modified as Russian employees' and leaders' interests change.

REFERENCES

Brookman, J. (1993, June). Signage. *The American Salesman,* 3-6.

Herrick, N. (1990). *Joint management and employee participation.* San Francisco: Jossey-Bass Inc. Publishers.

Kazemek, E., & Shomaker, B. (1990, August). Reducing turnover can bring bottom line results. *Healthcare Financial Management,* 80.

Montebello, A.,& Buzzota, V. (1993, March). Work teams that work. *Training and Development,* 59-64.

Resnick, H. (1992, July). Inspiring your work force. *Cellular Business,* 22-24.

Sailors, J.F., & Sylvestre, J. (1994, March-April). Reduce the cost of employee turnover. *Journal of Compensation and Benefits,* 32-34.

Serpa, R. (1991, April). Teamwork starts at the top. *Chief Executive,* 30-33.

Worman, D. (1991, October). Motivation by Stimulation. *Telemarketing,* 80-83.

THE *OTHER* SIDE OF JAPANESE LEADERSHIP

by
Stephanie Chaffins, Harold Fuqua, Jr.,
Joseph P. Cangemi, Stephanie Crabtree,
Jasmine Baali, Casimir J. Kowalski
R. Wilburn Clouse

Japanese leadership style has been regarded by many, particularly in the popular press, as being superior to American leadership style. In the 1950s, the legend "Made in Japan" left people snickering. U.S. markets were flooded with inferior products. Today, Japanese products command respect, especially in the automobile business and in electronics. The apparent success of the Japanese leadership style has led to the trade deficit between the United States and Japan (Katzenstein, 1991). Apparently, many believe if American companies would adopt Japanese leadership methods, they would produce a cure-all for the problems American firms have had to face in the recent past (Alston, 1985). It has become a common belief that adopting Japanese leadership principles within American firms would result in our ability to regain the edge once held in productivity and to improve quality and morale among employees. Wolf (1983) observed a flaw in this popular opinion which portrays Japanese leadership philosophy as superior to Western leadership philosophy. He asserted this philosophy was a distorted view of the true situation. This prevailing myth is portrayed by the lords of Japanese corporations. The Japanese use this myth to persuade others who are not Japanese that their leadership techniques are superior, when in fact this may be just an illusion (Wolf, 1983). While *some* components of Japanese leadership philosophy may work for *some* American firms, *attempted adoption of their overall philosophy would be a mistake* (Zemke, 1981).

Recently, the media has been depicting another side of Japanese leadership. Japan is neither the corporate utopia nor a working hell. Like any society, it has strengths and weaknesses. Newspaper stories tell us how eleven-year-old Japanese children are committing suicide (Death from Overwork) and how the Japanese family is breaking apart apparently due to working conditions, pressure, job transfers, and inflexible educational systems.

Less emphasized aspects of Japanese leadership will be reviewed in this article to explore difficulties and weaknesses of Japanese leadershship techniques, including decision-making processes and quality-control circles, seniority-based promotion, limited inter-organizational mobility and transfer, mandatory retirement, utilizing part-time/temporary employees, discrimination against females, and the psychological implications of such leadership behavior on employees.

The authors had one motive in researching and writing this article: to explore aspects of Japanese leadership behavior not commonly presented in either the popular or professional literature. No desire to detract from the many accomplishments of Japanese organizations, or their leaders, is intended.

IMAGE BUILDING VERSUS REALITY

According to Eberts and Eberts (1995), in Japan everyone is aware of the difference between *tatamae* (the image) and the *honne* (the reality). To the Japanese, the image often is more important and better than the reality; if the image is bad, then the reality must be worse. The image of Americans and other foreigners presented in films in Japan and presented to the Japanese people by the politicians generally is one of lack of discipline and laziness. Japanese leaders are well aware that these distorted images, plus the images of violence portrayed in American movies (often shown in prime time so Japanese children can view them), are developing powerful, negative images of Americans and other foreigners in the perception of both Japanese children and adults (Eberts & Eberts, 1995). The negative images of foreigners, particularly Americans, apparently are most beneficial when it comes to Japanese consumer practice, because these negative images affect the perception of the quality of foreign and American-made products and of the society in which they are made. How can a violent society such as the United States, as portrayed in such movies as *Robocop,* with its laziness and lack of discipline, produce quality products? Such image building deliberately created by Japanese leadership has lead Japanese citizens to avoid purchasing foreign-made products, to the benefit of Japanese industrialists and businesses.

Japanese leaders utilize *tatemae,* as mentioned above, quite effectively in keeping American and other foreign-made products out of Japan by creating the illusion that the Japanese products are better. This illusion is strengthened by obstacles, rules and regulations placed in the way of foreign-made products entering Japan and competing with Japanese products. The illusion of foreign-made products being inferior to Japanese-made products has been shown to be a manufactured myth contrived by Japan's political leaders because of the fear that many Japanese companies are, in reality, *not* competitive with foreign firms and would lose out to them if forced to compete with them (McCarron, 1994). Japanese leadership creates the image for the public that its markets are within an open market system, knowing full well the reality is quite different (Eberts & Eberts, 1995).

THE ILLUSION OF HARMONY AND THE YAKUSA

Many Japanese invest in the Japanese stock market, though not expecting to receive dividends as American investors do. The pay-off for Japanese investors is anticipated to come through appreciation in a stock's value when the stock is sold. This worked well in the past when the Japanese market flourished, but in recent time the value of many stocks plunged-causing, in all probability, distress among shareholders. Shareholders in Japan, however, are expected to be and stay happy. They are expected to invest in a company for the long term and to pay scant attention to quarterly losses. At annual shareholders' meetings, shareholders are expected to come in a happy frame of mind and so is the management of the company. Together they are expected to show a harmonious, happy relationship. Shareholders are not supposed to question the company's leadership or in any way do anything that would negate the image of a happy relationship between the parties. To insure that this does not happen, Japanese industrial leaders, on occasion, seek outside help by calling on the *yakusa,* the Japanese version of the *mafia,* to maintain the image of harmony between shareholders and company leadership. Japanese leaders do not wish to answer shareholders' inquiries or explain their decisions at these meetings. Should some shareholders become unhappy with this arrangement, the *yakusa* and other similar type groups are called upon to enforce the image of harmony and happiness (Van Wolferen, 1989). These groups set up "research institutes," and their members are "consultants." Company leadership pays to keep the "research institutes" in business, which in turn will send their "consultants" to a potentially disharmonizing and unhappy stockholder's home to encourage him, in a rather "gentlemanly" way, to adjust his attitude for the upcoming shareholders' meeting (Van Wolferen, 1989). This practice has given rise to an industry of extortion of Japanese leaders. These" research institutes" carry a big stick; if companies do not pay their demanded sum, then company leaders can be expected to be grilled for hours throughout shareholders' meetings, thereby destroying the image of harmony and happiness between shareholders and company leadership. Van Wolferen stated there were 6,300 such firms in Japan in the early 1980s.

DECISION MAKING PROCESS

The Japanese decision-making process has been heralded by many as the best one in the world. Hirowaka (1981) stated that Japanese organizations theoretically use a bottom-up procedure whereby many decisions are made in the lower and middle levels of the organization and then are passed on to the higher levels of leadership for the final decision to be reached by consensus. This process of consensus decision-making is much more time consuming than the process used in American firms by which a decision is made at the top and then "sold" to members of the organization. Kotin and Kishimoto (1986) asserted that "contrary to much bally-hooed notions about consensus decision-making, power within large Japanese organizations is highly concentrated at the top" (p. 58). Employees often are unwilling to reject a proposal from upper-level leadership or the group for fear of creating conflict and are pressured strongly to conform to the leader's or group's leaders or group's decision (Yoshimo, 1968; Kuramoto, 1983). Tanaka (1983) found that "few employees dare to voice a minority opinion in Japanese companies" (p. 23). It appears that consensus decision-making is the process utilized when the decisions to be made are of minor consequence and that top-down, group-pressured decisions are, in reality, the norm when the top leadership in the organization or the group wants a particular decision carried out. In Japanese firms, similar to what occurs in U.S. companies, most of the important decisions are made at the top and then *imposed* on the rest of the organization. We use the word "imposed" because in Japanese culture there pervades an incredibly strong attitude of deference toward leadership and toward the group (Doi, 1973; Jordan & Sullivan, 1995). It is entirely uncommon to voice dissent to one's leader or one's group. It would cause great emotional pain for a Japanese employee to tell his superior something contrary to what he knew was his leader's strong position (Feifer, 1992; Kuramoto, 1983). This point is more dramatically made in experiences recounted from World War ll when, in some instances, it was reported that wounded Japanese soldiers committed suicide rather than lose face with their superiors (Feifer, 1992; Kuramoto, 1983) with their families (Lomax, 1995). The appearance of consensus decision making deluded Admiral Yamamoto during World War II prior to the battle of Midway Island in 1942, causing him to make a disastrous decision, hence ending Japan's offensive posturing in the Pacific and requiring defensive posturing from this point on until the end of the war. Admiral Yamamoto made the decision to divide the Japanese fleet prior to the Battle of Midway, sending a large segment of the fleet to the Aleutian Islands and the other segment to Midway Island. His staff disagreed with the decision but chose not to differ with the admiral for fear of disappointing him, as he had let it be known ahead of time his preference for the split-fleet battle plan, allowing him, their leader, to make a most disastrous decision (Agawa, 1979; Chaffins et al., 1995; Jordan & Sullivan, 1995). This kind of thinking–obedience to authority and fear of disappointing and conflicting with authority–is still very much in evidence today in Japan. "Japanese subordinates do not stand up to their leaders and disagree with them face to face. They might disagree behind their back, but never to their face."* Nagase (Lomax, 1995) openly states, "There must be a break with all vestiges of the [Japanese] cult to obedience" (p. 272).

FLAWED DECISION MAKING

Japanese decision making is often flawed. Byham (1993) noted, "Japanese managers are delegated so little authority they have no choice but to negotiate with subordinates and peers through a consensus process to get anything done at all" (p. 13). He suggested that Japanese *lower level managers* admit that making decisions individually is too risky for them. This process leads to the group's sharing of responsibility for a decision which might lead to failure and avoids the single individual's losing face or taking responsibility for a decision which has failed (Byham, 1993).

It is a *myth* that Japanese corporations make better decisions than American firms. The Japanese process often is slow and inefficient. Business opportunities often are lost during the process of trying to reach a consensus. There are no quantifiable data available to suggest that the decision-making process in Japanese organizations is superior to the decision making process in American firms (Stewart et al., 1986). Johnson (1977) suggested that the Japanese firms in the United States which he studied *did not* practice more bottom-up communication than American firms.

> * Direct quote given by a leader to the authors with much experience in Japanese–owned organizations in the United States and abroad.

QUALITY CIRCLES

Quality control circles (QCC's), one of the highlights of Japanese leadership style, were actually developed by W. Edwards Deming, an American management consultant, to solve Japanese leadership problems (Tanaka, 1983). Though many believe that QCC's are efficient and helpful in increasing productivity and quality, some researchers have found different evidence. Ouchi (1981) observed QCC's involve from two to ten employees who are permanently assigned to circles. All employees, whether temporary or permanent, are "encouraged" to participate. Cole (1980) stated:

> QCC's do not always perform in Japanese companies as they do on paper. Because of Japan's remarkable economic success, we have a tendency to see the Japanese as miracle men who never make mistakes. Some of their common problems are: for all the emphasis on voluntarism in a QCC activity, there is a great deal of top-down control in many companies. A significant number of workers see the circle as a burden imposed on them by management rather than their own program. Thus, the circles often take on somewhat of a coercive aspect that is not the best incentive for motivating workers to produce innovative behavior. (p. 26)

In the U.S. and outside Japan, the achievements of quality circles are more limited and do not produce the results proclaimed by many consultants and enthusiastic organizational members (Zemke, 1981). Alston (1986) found that one third of QCC's contributed little or nothing toward improving the company and relatively few are, in fact, effective. From this we can infer QCC's are not all that mangers and authors have made them out to be.

Total quality must be a virtue everyone acknowledges in today's companies. Miller and Cangemi (1993) pointed out that quality circles and total quality management often fail in organizations because managers cannot delegate quality. Every employee in the organization must have a positive attitude relative to quality. Quality cannot be the responsibility of one department or a few circles trying to produce quality for the entire organization. The attitude which prevails among managers relieves them from accountability to increase quality. Miller and Cangemi (1993) further argued that "many managers simply fail to recognize that quality really must be the foundation of their company's strategy and strategic planning, as well as its daily operations" (p. 42).

Most of the experiences within quality circles in the U.S. have been shallow. Few firms have had this system in operation for more than a few years, which makes it impossible to determine if QCC's are compatible with American firms. QCC's will fail in the U.S. unless they are adjusted to meet American conditions. They will have to be adapted to meet the unique needs of American workers and leaders in order to have a chance to work in American corporations (Cole, 1980).

LIFETIME EMPLOYMENT: THE DOWNSIDE

Another negative aspect of Japanese leadership is the employment system known as *Nenko,* which dates back to World War II. Many organizations, particularly the most prestigious and powerful, recruit young high school or college graduates who are paid entry level wages and are promoted *based upon seniority rather than performance.* Employees of these companies are expected to remain with them throughout their careers. Not only are they dependent upon them for their incomes but also for housing and recreation (Tanaka, 1983). This seniority system reduces vertical competition and increases loyalty among employees. The *Nenko* system was summarized by Fujida in this manner:

> During the first half of their working life, employees under the Nenko system are underpaid for the work they have performed, so in order to collect all their rightful wages, they must work until retirement, during which time overpayment for work performed well will compensate for their prior underpayment. (Fujida, 1962)

The *Nenko* system, however, is operative only in the larger Japanese firms, which employ less than 30 percent of Japanese workers (Oh, 1975).

Promotion based primarily upon seniority has led to a new generation of less-committed employees. Seniority is not a good predictor of productivity, according to Lucier et al. (1992). Employees feel they have little individual control in an automatic progression up the corporate hierarchy (Baali et al., 1993). Younger Japanese today are more self-oriented and less concerned about work (Kotkin & Krugman, 1990), are displaying a growing distaste for hard, industrial work, and are moving into non-technical fields. According to Kotkin and Krugman (1990), "One of the basic values clearly in decline is the much commented upon work ethic of the conventional Japanese salary-man" (p. 38). The seniority system has had an increasingly negative effect upon employees. Laver (1991) declared, "Younger Japanese, whose parents and grandparents willingly toiled twelve hours a day, seven days a week, are now seeking jobs that offer shorter working hours, two-day weekends, and greater scope for individual creativity" (p. 48). Motivation and productivity are less important today; hence, employees have become less productive knowing they will be promoted regardless (Lucier et al., 1992).

Lifetime employment creates a surplus of older workers who, if terminated, cannot find other jobs. Employers are forced to "find them something to do" (Tanaka, 1983). Researchers also have found that younger people want to avoid being tied to one company and are willing to work at temporary or part-time jobs to increase their experience and abilities (Yoji, 1988). Fox (1977) proclaimed, "Younger employees are not as conscientious about quality or as willing to be inconvenienced by non-routine demands" (p. 83). He also felt that traditional Japanese firms have "exploited the unique personal selflessness created by their society" (p. 84). In attempting to create a more positive employment system by which employees would feel more secure in their occupations, *it appears the Japanese have evolved into a workforce that is less dedicated, less hard-working, and less submissive.*

Contrary to what many believe, most Japanese are not guaranteed lifetime employment. Only about 30% of the Japanese workers (men) are employed full-time by Japan's larger companies. The remaining 70%, including women and part-time employees, may find themselves working 30 hours per week with no guarantee of lifetime employment. Also, most Japanese workers are forced to retire between the ages of 55 and 60 and have no guarantee for work after retirement (Katzenstein, 1991).

Clive Morton (1994) stated that Western business people have three choices in world wide competition: (1) blind faith, (2) ruthless, short-term exploitation of the market, or (3) world-class performance which gives long-term competitiveness. Morton challenges the bottom-line benefits of applying Japanese style management and techniques to Western factories, especially in the United Kingdom. Morton cites several Japanese companies, such as Mazda, Yamaha, and Mitsubishi, as failing to achieve their aspirations for corporate renewal. Furthermore,

Morton discusses the contrast between "group think" in Japan and "individualism" in the United Kingdom and in the United States.

A CAREER MOVE TO ANOTHER ORGANIZATION–ALMOST IMPOSSIBLE

With promotion based upon seniority, it is difficult to move from one organization to another during one's career. Hence, older employees are discouraged from attempting to switch firms. One who leaves a job is viewed with suspicion by prospective employers because of his/her "lack of loyalty" to the former group. Such an individual would be considered an intruder in a new organization (Tanaka, 1983). Lucier et al. (1992) found switching firms to be an unrealistic alternative. The stigma of lack of loyalty to one's former organization attached to one who attempts to move into a new organization is difficult to overcome.

Within the *Nenko* employment system, mandatory retirement at age 55 also has proven to be a negative aspect of Japanese leadership (Wright, 1979). Employees are forced to resign at the specified age but often are rehired as part-time or temporary workers at reduced wages under yearly contracts (Oh, 1975). Retired workers, called "special employees," lose their access to housing upon termination and are forced to live on much less income than that to which they have been accustomed.

Permanent employees are only one of four types of employees found within Japanese organizations. Retired workers, temporary workers, and subcontract/daily workers also are employed. Temporary workers make up 33 percent of Japan's work force, are paid 50 percent less than permanent employees, and are given no fringe benefits or job guarantees. Subcontract/daily workers are contracted from larger firms to supply labor to smaller firms. They have an even lower status and receive even lower pay (Oh, 1975). Overall, permanent workers affected by the *Nenko* system are very few.

JAPANESE DISCRIMINATION AGAINST FEMALES

Japanese employers have historically discriminated against females. Reddy et al. (1987) observed that American organizations do not exploit women as do Japanese firms. Japanese organizations manipulate their female employees by overworking and underpaying them. In 1992, 69.9% of all temporary workers in Japan were female (Breton, 1995), suggesting limited full-time opportunities for Japanese women. Japanese women rarely are promoted to management positions. Women often are misused to reduce production costs (Ready et al., 1987). Helm et al. (1985) stated, "Over the past decade, Western admirers have extolled the advances of management, manufacturing, and labor relations which have made Japan a formidable worldwide competitor. But they have overlooked one key factor, exploitation of women" (pp. 54-55).

Harper (1988) believed the Japanese system of leadership has drawbacks, which include the negative treatment of women. According to Johnson (1988) there are signs Japanese leadership behaviors cannot be transferred to the United States without some or even considerable modification. Currently, there are six or more anti-discrimination suits involving major Japanese companies doing business in California. Each of these suits raises questions that were not resolved in a case involving the Sumitomo Corporation in 1981, whereby the Supreme Court decided that as long as Sumimoto Trading Company was incorporated in the United States, it was not entitled to protection under the terms of the U.S.–Japan Friendship, Commerce, and Navigation Treaty. Portions of that treaty gave Japanese companies operating in the United States the legal right to discriminate in employment practices, favoring Japanese personnel. However, in the Sumitomo case, the Court judged the company's blatant acts of discrimination toward American women violated Title VII of the Civil Rights Act of 1964, (Johnson, 1988). further observed that some Japanese firms operating in the United States have become so concerned about being involved in gender and racial struggles they will not promote Americans, whether they are male or female, into top-level management positions even though they have concluded that advancing American men and women would improve their overall efficiency, performance and image.

Another way in which Japanese organizations discriminate against women is by forcing them to resign when they get married. Laver (1991) remarked that four in ten Japanese workers are female and many Japanese corporations force their women employees to resign from their jobs when they marry or have children. Japanese women are socialized from birth with the self-perception that a wife's duties are to perform domestic chores, such as cooking, cleaning house, caring for children, and catering to the needs of her husband. Few Japanese women violate these rules of conduct. Japanese women who do try to combine career and marriage often find their goals are hindered by employers and husbands alike who are unwilling to accept their desire for a career (Laver, 1991). Laver (1991) further asserted that, in Japan, "In theory, at least, companies are prohibited from firing women on the basis of marital status. The 1986 Equal Employment Opportunity Law forbids sexual discrimination in hiring and promotions. But there are no penalties for firms that break the law (p. 50)." The same information about the illegal aspects of discrimination against females was recently reported by the Embassy of Japan (Breton,1995). Hellriegel & Slocum (1989) suggested Japanese society expects women to work until they are married, quit their jobs in order to rear their children, and then return to the workforce after the age of 40. After age 60, they are used mostly to fill lower-level, part-time positions. This practice reduces the size of Japanese corporations (Hellriegel & Slocum, 1989). With regard to the discrimination practices against women in Japan, Japanese leadership is not a viable alternative to adopt in U.S.Commercial organizations (Chaffins et al., 1995). Although American women still face discrimination in the United States, they are treated with more dignity and respect in U.S. organizations and have more opportunities for career advancement (Herklemann et al., 1993).

Japanese women represent approximately 40% of the working population but are grouped into a narrow range of jobs. These include nurses, teachers, maids, and waitresses. Less than 20% of technical/ professional positions (doctors, dentists, professors) were held by women in 1975. These women earned 56% as much as men in the same occupations (Woronff, 1982). This author proclaimed, "If Japan keeps on neglecting more than one third of its labor force while other countries offer women a more useful role, it is going to be a loser" (p. 116). The situation has not improved much as of 1996.

Seventy-three percent of companies provide different starting salaries for men and women-justified by different job descriptions and content of work. Wolf (1983) noted, "Japanese male workers are often exploited, but many women in the workplace suffer even greater indigni-ties." As recently as 1981, the public policy of *Sohyo,* the Japanese union council, toward women read like the Japanese version of the Dread Scott Decision: "Women are entitled neither to lifetime employment, nor to seniority wage rates, and are customarily considered to have resigned the day they marry" (Wolf, 1983, p. 261). How much has *really* changed as of 1996?

JAPAN'S WASTED WORKERS

As stated previously, many of Japan's workers actually are being exploited by the companies for which they work. Wolf (1983) noted, "The fact is that underpinning Japan's economic system are legions of exploited workers who give far more to their nation's effort than they receive. They work hard, they march to management's cadence, but they are not, as some have suggested, happy drones." In fact, a 1983 Indiana University study revealed they are a relatively dissatisfied, if submissive, army. Only 53 percent of Japan's workers said they were relatively satisfied with their jobs, in comparison with 81 percent of American workers (Wolf, 1983, pp. 231-232). Wolf observed that Japan's workers are loyal to their corporations from assembly line workers to top management in the sense of *obedient servants to the state industrial complex.*

Another flaw in Japanese corporations is related to the use of part-time workers. Wolf (1983) remarked that "perhaps the most common exploiting of Japanese workers is to use them as part-timers, making them ineligible for extensive fringe benefits. Over four million of Japan's 58.3 million workers are part-timers, an increase of 21 percent from 1978" (p. 252). Wolf suggested, in a survey by Jensen Domei, a Japanese business organization, 70 percent of "part-time" workers work a full day, but do not receive fringe benefits. They only receive 65 percent of what permanent workers receive when they do the same job. Part-time workers actually lose benefits and do not have the hope of ever becoming "permanent employees" (p. 255).

TIME OFF EXPLOITED

Many Japanese firms do not allow their workers to take off two days a week and many do not allow vacation time during production periods. Wolf (1983) suggested Japanese workers often work hard for lower wages but they also get less rest than most Western laborers. Less than 10% of Japanese corporations allow their workers to receive a two-day weekend. During times of pressure to get production out, national holidays are ignored (Wolf, 1983).

A knowledgeable leader speaking to the authors as an anonymous source (in 1995) stated:

Japanese leaders do not like change no matter how much they publicly proclaim this to the contrary. Japanese workers are obedient to their superiors. They demonstrate enormous fear of them, particularly in their non-verbal behavior. Japanese leaders do not compliment their workers for doing a good job. Japanese corporations resist promoting women into higher level management positions, even Japanese companies in the United States. Only 20% of Japanese corporations in the United States practice Kaizan, which emphasizes continual improvement techniques. Those companies that do practice continual improvement techniques essentially are located in Tokyo.

CONCLUSION

Critical observations of the effectiveness of Japanese leadership behavior are beginning to emerge. Japanese leadership practices that have been accepted unquestioningly for a generation as superior only now are becoming scrutinized and criticized. Though many Japanese leadership concepts have proved successful in the past in Japan, it appears they will not be necessarily so in the future without modification. Transporting Japanese leadership practices to the United States is yet another quagmire. Another anonymous source, highly placed in a Japanese/American enterprise, stated to one of the authors it would take at least seven years for a Japanese company, with its concomitant cultural values, to integrate with an American company and its inherent values—if *ever!*

The Japanese management style seems somewhat ruthlessly dedicated to catching up to and overtaking other economies. This strategy may have worked in early post World War II where countries were developing into an information society. However, a strategy engineered for developing economies is likely to not work as effectively in today's mature international economy.

While there are many good things to be said about the Japanese leadership system, there is at least one fatal weakness—it does not appear to foster bold, innovative, creative management styles. As stated by Ogura (1995) "When stormy weather comes, the company battens down the hatches, puts everyone on half-rations, and waits for the storm to pass—when some might say it should really be building a new ship."

The purpose of this article has not been to discredit Japan, the Japanese, their culture, or their leadership practices. Rather, the purpose has been to more clearly focus on some aspects of Japanese leadership practices and organizational behavior that demonstrate their less known, less emphasized and more problematic side. The authors have only the highest regard for the Japanese, their value system, and their economic success.

REFERENCES

Agawa, H. (1979). *The reluctant admiral.* San Francisco: Kondansha
     International USA.

Alston, J. (1985). *The American samurai: Blending American managerial
     practices.* New York: Walter de Gruyter.

Baali, J.C., Crabtree, S.K, & Cangemi, J.P. (1993). *Japanese management:
     Some negative aspects.* Unpublished manuscript.

Breton, M. (1995, October). *Embassy of Japan. Economic
     Section.* (Facsimile Transmission).

Byham, W. (1993). *Shogun management.* New York: Harper Collins.

Chaffins, S., Forbes, M., Fuqua, H.E., & Cangemi, J. (1995). The glass
     ceiling: Are women where they should be? *Education. 115*
     (41), 380-386.

Cole, R.E. (1980). Learning from the Japanese: Prospects and pitfalls.
     Management Review, 69, 22-42.

Doi, T. (1973). *The anatomy of dependence.* San Francisco: Kodansha
     International/USA Ltd.

Eberts, R., & Eberts, C. (1995). *The myth of Japanese quality.* N.J.:
     Prentice Hall.

Feifer, G. (1992). *Tennozan.* New York: Ticknor and Fields.

Fox, W.M. (1977, August). Japanese management: Tradition under strain.
     Business Horizons, 76-85.

Fujida, W. (1962). *Labor union organization and activities (Rodo Kumiai
     no Soshiki to undo).* Kyoto, Japan: Minerva.

Fuqua, E., Chaffins, S., Cangemi, J., & Kowalski, C. (1995). Group think:
     A hindrance to effective decision making in organizations.
     National Forum of Administration and Supervision Journal, 13
     (1), 47-59.

Harper, S.C. (1998). Now that the dust has settled: Learning from
     Japanese management. *Business Horizons, 43-51.*

Harries, M., & Harries, S. (1991). *Soldiers of the sun.* New York:
     Random House.

Hellriegel, D., & Slocum, Jr., J.W. (1989). *Management.* Reading, MA:
     AddisonWesley.

Helm, L., Takahasi, K., & Arnold, B. (1985, March 4). Japan's secret
     weapon: Exploited women. *Business Week,* 54-55.

Herkelmann, K., Dennison, T., Branham, R., Bush, M., Pope, K.H., & Cangemi, J.P. (1993). Women in transition: Choices and conflicts. *Education. 114,* 127-144.

Hirokawa, R.Y. (1981). Improving intra-organizational communication: A lesson from Japanese management. *Communication Quarterly. 30,* 35-40.'

Johnson, R.T. (1977, Spring). Success and failure of Japan subsidiaries in America. *Columbia Journal of World Business,* 30-37.

Johnson, R.T. (1988). Japanese style management in America. *California Management Review, 69,* 34-35.

Jordan, M., & Sullivan, K. (1995, September 10). Helping people save face rings up profits in Japan. *The Sunday Oregonian,* p. A9.

Katzenstein, G. (1991). Japanese management style: Beyond the hype– What to try, what to toss. *Working Women, 49.*

Kotkin, J., & Kishimoto, Y. (1986, April). Theory F. *Inc,* 53-60.

Kotkin, J., & Krugman, P. (1990, Summer). Beyond Japan, Inc. *NPO,* 36-45.

Kuramoto, J. (1983). Conversation between J. Kuramoto and J. Cangemi regarding the psychological foundation of Japanese leadership behavior, in Osaka, Japan.

Lomax, E. (1995). *The railway man.* New York: W.W. Norton.

Laver, R. (1991, November). Will the steam run out? *Maclean Magazine,* 48-54.

Lucier, C., Boucher, M., White, J., Cangemi, J., & Kowalski, C. (1992). Exploring values of Japanese & American management systems. *Education. 112,* 487-498.

McCarron, J. (1994, November 6). The Medicine Japan is afraid to take. *Chicago Tribune.*

Miller, R.L., & Cangemi, J.P. (1993). Why total quality management fails: Perspective of top management. *Journal of Management Development,12,* 40-50.

Morton, C. (1994). The best of both worlds. *Personnel Management.*

Ogura, M. (1995). Heavy listings: S.S. Japan Incorporated heads for the rocks. *Tokyo Business.*

Oh, T. (1976). Japanese management—A critical review. *Management Review, 1,*14-25.

Ouchi, W.G. (1981). An elaboration of methodology and findings. *Journal of Contemporary Business, 11,* 27-41.

Reddy, A.C., Owens, S.L.O., Rao, C.P., & Elkins, C. (1987). Is Japanese management a solution or a myth? *International Journal of Management, I,* 14-23.

Stewart, L.P., GudyKunst, W.B., Ting-Toomey, S., & Misida, T. (1986, September).The effects of decision-making style on openness and satisfaction within Japanese-organizations. *Communication Monographs, 53,* 236-251.

Tanaka, F.J. (1983, March). Japan's management illusion. *USA Today,* 20-24.

Wolf, M. (1983). *The Japanese conspiracy.* New York: Harper & Row.

Woronff, J. (1982). *Japan's wasted workers.* Tokyo: Lotus Press.

Wright, R.W. (1979, Spring). Joint venture problems in Japan. *Columbia Journal of World Business,* 25-31.

Yoji, I. (1988). The 1988 job market for recent graduates. *Japan Ouarterly,* 196-200.

Yoshimo, M.Y. (1968). *Japan's managerial system.* Cambridge, MA: MIT Press.

Zemke, R. (1981). What's good for Japan may not be best for America. *Training/Human Resource Development,18,* 62-65.

Van Wolferen, K. (1989). *The enigma of Japanese power: People and politics in a stateless nation.* New York: Knopf.

WOMEN AS LEADERS

By
Kay E. Payne
Harold E. Fuqua, Jr.
Joseph P. Cangemi

In the competitive children's game of paper-rock-scissors, the goal centers around outguessing the opponents by trying to choose one of the three (paper, scissors or rock) which would dominate the opponent. In this game, since what opponents might choose is unknown, a person simply has to take his or her chances in hopes of becoming the dominant player. Without training, leaders may operate in a similar fashion, by simply trying to guess what strategy would outdo their opponents so they can accomplish their goals, be in control, and dominate others. To a certain extent, having power and using it to accomplish an organizational vision often involves goals to dominate. The desire to be in a dominant position, or to have power, emanates from a variety of sources, but usually relies on task accomplishment, and competitiveness, often manifesting itself in hierarchical authority, generating respect but not having as a central goal "to be liked," facilitating high control for the leader and unemotional, analytic problem solving, usually accompanied by a tough attitude. Some of the most famous and wealthy business persons of our time have operated in this way. In fact, norms for leadership practices in institutions were established using these male patterns, and people who do not use them often experience domination by others, much like in the paper-scissors-rock game.

McGregor (1960) first identified attitudes about power and control held by managers, portraying them as either pessimistic about employees (Theory X) or optimistic about employees (Theory Y). Among other things, theory X assumptions indicate a subordinate needs direction and control and has little desire for responsibility, while Theory Y assumptions facilitate employee trust and empowerment. Curiously, Donnell and Hall (1980) found high achieving females scored higher than low achieving females on McGregor's (1960) Theory X assumptions, while for males the findings were reversed. We can speculate about the reasons why high achieving women have often believed their success depended on acting in ways which made them appear "more like a man." To compensate for the stereotypical attitude that women are the weaker sex may, in part, explain why some women leaders have adopted this masculine style. It may be that high achieving females have achieved, but paid the price interpersonally because they believed personal relationships might jeopardize their success.

The dominant and control style of leadership may have contributed to the "glass ceiling" effect experienced by many high achieving women. Because acting masculine goes against stereotypical expectations for women, high achieving women may have breached interpersonal alliances by acting masculine. Also, acting masculine opposes what we now know about the stereotypical leadership style of women. Researchers indicate that what comes "naturally" to women involves the use of strategies pertaining to nurturing, helping, and encouraging, all of which enable *others* to achieve their goals. Even so, no one ideal kind of leadership behavior exists which achieves optimum performance under all conditions, and women can certainly use with great success other more task-oriented strategies.

Development of organizational leaders has long been a subject of study. Professional socialization has recently become an area of extensive research. The purpose of this research will be to organize professional socialization and organizational leadership around women as leaders. Our interest in this inquiry stems from examining the combination of socialization of women and the changing climate of organizations which together create a uniquely positive situation for women as leaders in the 21st century. Our inquiry will examine the socialization of women as leaders. Also, we will discuss the necessary skills for successful "women as leaders" including: communicating anger, competitiveness, persuasiveness, assertiveness, and listening as qualities necessary for successful leadership in the future. The underlying philosophical basis for this inquiry includes the belief which says women and men do not differ in leadership style when they have been trained, but differ along stereotypical lines when untrained. Leaders can be trained to incorporate both task and consideration in their leadership styles, but *males will use task* as a backup style, *while females will use consideration* as a backup style.

SOCIALIZATION

Society: One of the greatest reasons women do not occupy more leadership positions in organizations stems from the socialization of women into specific gender roles. Gender expectations emerge from socialization in society, family, educational institutions and religious institutions. These sources have the most profound influences upon the development of both males and females in American society. As a result of these influences, women often enter the workforce believing men exhibit more qualifications for leadership than do women.

Fagerson (1990) argued that women in our society may not be seen as promotable leaders due to an image based on false assumptions. Characteristics of early workplace organizations used a masculine norm to compare employees for promotions. Consequently, we now find females being evaluated by masculine norms such as aggressiveness, forcefulness, rationalness, competitiveness, decisiveness, body size and strength, self-confidence and independence (Fagerson, 1990). Fagerson (1990) further believed women have been characterized as submissive and non-rational in their social encounters by qualities such as kindness, unselfishness and warmth. Consequently, these traits often put women at a disadvantage when it comes to evaluations for leadership promotions. Chaffins, Forbes, Fuqua, & Cangemi (1995, p.381) asserted "societal norms and beliefs in relation to women often inhibit females from entering managerial positions in corporations." Terborg (1977) agreed with the existence of a male managerial model inhibiting women from being successful in leadership positions.

FAMILY

In the home, parents rear their children to conform to the roles expected by society. Bartleson and Cangemi (1983) argued males receive more affection, more attention, and more nurturing in the family. The concept of male superiority begins at birth and continues throughout adult life. Parents teach and train male children to be aggressive while female children learn passiveness. Women learn to accept male authorities from the beginning of their lives. Henning and Jardin (1976) claimed daughters who identify more closely with their fathers, rather than their mothers, develop interests in traditionally male careers and utilize more masculine personality characteristics. Berryman-Fink (1985, p.308) noted, "the gender typical behaviors which socialized females exhibit may, in fact, be incompatible with traditional organizational definitions of managerial effectiveness." Terborg (1977) believed when families and society pressure and discourage women from seeking nontraditional occupations, such as leadership, they refrain from seeking such positions.

EDUCATION

Educational institutions socialize females to accept society's perspective about gender differences in leadership style. Sadker and Sadker (1985) asserted that in school, boys receive positive reinforcement for assertiveness and active learning behavior, while girls receive positive reinforcement for passive, quiet learning behavior. Pearson, Turner, and Mancillas (1985) argued, "several researchers have found boys generally receive more favorable attention in school than girls." Terborg (1977) said vocational counselors gave different advice to females who desired to enter medical school than they gave to males. Males received more encouragement to reapply to more schools or to consider Ph. D. programs in related fields while females heard warnings about the difficulties of medical school and Ph. D. programs. Vocational counselors encouraged females to shift their desires toward those more compatible with sex-role stereotyped professions such as nursing.

RELIGION

In most religious denominations in America the patriarchal order of male as head of the family and female, as second-in-charge who submits to his authority, acts as the norm. The distribution of relational power becomes tense as couples attempt to live out their sex-roles, often misinterpreting the patriarchal order to cover the gamut of all males as head, in all of society. Feminists argue the patriarchal order causes women to experience a lack of self-esteem, a necessary component of leadership (Prayer, 1983). Persons who believe they control the outcome of incidents in their own lives tend to characterize themselves as having an *internal locus of control*. Those who attribute the outcome of incidents in their own lives to luck, chance, powerful others, or other factors outside their control characterize themselves as at the mercy of an *external locus of control*. As most females grow up in the church they learn to accept male authority, which places them in a position where control comes from outside themselves, or an external locus of control.

ATTRIBUTES FOR WOMEN AS LEADERS

Once trained, managers differ not so much along gender lines, but rather between high achievers and low achievers. Women who plan careers in male dominated occupations have higher career aspirations than women who desire careers in female dominated occupations. They also experience more traditional attitudes toward the tensions between work and home/children. The existence of different expectations for women as leaders appears to be a bigger problem for women, a finding which has been documented in extensive research on gender (Broverman, Vogel, Broverman, Clarkson, & Rosenkrantz, 1972; Deaux & Lewis, 1983; Eagly & Karau, 1984; & Ruble, 1983). In summary, they believed gender-role expectations would result in behaviors consistent with those expectations. Consequently, women as leaders experience an extensive hazing period within the context of their role in the organization before subordinates will accept them as leaders. Eagly and Johnson (1990) said because people have differing expectations, gender roles may, to some extent, contaminate organizational roles. Eagly and Karau (1991) argued effective leadership more closely conforms to task-oriented contributions. Cann and Siegfried (1990) found superiors valued "masculine" traits in leaders who were their subordinates, while "feminine" traits were more highly valued by subordinates. Contributions to group morale and harmony make a contribution to the effectiveness of task-oriented groups, but may not be recognized as leadership by many members of the group. Interestingly, as task-relevant competence diminishes over time, and as skills increase and group members become aware of each others' competencies, or as social interactions become more complex, the tendency for women to emerge as leaders strengthens.

ANGER

No person who harbors a deeply-felt anger toward the opposite or same sex should occupy a position of leadership. Such angry people become disruptive of the collaborative processes necessary to building strong organizations. Often these people will use the organization to fulfill their own neurotic problems. Aside from these neuroses, women as leaders often experience and express normal every day anger in ways which may confuse organizational members, and may lead to misunderstandings. For example, females become angry when others treat them with a condescending and insensitive attitude. They do not like being referred to as promiscuous, nor do they appreciate it when others act dismissive toward them. Further, women become angry when others treat them with a patronizing attitude, or when others fail to listen to them and accept their ideas as worthwhile. These anger-producing phenomena frustrate women and cause anxiety, because the expression of anger has been described as socially prohibited for women (Kagan & Moss, 1962).

Current research on the role of appropriate emotional expression at work suggests that gender plays an important part in the assessment and interpretation of anger displays (Blier, Blier, & Wilson,1989;

Chiauzzi, Heimberg, & Doty, 1982; Hochschild, 1983; Tavris, 1982). In the case of Ann Hopkins vs. Price Waterhouse (Seligman, 1988), Ann Hopkins was denied full partnership in the firm because of her overbearing and abrasive personality. Women as leaders acknowledge higher evaluations when they act out their anger through consideration rather than through structuring behaviors (Bartol & Butterfield, 1976). Tannen (1994) reported when women get angry, they typically just walk away, shed a few tears alone, and then return to a conversation pretending like nothing happened. Acting angry contradicts the "wanting to be liked" phenomenon. Consequently, women as leaders often act "extra nice," attempting to assure others they would not throw their weight around. Their unexpressed anger may build up to later expel in the form of "gunny-sacking" whereby grievances number so high they overwhelm both parties. Kopper (1993) reported a high level of "anger-in" for women as leaders. Anger-in refers to efforts of controlling the expression of anger. Consequently, women leaders need help with controlling depression and anxiety. In the last 30 years, feminists have encouraged women to get in touch with and express their anger, even though we often think of anger as a male emotion (Shields, 1987; Sharkin, 1993). Fischer et al., (1993) reported women may have succeeded, challenging earlier stereotypes by saying that women are learning to experience and express anger, but may be doing so in unexpected ways. Research on communication behaviors (Blier, Blier, & Wilson,1989; Chiauzzi et al., 1982) argue females express negative feelings with great difficulty. They experience anxiety about aggression and disagreement with others during discussions involving collaboration (Frodi, Macauley, & Thorme, 1977). Women believe and judge their own angry displays as costly to their interpersonal relationships. Since angry displays act as a policing function (Tavris, 1982) which help regulate social relations, they help express messages of how one ought to behave. In other words, the use of anger displays can be a legitimate part of a supervisory role. If women have trouble expressing anger, this may put them at a disadvantage in a leadership role.

The extent to which we identify aggressive and dominant behavior (Condry & Condry, 1976; Shields, 1987; Tavris, 1982) may be closely aligned with the masculine gender role and the degree to which an individual identifies with that role (Kogut, Langley & O'Neal, 1992). Women higher in masculinity were more aggressive than were those in the low masculinity group. In an unpublished research project using the Bem Sex Role Inventory on university students, the author found more females self-scored themselves as masculine in gender role. This finding suggests women are moving from a dependent, submissive, feminine role in the workplace, to one of more independence, assertiveness, and competitiveness in efforts to achieve higher status. Consistent with that notion, Tavris (1982) argued that anger expression may be more of a status-related emotion. High group status produces feelings of power and expectations of competence for oneself (Webster & Foschi, 1988). Russel and Mehrabian (1974, p. 79) conceptualized dominance as "the degree to which a person feels powerful or in control of a situation" and, therefore, entitles that individual to the expression of anger (Novaco, 1976). Powerlessness, on the other hand, acts to create anxiety, which Russel and Mehrabian (1979) described as the bipolar opposite of anger along the dimension of dominance. According to Smith and Ellsworth (1985), however, the perception of being in control should diminish rather than encourage the expression and feeling of anger, while the reverse should be true for people who experience lower power and status.

Curiously, we generally view females as emotionally expressive, with the exception of anger, while we view males as emotionally inexpressive, with the exception of anger. Consequently, *the presence of males in an organization creates an awareness of the possibility of violence,* the knowledge that some men will resort to violence against women. However vague and in the background the threat of violence lurks, women recognize it could happen, even though it probably never will. Intimidation describes the feeling best, even among women who recognize their own dominance and strength. Given this intimidation, expressions of legitimate anger and protest from women produce the risk of reprisal, or at the least the risk of standing alone, disapproval and loss of love from others. For women as leaders, this requires a particular degree of courage and autonomy. Women leaders who recognize this take responsibility for their own choices, decide their own risks, and assume the challenge for their own growth and development.

COMPETITION

Leader effectiveness depends to a large extent on the competition for social influence. Competing for social influence involves vying for status and dominance, making opinions known, and appreciating the value of agreement in conversation. Conflicting evidence supports the notion that women typically display fewer influence strategies than males (Eagly, 1978), but may be more easily influenced. Also, Rosenfeld and Fowler (1976) found highly dominant personalities always assumed the leader role, except when a high dominant female paired with a low dominant male, in which case the male assumed the role of leader.

Vying for status involves competition between two people for the same position or object. Women do not typically like to compete with other women, but do not mind doing so with men (McCarrick, Manderscheid, & Silbergeld, 1981). Women may view competing for status as a way of establishing connection (Tanner, 1994), as in the case of sports and popularity contests. Rather than thinking of status and connection at opposite ends of a continuum, women often see them as intertwined. Establishing relationships with people helps us to know who to call on when we need to get around rules, or when we need support on an important issue. Dominance, on the other hand, involves control through superior power or influence (McCarrick, Manderscheid, & Silbergeld, 1981). Dominance strongly relates to a role relationship of people, defining who is in charge, while competition relates to the context of the interaction (McCarrick et al., 1981). Interrupting, interrupting back, talking over, topic control, one down and one up comments, and overlaps— all constitute communication strategies of dominance.

Competing for status, a legitimate activity for high-status group members but illegitimate for low-status members, acts to keep low-status members down. Women often see themselves as lower in status than males in organizations. Discouraged from competing for status, low-status group members, such as women, may make an effort to roust more influence by using indirect strategies. One indirect strategy, for example, may be not disagreeing publicly, but operating behind the scenes either before or after a meeting, to rally support for a project or to oppose an issue. Or, low-status people may make greater use of referent power, relying on their similarity to others and being likable, while higher-status individuals use more expert power, relying on perceived knowledge and skill (Raven, Centers, & Rodriguez, 1975). Consequently, higher-status group members operate with greater confidence and appear more competent; they receive more opportunities to make task contributions and rally more support for their contributions (Berger, Cohen, & Zelditch, 1972: Berger & Fisek, 1974; Berger, Fisek, Norman & Zelditch, 1977; Berger, Rosenholtz, & Zelditch, 1980).

Eagly and Carli (1981) argued that women may not always display the realities of their private opinions, in part because of their strong value to maintain at least the appearance of a "relationship orientation." In efforts to maintain the "relationship orientation" women often exhibit a greater amount of positive social behaviors, such as relieving group tension and showing group solidarity, just to be polite. Consequently, women often may act in contradictory ways, or be perceived as sneaky, back-stabbing, unpredictable, two-faced, or even clandestine. This apparent contradiction can work against a woman as leader because subordinates may not understand why she did not speak up, or speak more directly. People who understand this phenomenon will recognize and provide support for a female leader who may be experiencing a contradiction between private opinion and social rules.

Another strategy for gaining status in groups often involves task behaviors such as giving opinions, suggestions, and directions (Aries, 1982; Carli, 1981; Heiss, 1962; Piliavin & Martin, 1978; Strodbeck & Mann, 1956; Zelditch, 1955). Challenging the notion that task behaviors solicited more status, Carli (1989) found instead that agreement and disagreement directly predicted influence. Carli (1989) found agreements on the part of the partner increased their influence, and disagreements decreased it. This finding opposes earlier studies which claim more disagreement elicited influence. Further, partner's gender rather than own gender influenced the use of agreement over disagreement. When interacting with females, both males and females tended to be more agreeable. When people agree with us, we tend to think of them as supportive, and we want to support them in return, thus generating a reciprocal system of influence.

The major thrust of participative management involves a reciprocal system of trust and influence. It involves joint participation in the making of work-related decisions. This style of leading people revolves around the collaborative process characterized in group discussion. Kohn (1986) suggested debate exemplifies competitiveness with the goal to score points and win. In competition, the enhancement of one's own power and the minimization of the legitimacy of the other side's interests in a situation become the objectives. On the other hand, when one seeks to resolve conflict by arriving at consensus, the objective involves searching for a solution that responds to the needs of others. This style of resolving conflict prevails in group discussion, the hallmark of participative management. Consideration of other peoples needs, characteristic of women's style of leading, enhances the collaborative process in participative management.

After examining the notion of the "fear of success," Sassen (1980) claimed women did not fear success, but rather they experienced anxiety within a climate of competition. She advocated against teaching women to compete but rather called for a restructuring of institutions so that competition acts as only one avenue to success. The cost of competing for success involves alienating all those who fail. *Capitalist organizations historically have used a system of competition rather than participative strategies for organizing.* Maccoby (1976) and Slater (1970) claimed capitalist organizations need a reorganization of their structures, human relations, political climates, and symbols to recreate new kinds of organizations. To reduce the win-orientation and replace it with an achievement-orientation would cause people to reach down from within themselves to compete *with themselves* rather than competing *with others.* Weaver (1995) claimed women leaders already tend to share information and power by inspiring good work through interacting with others, encouraging member participation, and showing how member goals relate to group goals.

PERSUASION

Exerting influence over one's employees represents a crucial and pervasive aspect of the daily activities of leadership, motivation, and satisfaction. In this section, we will discuss how women as leaders influence others, and how they act as the targets of influence from others. Harper and Hirokawa (1988) looked at persuasive strategies used by women and found female managers relied on direct requests, altruism, and rationale based strategies, indicating a preference for counsel ("Is there anything I can do to help?") or explanation ("You need to do this because...") when attempting to persuade and convince a subordinate to comply with requests. If the organization sanctioned a request, women tended to influence by using reward or punishment, but employed non-authoritative influence strategies when the organization had not sanctioned the request. Consequently, when a problem arose, one could find women as leaders attempting to influence the organization to sanction a punishment or reward for the "next time" something irregular occurred.

In a study by Andrews (1987) females expressed low confidence in their ability to communicate their arguments persuasively. When successful at persuasion, women tended to attribute their success to circumstance (Henning & Jardim, 1976), but they attributed their failure to themselves. The kinds of arguments used to persuade reveal something of a person's values, and women tended to use persuasive strategies based on more equitable or humane decisions. Their arguments focused on social contributions to society and the theme of maintaining family relationships. Burgoon et al., (1983) suggested individuals develop expectations about appropriateness of communication behavior, and when speakers did not meet those expectations it resulted in weakened influence strategies. Consequently, female leaders will achieve maximum persuasion when they use message strategies, as well as language choices which audiences expect them to use. The strategies considered most feminine included promise, pre-giving, positive moral appeal, altruism, and liking, which when not used by women decreased their persuasive appeal. It is said females use more prosocial message strategies, use less verbal aggressiveness and receive penalties for deviations from the expected strategies. That does not mean women cannot be effective using more task oriented persuasive strategies, it merely means they have to work up to those strategies by slowly preparing their audience to expect them.

To become more influential, women can elect to participate in projects which will help them make a name for themselves, gain respect and recognition. *To be noticed, people have to do more than what their job description provides.* Initiative, rather than conformity, causes women to be promoted into leadership positions. Proving to be a reliable source of information, one who knows how to anticipate the reactions of others, who can warn superiors about "land mines," and who brings potential problems to the boss's attention will likely become a valued and trusted person. Defending and supporting the boss' decisions to organizational peers also provides a forum from which superiors notice and promote. It does a woman no good to work hard and "suffer in silence" while those around her are completely oblivious to her efforts and her need for reciprocity. At the very least she should initiate a direct conversation in which she asks bluntly, but politely, if her view that reciprocity is being ignored matches theirs.

Women as leaders often enjoy the compliment "she is approach-able." Perhaps women leaders receive this compliment because of the widely held idea of women being highly persuadable (Scheidel, 1963). Kanter (1977) said women typically employ communication strategies which connote open-mindedness and nurturance. Another reason for this perception might result from women freely self-disclosing, which leads to the reduction of psychological distance between self and others. In any case, Sistrunk and McDavid (1971) found, in certain circumstances, females reacted susceptibly to social pressures and therefore acted more persuasible. Further, they agreed, the control of an increasing number of other factors, such as personality, content of the task, sex of the influencer, and motivation, influenced susceptibility to persuasion more than sex. Montgomery and Burgoon (1980), Infante and Grimmett (1986), and Nord (1969) suggested feminine females, especially those with lower levels of self-esteem and aggressiveness, reacted to persuasion with less motivation to produce counter-arguments to defend their own positions. Nord (1969) explained this, in part, by suggesting women have a high need for affiliation and achievement. But, Donnell and Hall (1980) claimed women reported lower basic needs and higher needs for self-actualization, especially women who are leaders. Interestingly, all other females, including masculine and androgynous women, in the Montgomery and Burgoon (1980) study, demonstrated resistance to persuasion. When trained in critical methods (analysis of fallacies in argument), female listeners became less persuaded, probably due to learning to discover their own refutational arguments (Infante & Grimmet, 1986). They suggested female leaders concerned themselves more with opportunities for growth, autonomy, and challenge; they experienced less concern with work environment, pay, and strain avoidance. Goal achievement appears to persuade women as leaders more than any other variable (Gill, 1988). Contrary to popular belief, Donnell and Hall (1980) claimed females do not have a great need to belong, as previous research has suggested. Beh (1994) argued these findings indicated a change in performance and represented a significant shift in attitudes toward the acceptance of equality of roles for women as leaders.

ASSERTIVENESS

Infante & Grimmett (1986) described aggressiveness in interpersonal communication along a continuum as either constructive or destructive. Constructive types included assertiveness and argumentativeness which lead to satisfaction and enhanced interpersonal relationships. Destructive types included hostility and verbal aggressiveness which lead to dissatisfaction and relationship deterioration. On the positive side, assertiveness consisted of an individual's "general tendency to be interpersonally dominant, ascendant, and forceful" (Infante, 1989, p. 165). Assertive individuals state their point and respect the right of others to express their position. Argumentativeness refers to a generally stable trait which predisposes an individual to advocate positions on controversial issues and verbally attack the positions other people take on these issues (Infante & Rancer, 1982). Inherently interesting, verbal conflict leads to advocacy and refutation. On the negative side, hostility includes irritability, negativism, resentment, and suspicion (Infante, 1989). Hostility is usually aroused by frustration, otherwise it may remain latent. *Verbally aggressive individuals attack the self-concepts of individuals, in order to make them feel psychological pain. Examples include: Character attacks, competence attacks, insults, maledictions, teasing, ridicule, profanity, and nonverbal emblems* (Infante &Wrigley, 1986). Even some nonverbal behaviors have become functionally equivalent to aggressive words (Ekman & Friesen, 1967).

The effect of verbal aggressive talk is self-concept damage (Infante, Treblin, Shepherd & Seeds, 1984). Sometimes, verbally aggressive talk escalates into violence (Patterson & Cobb, 1973). Several reasons for verbal aggression include: frustration, social learning, psychopathology, and argumentative skill deficiency. Verbally aggressive individuals may also attack their opponents position on controversial issues (Infante & Wrigley, 1986), just like argumentative individuals, but the difference occurs when *they want to win so much they cross the psychological boundary to actually wound their victim.* The negative consequences of verbal aggressiveness include lower marital satisfaction (Rancer, Baukus, & Amato, 1986), greater interspousal violence (Infante, Chandler, & Rudd, 1989; Infante, Sabourin, Rudd, & Shannon, 1990), depression, especially among husbands whose wives are verbally aggressive (Segrin & Fitzpatrick, 1992; Millar & Rogers, 1987) and unfavorable organizational interactions (Infante & Gorden, 1991). On the other hand, research on argumentativeness reveals a number of benefits.

Arguing acts to stimulate curiosity and learning. People learn more about positions on controversial issues which disagree from their own, thereby reducing egocentric thinking, while increasing multiple perspectives on issues (Johnson & Johnson, 1979). People who enjoy arguing communicate with more dynamism, seem more interested, more verbose, exert a greater effort to win, are more task oriented and more inflexible than people who prefer to argue less (Infante, 1981). In terms of credibility, people who enjoy arguing appear more enthusiastic, persuasive, confident, and certain by reflecting energy and boldness of presentation (Berlo, Lemert, & Mertz, 1969-70).

Males score higher than females on scales measuring both argumentativeness (Infante, 1985; Schultz & Anderson, 1982) and verbal aggressiveness (Burgoon, Dillard, & Doran, 1983; Infante, Wall, Leap, & Danielson, 1984; Roloff & Greenberg, 1979; Whatley, 1982). However, Canary et al., (1988) suggested females may be more aggressive than males in familiar contexts, using tactics to seek personal gain through coercion, criticism, and intimidation. Interestingly, Rancer and Dierks-Stewart (1985) explored biological (sex) and psychological (gender) differences in argumentativeness and found no biological sex differences. However, significant differences were found in argumentativeness when subjects were classified according to psychological gender. Subjects classified as masculine (instrumental) rated higher in argumentativeness than those classified as feminine (expressive), androgynous, or undifferentiated, no matter what their sex. In other words, people "with a traditional masculine psychological sex-role orientation exceeded all others in argumentativeness" (Nicotera & Rancer, 1994, p. 287). When adversaries used verbal aggression to provoke males they responded with verbal aggression while females responded by becoming more argumentative and rational (Infante, 1989). In that same study Infante (1989) found a highly argumentative individual able to influence whether he or she was the recipient of argument or verbal aggression. People who like to argue indicated they believe arguing acts to produce enjoyment and functional, pragmatic outcomes; it has a positive impact on self-concept, and creates high ego involvement. People who do not like to argue indicated they believe arguing acts to produce a negative impact on self-concept, creates dysfunctional outcomes, has little ego involvement with corresponding little enjoyment or pragmatic outcomes (Rancer, Kosberg, & Baukus, 1992).

Stereotypical sex-role expectations for females discourage them from both argumentative and verbally aggressive behavior, and they often view arguments as stressful events. People with a low desire to argue are more socially oriented, prefer to shift the focus of interaction from a controversial issue to a social-emotional matter (Infante, 1981), or concede with premature agreement, which correlates with stereotypical feminine communication expectations. When females violate these expectations communication outcomes (Burgoon et al., 1983) often are affected. For example, if a woman acts more aggressive than expected she might experience social disapproval and be called *a bitch;* while if a man acts less aggressive than expected he might experience the same social disapproval but be called a *wimp.* Even so, males who act more aggressive than socially expected often receive the label of *bastard.* If women in organizations see argumentativeness as negative, they probably will not argue, and will therefore be seen as less competent (Onyekwere, Rubin, & Infante, 1991).

Female leaders who use an assertive communication style more quickly overcome negative stereotypes commonly associated with submissiveness, weakness, and passiveness (Bradley, 1981). Associates take assertive women more seriously as they appear more competent and influential in male-dominated leadership decision-making groups (Bradley, 1981). Bradley (1981) further said, due largely to socialization processes in the American society, women using a passive style of communication also appear less direct and certain than their male counterparts. The task involves educating women in effective workplace communication styles consistent with the male norm. Harragan (1992) noted male managers stereotypically operate using an assertive style more often than female managers. By directly communicating their legitimate needs, feelings, thoughts, and ideas to their bosses, as well as to their employees, female leaders accomplish a credibility leap (Harragan, 1992). Aggressive communication often initiates questioning which begins with words such as the following: who, what, where, when, and how. Both male and female leaders should avoid using negative aggressiveness often associated with hostility, irritability, negativism, resentment, and suspicion (Infante, 1986).

LISTENING

Listening engages an enormous amount of one's time. Berko et al., (1994) found an average person spends 50 to 80 percent of a day listening. Further, *individuals understand only about a fourth and remember even less.* This alarming finding prompted corporations to spend millions of dollars to promote good listening skills (Goldhaber, 1986). From a social perspective, women generally perceive men as poor listeners. However, research attempting to determine who listens better, men or women, suggests conflicting evidence exists. Tannen (1990) argued men and women may listen differently, with *men listening to find out how to solve problems,* while *women listen to understand and maintain relationships.* Halley (1975) discovered males extract more information when listening than women. As males listen they appear to restructure the situation to fit with their own goals. Women, on the other hand, may become distracted by competing details within a story, but accept the pattern while attempting to determine relationships between details. Females allow emotions and unclear impressions to determine what they select to hear more than male listeners. Yet, women appear to hear more of a message because they reject less of it, while men derive more coherent meaning from the message because they build the structure of the general message as they listen.

Listening directly relates to empathy. People who choose employment which demands empathy, male or female, usually become skilled at nurturing, expressiveness, or artistic ability (Rosenthal et al., 1974). People employed in these types of positions need to gather more data from speakers in order to establish empathy. Hughey (1984) claimed males and females achieve empathy in different ways. After adapting to and getting to know their partner, males empathize with greater success. For females, gaining a speaker's trust results in the greatest likelihood for achieving empathy. In any case, the unempathic woman receives social condemnation, while men are viewed as quite normal in our society when they do not express empathy (Gardiner, 1987).

Leaders will not succeed without good listening skills, whether they listen with empathy or not. Stewart and Clake-Kudless (1993) found better listening skills among female rather than male leaders. Using an open door policy, both male and female leaders encourage workers to come in and engage in conversation. Using an active listening style generates more talk. Employees in today's workplace appreciate leadership based on greater openness and interaction from leaders to employees. This requires leaders to hear both direct and indirect communication from their employees, as well as to act on what they hear (Nelson, 1991). Women may not only hear direct and indirect communication, but usually read nonverbal cues with greater astuteness than men (Berman & Smith, 1984).

CONCLUSION

The combination of society, the family, education and religion all influence the way women think about their role in society. These influences often create tensions between the way women may instinctively lead and the expectations organizations have about leadership. As a result of socialization women tend to lead with a "consideration" style. As we approach the 21st century and the changing climate of organizations—moving away from authoritarian toward more participative styles—a uniquely positive situation is created for women as leaders. This article described research about women and anger, competition, persuasion, assertiveness, and listening. The research suggests men and women do not differ in leadership style when they have been trained, but differ along stereotypical lines when untrained. Leaders can be trained to incorporate both task and consideration in their leadership style, but males will use task as a backup style, while females will use consideration as a backup style.

REFERENCES

Andrews, P. H. (1987). Gender differences in persuasive communication and attribution of success and failure. *Human Communication Research, 13,* (3), 372-385.

Aries, E.J. (1982). Verbal and nonverbal behavior in single-sex and mixed-sex groups: Are traditional sex roles changing? *Psychological Reports, 51,* 127-134.

Bartleson, F., & Cangemi, J. (1983). A brief psychology of discrimination against women. *Journal of Instructional Psychology, 10,* 3-8.

Bartol, K. M., & Butterfield, D.A. (1976). Sex effects in evaluating leaders. *Journal of Applied Psychology, 61,* 446-454.

Beh, H. C. (1994). Gender rivalry and attitudes toward sex roles: Changes over a fifteen year period. *Psychological Reports, 74,* 188-190.

Berger, J., Cohen, B.P., & Zelditch Jr., M. (1972). Status characteristics and social interaction. *American Sociological Review, 37,* 241-255.

Berger, J., & Fisek, M.H. (1974). A generalization of the status characteristics and expectation states theory. In J. Berger, T.L. Conner, & M.J. Fisek (Eds.), *Expectations states theory: A theoretical research program* (pp. l6-205). Cambridge, MA: Winthrop.

Berger, J., Fisek, H.M., Norman, R.Z., & Zelditch Jr., M. (1977). *Status characteristics and social interaction: An expectation states approach.* New York: American Elsevier.

Berger, J., Rosenholtz, S.J., & Zelditch Jr., M. (1980). Status organizing processes. In A. Inkeles, N.J. Smelser, & R.H.Turner (Eds.), *Annual Review of Sociology, 6,* pp. 479-508. Palo Alto, CA: Annual Reviews.

Berko, R.M., Rosenfeld, L.B., & Samovar, L.A. (1994). *Connecting: A culture sensitive approach to interpersonal communication competency.* Ft. Worth, TX: Harcourt Brace.

Berlo, D. K., Lemert, J.B., & Mertz, R.J. (1969-70). Dimensions for evaluating the acceptability of message sources. *Public Opinion Quarterly, 13,* 563-76.

Berman, P. W., & Smith, V.L. (1984). Gender and situational differences in children's smiles, touch and proxemics. Sex *Roles, 10,* 347-56.

Berryman-Fink, C., (1985). Male and female manager's views of the communication skills and training needs of women in management. *Public Personnel Management, 14,* 307-385.

Blier, M.J., Blier, I., & Wilson, L.A. (1989). Gender differences in self-rated emotional expressiveness. *Sex Roles, 21,* 287-295.

Bradley, P.H. (1981). The folk-linguistics of women's speech: An empirical examination. *Communication Monographs, 48,* 74-90.

Broverman, I.K., Vogel, S.R., Broverman, D.M., Clarkson, F.E., & Rosenkrantz, PS. (1972). Sex role stereotypes: A current appraisal. *Journal* of *Social Issues, 128,* 59-78.

Burgoon, M., Dillard, J.P., & Doran, N.E. (1983, Winter). Friendly or unfriendly persuasion: The effects of violations of expectations by males and females. *Human Communication Research, 10,* (2), 283-194.

Canary, D.J., Cunningham, E.M., & Cody, M.J. (1988). Goal types, gender, and locus of control in managing interpersonal conflict. *Communication Research, 15,* 426-446.

Cann, A., Siegfried, W.D. (l990). Gender stereotypes and dimensions of effective leader behavior. *Sex Roles, 23,* (7/8),413-419.

Carli, L. L. (1981, August). *Sex differences* in *small group interaction.* Paper presented at the 89th annual meeting of the American Psychological Association, Los Angeles.

Carli, L. L. (1989). Gender differences in interaction style and influence. *Journal of Personality and Social Psychology, 56,* 565-576.

Chaffins, S., Forbes, M., Fuqua, H., & Cangemi J.P. (1995). The glass ceiling: Are women where they should be? *Education, 155,* 380-385.

Chiauzzi E., Heimberg, R.G., & Doty, D. (1982). Task analysis of assertiveness behavior revisited: The role of situational variables with female college students. *Behavioral Counseling Quarterly, 2,* 42-50.

Condry, J., & Condry, S. (1976). Sex differences: A study of the eye of the beholder. *Child Development, 47,* 812-819.

Deaux, K., & Lewis, L.L. (1983). Components of gender stereotypes. *Psychological Documents, 13,* (25) (NIB. No. 2583).

Donnell, S. M., & Hall, J. (1980, Spring). Men and women as managers: A significant case of no significant difference. *Organizational Dynamics.*

Eagly, A.J (1978). Sex differences in influenceability. *Psychological Bulletin, 85,* 86.

Eagly, A.H., & Carli L.L. (1981). Sex of researchers and sex-typed communications as determinants of sex differences in influenceability: A meta-analysis of social influence studies. *Psychological Bulletin, 90,* 1-20.

Eagly, A. H., & Johnson, B.T. (1990). Gender and leadership style: A meta-analysis. *Psychological Bulletin, 108,* (2), 233-256.

Eagly, A. H., & Karau, S.J. (1991). Gender and the emergence of leaders: A meta-analysis. *Journal of Personality and Social Psychology, 60,* (5), 685-710.

Ekman, P., & Friesen, W.V. (1967). Head and body cues in the judgment of emotion: A reformulation. *Perceptual and Motor Skills, 94,* 711-24.

Fagerson, A.E. (1990). At the heart of women management research: Theoretical and methodological perspectives. *Journal of Business Ethics, 9,* 267-274.

Fischer, P. C., Smith, R. J., Leonard, E., Fuqua, D.R., Campbell, J.L., & Masters, M.A. (1993, March/April) Sex differences on affective dimensions: Continuing examination. *Journal of Counseling and Development, 71,* 440-443.

Frodi, A., Macauley, J., & Thome, P.R. (1977). Are women less aggressive than men? A review of the experimental literature. *Psychological Bulletin, 84,* 634-660.

Gardiner, J.K. (1987). Self psychology as feminist theory. *Signs, 12,* 761-780.

Gill, Diane L. (1988). Gender differences in competitive orientation and sport participation. *International Journal of Sports Psychology, 19,* 145-159.

Goldhaber, G.M. (1968). *Organizational communication.* Dubuque, IA: Wm. C. Brown.

Halley, R.D. (1975). Distractibility of males and females in competing aural message situations: A research note. *Human Communication Research, 2,* 79-82.

Harper, N. L., & Hirokawa, R.Y. (1988, Spring). A comparison of persuasive strategies used by female and male managers: An examination of downward influence. *Communication Quarterly, 36,* (2),157-168.

Harragan, B. (1992). *Games mother never taught you.* New York: Warner Books, Inc.

Heiss, J.S. (1962). Degree of intimacy and male-female interaction. *Sociometry, 25,* 197-208.

Henning, M., & Jardim, A. (1976). *The managerial woman.* New York: Pocket Books.

Hochschild, A.R. (1983). *The managed heart: Commercialization of human feeling.* Berkeley: University of California Press.

Hughey, J.D. (1984). *Communication confirmation, surprises, and specu-
lations.* Paper presented to the annual conference of the International Communication Association, San Francisco, CA.

Infante, D.A. (1981). Trait argumentativeness as a predictor of communi-
cative behavior in situations requiring argument. *Central States
Speech Journal, 32,* 265-272.

Infante, D.A. (1985). Inducing women to be more argumentative: Source
credibility effects. *Journal of Applied Communication Research,
13,* 33-44.

Infante, D.A. (1986). Aggressiveness and interpersonal communication.
In J. C. McCroskey & J. A. Daly (Eds.), *Personality and interpersonal communication.* Beverly Hills, CA: Sage Publications.

Infante, D.A. (1989). Response to high argumentatives: Message and sex
differences. *The Southern Communication Journal, 54,* 159-170.

Infante, D.A., Chandler, T.A., & Rudd, J.E. (1989). Test of an argumentative skill deficiency model of interspousal violence. *Communication Monographs, 56,* 163-177.

Infante, D.A., & Gorden, W.I. (1991). How employees see the boss: Test
of an argumentative and affirming model of superiors' commu-
nicative behavior. *Western Journal of Speech Communication,
55,* 294-304.

Infante, D. A., & Grimmett, R.A. (1986). Attitudinal effects of utilizing a
critical method of analysis. *Central States Speech Journal, 50,*
213-217.

Infante, D.A., & Rancer, A.S. (1982). A conceptualization and measure
of argumentativeness. *Journal of Personality Assessment, 46,*
72-80.

Infante, D.A., Sabourin, T.C., Rudd, J.E., & Shannon, E.A. (1990). Verbal
aggression in violent and nonviolent marital disputes. *Communication Quarterly, 38,* 361- 371.

Infante, D.A., Trebling, J.D., Shepherd, P.E., & Seeds, D.E. (1984). The
relationship of argumentativeness to verbal aggression. *Southern Speech Communication Journal, 50,* 67-77.

Infante, D.A., Wall, C.H., Leap, C.J., & Danielson, K. (1984). Verbal
aggression as a function of the receiver's argumentativeness.
Communication Research Reports, 1, 33-37.

Infante, D.A., & Wiley; C.J., III. (1986, March). Verbal aggressiveness:
An interpersonal model and measure. *Communication 'Monographs, 54,* 61-69.

Johnson, D.W., & Johnson, R.T. (1979). Conflict in the classroom: Controversy and learning. *Review of Educational Research, 49,* 51-70.

Kagan, J., & Moss, H.A. *(1983). Birth to maturity: A study in psychological development, (2nd ed).* New Haven: Yale University Press.

Kanter, R.M. (1977). *Men and women of the corporation.* New York: Basic Books.

Kogut, D., Langley, T., & O'Neal, E.C. (1992). Gender role masculinity and angry aggression in women. *Sex Roles, 26,* (9-10), 355-368.

Kohn, A. (1986). *No contest: The case against competition.* Boston: Houghton Mifflin.

Kopper, B. A. (1993). Role of gender, sex role identity, and type A behavior in anger expression and mental health functioning. *Journal of Counseling Psychology, 40,* (2), 232-237.

Maccoby, M. (1976). *The gamesman.* New York: Simon & Schuster.

Mast, D.L., & Herron, W.G. (1986). The sex-role antecedents scales. *Perceptual and Motor Skills, 63,* 27-56.

McCarrick, A. K., Manderscheid, R.W., & Silbergeld, S. (1981). Gender differences in competition and dominance during married couples group therapy. *Social Psychology Quarterly, 44,* (3), 164-177.

McGregor, D. (1960). *The human side of enterprise.* New York: McGraw-Hill.

Millar, F.E., & Rogers, L.E. (1987). Relational dimensions of interpersonal dynamics. In M.E. Roloff & G. Millar (Eds.), *Interpersonal Processes* (pp. 117-139). Newbury Park, Ca: Sage.

Montgomery, C. L., & Burgoon, M. (1980, March). The effects of androgyny and message expectations on resistance to persuasive communication. *Communication Monograph, 47.*

Morrison, R.F., & Sebald, M. (1974). Personal characteristics differentiating female executives from female non-executives. *Personnel: Journal of Applied Psychology, 59,* 656-659.

Nelton, S. (1991). Men, women, and leadership. *Nation's Business,* pp. 16-22.

Nicotera, A.M., & Rancer, A.S. (1994, Fall). The influence of sex on self-perceptions and social stereotyping of aggressive communication predispositions. *Western Journal of Communication, 58,* 283-307.

Nord, W.R. (1969). Social exchange theory: An integrative approach to social conformity. *Psychological Bulletin, 71,* 174-208.

Novaco, R.C. (1976). The function and regulation of the arousal of anger. *American Journal of Psychiatry, 133,* 1124-1128.

Onyekwere, E.O., Rubin, R.B., & Infante, D.A. (1991). Interpersonal perception and communication satisfaction as a function of argumentativeness and ego involvement. *Communication, Quarterly, 39,* 35-47.

Patterson, G.R., & Cobb, J.A. (1973). Stimulus control for classes of noxious behaviors. In J.F. Knutson (Ed.), *The control of aggression: Implications from basic research* (pp. 145-194). Chicago: Aldine.

Pearson,J.C., Turner, L.H., & Mancillas, W.T. (1985). *Gender and Commnunication.* Dubuque: Wm. C. Brown.

Piliavin, J.A., & Martin, R.R. (1978). The effects of the sex composition of groups on the style of social interaction. *Sex Roles, 4,* 281-296.

Prager, K.J. (1983). Identity status, sex-role orientation, and self-esteem in adulthood. *International Journal of Aging and Human Development, 12,* 129-138.

Rancer, A.S., Baukus, R.A., & Amato, P.P. (1986). Argumentativeness, verbal aggressiveness, and marital satisfaction. *Communication Research Reports, 3,* 28-32.

Rancer, A.S., & Dierks-Stewart, K.J. (1985). The influence of sex and sex-role orientation on trait argumentativeness. *Journal of Personality Assessment, 49,* 69-70.

Rancer, A.S., Kosberg, R.L., & Baukus, R.A. (1992, October). Beliefs about arguing as predictors of trait argumentativeness: Implications for training in argument and conflict management. *Communication Education, 41,* 375-387.

Raven, B.H., Centers, R., & Rodriguez, A. (1975). The bases of conjugal power. In R.E. Cromwell & D.H. Olson (Eds.), *Power in families* (pp. 217-232). New York: Wiley.

Roloff, M.E., & Greenberg, B.S. (1979). Sex differences in choice of modes in conflict resolution in real-life and television. *Communication Quarterly, 2,* 3-12.

Rosenfeld, L.B., & Fowler, G.D. (1976). Personality, sex, and leadership style. *Communication Monographs, 43,* 320-2324.

Rosenthal, R., Archer, D., Di Matteo, M.J., Koivumaki, J.H., & Rogers, P.L. (1974). Body talk and tone of voice: The language without words. *Psychology Today, 8,* 64-68.

Ruble, R.L. (1983). Sex stereotypes: Issues of change in the 1970s. *Sex Roles, 9,* 397-402.

Russell, J.A., & Mehrabian, A. (1974). Distinguishing anger and anxiety in terms of emotional response factors. *Journal of Consulting and Clinical Psychology, 42,*79-83.

Sadker, M.P., & Sadker, D.M. (1985, March). Sexism in the classroom of the 80's. *Psychology Today, 54,* (56, 57).

Sassen, G. (1980). Success anxiety in women: A constructivist interpretation of its source and its significance. *Harvard Educational Review, 50,* (1), 13-24.

Scheidel, T. M. (1963). Sex and Persuasibility. *Speech Monographs, 30,* 353-358.

Schultz, B., & Anderson, J. (1982, May). *Learning to negotiate: The role of argument.* Paper presented at the annual meeting of the Eastern Communication Association, Hartford, CT.

Segrin, C., & Fitzpatrick, M.A. (1992). Depression and verbal aggressiveness in different marital couple types. *Communication Studies, 43,* 79-91.

Seligman, D. (1988). The case of the profane lady. *Fortune, 118,* (2),11.

Sharkin, B. S. (1993, March/April). Anger and gender: Theory, research, and implications. *Journal of Counseling and Development, 1,* 386-389.

Shields, S. (1987). The dilemma of emotion. In P. Shave & C. Hendrick (Eds.), *Sex and gender.* Newbury Park, CA: Sage.

Sistrunk, F., & McDavid, J.W. (1971). Sex variable in conforming behavior. *Journal of Personality and Social Psychology, 17,* (2), 200-207.

Slater, P. (1970). *The pursuit of loneliness.* Boston: Beacon Press.

Smith, C.A., & Ellsworth, P.C. (1985). Patterns of cognitive appraisal in emotion. *Journal of Personality and Social Psychology, 48,* 813-838.

Stewart, P., & Clake-Kudless, D. (1993). *Communication* in *corporate settings: Women and men communicating.* Fort Worth: Harcourt Brace Jovanovich College Pub.

Strodtbeck, F.L., & Mann, R.D. (1956). Sex role differentiation in jury deliberations. *Sociometry, 29,* 3-11.

Tannen, D. (1990). *You just don't understand: Women and men in conversation.* New York: Ballantine Books.

Tannen, D. (1994). *Talking 9 to 5.* New York: William Morrow.

Tavris, C. *(1982). Anger: The misunderstood emotion.* New York: Simon & Schuster.

Terborg, J.R. (1977). Women in management: A research review. *Journal of Applied Psychology, 6,* 647-644.

Weaver, R. L. (1995, February 11). Leadership for the future: A new set of priorities. *Vital Speeches of the Day.*

Webster, M., & Foschi, M. *(1988). Status generalization: New theory and research.* Palo Alto, CA: Stanford University Press.

Whatley, A.B. (1982). Televised violence and related variables as predictors of self reported verbal aggression. *Central States Speech Journal, 33,* 490-497.

Zelditch, M., Jr. (1955). Role differentiation in the nuclear family: A comparative study. In T. Parsons & R.F. Bales. (Eds.), *Family socialization and interaction process* (pp. 307-352). New York: Free Press.

HUMANISTIC LEADERSHIP FOR THE TWENTY-FIRST CENTURY

By
Marti Tamm Loring

The 90's have brought significant changes in our world. A greater degree of freedom in Russia and elsewhere characterize a decade in which many people are stretching the leadership and creativity standards away from an authoritarian and dictatorial style. A prevailing climate exists in which many people treasure the freedom of individual style, production, and leadership.

The search for ideal styles of leadership continues in the business and professional communities. Differences in style of leadership between men and women is one important focus of study prior to and during this shifting world climate. Exploration into the possibilities of combining the most effective components of various leadership styles is another quest, as is the identification of abusive leadership styles. This search for leadership style seems to mirror the worldwide search for peace, cooperation, and mutual interdependence in an otherwise violent world. The violence stems from international terrorism, national strife and conflict, and even interfamily violence in which a family member kills a loved one in the supposed security of a family system. In contrast, the literature reflects aspirations for a workplace in which leadership begets excellence in products and human relationships. This aspiration is a microcosm of our hopes for a productive, caring, nonabrasive world.

GENDER CHARACTERISTICS OF LEADERSHIP STYLES

There has been considerable attention focused on leadership styles in the corporate world. For example, Goh (1991) examined the perceptions of female and male MBA students in regard to their interpersonal work style, career emphasis, supervisory behavior, and job satisfaction based on current or recent work experience. Goh affirmed that women perceived themselves as less assertive in work situations, emphasized home life over their career success and advancement, and perceived male supervisors as less monitoring toward them than toward males. Thus, these women were described as having lower job satisfaction than the males who were under male supervision in this study.

Another area of investigation has been autocratic versus democratic styles of leadership. A review of the literature (Eagly & Johnson, 1990) indicates that evidence exists for both the presence and absence of differences between the sexes, but the assumption that women lead in an interpersonally-oriented style and men in a task-oriented style did not appear to be valid. Yet, women tended to adopt more of a democratic leadership style involving participation and less autocracy, while men tended to be more directive in their leadership styles, much as they have been socialized in many countries.

Are there different expectations regarding women versus male leadership? Russell, Rush, and Herd (1988) explored whether an effective female leader would be expected to demonstrate greater consideration towards others, and whether an effective male leader would, in contrast, be expected to exhibit more behaviors in the area of initiating structure and production. They concluded that there was only partial support for this sex-role congruency theory because an effective female leader was found to be expected to not only be considerate but also to initiate structure. They found no sex differences in regard to the role assumption of productive behaviors.

Statham (1987) has argued that research on leadership styles of men and women in America has tended to focus on and measure behavior. She suggested that it is difficult to separate out-come from style differences. It may be that women managers are equally effective in accomplishing desired ends (hence looking similar to men on specific behavioral indices), yet use somewhat different styles to accomplish those ends (p. 411).

TASK-ORIENTED VERSUS PEOPLE-ORIENTED LEADERSHIP STYLES

Meeker and Weitizel-O'Neil (1977) found that women were as effective as men in leadership when it came to leading a group toward its goal. Yet, these same women were perceived as less effective because of their style or behavior differences. Some of these differences in style have been described by Statham as women being more people-oriented, stressing their concern with subordinates as very important, and calling themselves teachers. However, Statham asserted that these women were also task oriented in that getting the job done was very important to them. In fact, Statham described the people-orientation of the women as effective strategy in that the people-skills contributed toward task accomplishment by, for one thing, motivating subordinates.

On the other hand, Statham affirmed that the men in her study, unlike the women who focused on using their people orientation to accomplish a task, tended to be "image engrossed." This involved the men's focusing on the importance of their jobs for the organization and for society, as well as focusing on their control over crucial resources, such as moving dollars around.

According to Statham's analysis, men delegated and then tended to back off from a project, while women who delegated stayed involved, apparently enjoying the involvement with their subordinates more than did the men. Statham suggested that men viewed good management as not being involved in their subordinates' behavior.

INTEGRATIVE STYLE OF LEADERSHIP

Lipman-Blumen (1992) argued in favor of women having an integrative style of leadership that combines direct, competitive leadership with the more connective types of instrumental and rational leadership. This *instrumental leadership* includes *personal instrumental style* involving the utilization of intelligence, wit, compassion, humor, family background, previous accomplishments and defeats, courage, physical appearance, and sexual appeal to connect themselves to those whose commitment and help they seek to engage (p. 193). An example of this style is Frank, who came to me for a consultation regarding his leadership style and effectiveness. (Similarly, other examples discussed in this article are taken from the author's own experiences in consulting and counseling in the business community.) Frank is a manager in a telephone company. He needed to mobilize a large number of technicians for repair work during an earthquake, but a large number of the employees were scheduled for vacation and weekend time-off. Rather than requiring that all time-off be temporarily cancelled, Frank telephoned each technician individually, praising each one for past accomplishments and requesting a delay in their time-off because of numerous problems which Frank described to them as having been caused by the earthquake. All of the technicians (over thirty) agreed to immediately return to work. After the disaster was over' several of them credited Frank's personal approach, humor, and compassion as one of the reasons for their voluntary return to work.

Another type of instrumental leadership is *social instrumental style,* which is characterized by an appreciation of informal processes and relationships as vital and legitimate conduits for accomplishing goals. These leaders "do things through other people, selecting specific individuals for specific tasks" (p.194).

Ann was a vice president of a bank. In order to have greater influence in decisions, she learned skills in golf and tennis. Subsequently, she initiated a number of tennis and golf games with the other vice-presidents and the bank president. Ann's involvement in these informal contacts enabled her to participate in business discussions and give input beyond what had been possible through more formal contacts at the bank.

The third kind of instrumental style is *entrusting instrumental style* where the leader comfortably relies on everyone, not just specifically chosen individuals, to accomplish their tasks...are adept at attracting others over whom they have no formal authority to help them realize their goals (p. 195).

For Denise, the CEO of a large company, an "open door" idea included a few hours of discussions weekly with all employees who wished to visit her office and discuss new ideas for products, marketing, and public relations, as well as any problems. She also sought consultation in the community on such matters as race relations, child care provisions, and work/environment provisions for disabled employees. Her openness to input from those under her formal authority and others not under her authority, in the areas of problem-solving and prevention, helped to maintain a cooperative and problem-free climate in her company.

This instrumental style is in contrast with the *power direct style* involving command, delegation, and control over implementation. And this power style is in contrast with a *relational style* that emphasizes 1) collaboration in joining forces with others to accomplish tasks, 2) contributory emphasis in helping others, and 3) a focus on monitoring and taking pleasure in the accomplishments of others.

Lipman-Blumen (1992) appeals for leadership styles in the workplace today to be responsive to the needs of our larger world:

> Global interdependence increases the urgency of America's leadership problem. Fostering connective leadership demanded by the global environment requires integrating the other two, more appropriate sets of achieving styles–more feminine behaviors–with the traditional American direct styles (p. 192).

MOVING TOWARD ABUSE-FREE LEADERSHIP IN A VIOLENT-FREE WORLD

NiCarthy, Gottlieb, and Coffman (1993) analyze abusive styles of leadership in the workplace. There is the *leadership style of manipulators* who hide their errors, blame others, misrepresent subordinate's responsibilities, seem uncaring regarding subordinate's needs, and manipulate subordinate's into finishing off their own details–often denying their own mistreatment of employees and looking the other way while others abuse their subordinates. An administrator in a large power plant, Amy was perceived as uncaring and blaming, often indicating to higher authorities that mistakes were caused by others when she, herself, had committed the errors. There was a large number of resignations in the work force, since people were not happy working for her.

In addition, individuals utilizing the *dictating style of leadership* respond to complaints by advising subordinates to leave the job and indicating that they are dispensable. These leaders view subordinates as a means to an end–getting out the product–with no regard to their feelings. Jeff, an executive of a paper company, would frequently order employees to obey his commands to attend meetings, with no regard for their personal time or family needs. As a result, many of these same employees did not feel or demonstrate loyalty toward him in meeting deadlines that impinged on their leisure time.

An *admiral-type of leadership* involves super-organization while focusing on image, although the need for efficiency clouds the actual treatment of subordinates. How the work environment impacts the employees is not considered important. Sheil, head of a large firm of lawyers, focused on the image of the firm in accepting cases, making assignments of cases and demanding long work hours with no regard for the family needs or special interests of various lawyers. The firm did not draw the more talented attorneys because of its reputation for image over service and caring.

Further, the *pseudo-democratic style* of leadership involves delegation and rewards although, when the pressure is on, the style changes to harassment and abuse with a frantic attempt to get the job done while racing for a deadline. This kind of leadership can also switch back and forth to a dictatorial style. Jeff, who was mentioned previously, occasionally asked for employee input, but–under pressure–increased his demands and commands.

These authors (NiCarthy, Gottlieb, & Coffman, 1993) also describe an *unpredictable style of leadership* that involves a back and forth between praise altered with yelling or criticism. This can involve both praise and humiliation on the same day and often includes decisions that do not allow for input from others. Jason was the owner's son in a sports products design and manufacturing business. He would alternate between complementing employees and criticizing them, never taking their ideas into consideration even when designers warned him about changes in the industry. Consequently, his company was often lagging behind others in pursuing new directions and product development.

In addition, a *crisis management style of leadership* is characterized by constant crises. There is a void of thoughtful planning in the midst of reaction to crisis situations. With this style, there are often apologies in private after public humiliations from the leaders. Sam, the president of a clothing company, lagged behind his competitors and had difficulty keeping key leadership personnel because of continuous crises with little opportunity for planning.

Lastly, the *combination style of leadership* involves a combination of two or more styles described previously. An example of this combination style of leadership is seen in Joan, an executive with a large American corporation. Joan, a state official in charge of a large number of employees, made a pretense of encouraging others' input while, shortly afterwards, she would make decisions that did not integrate this input. She criticized and humiliated her subordinates, while rewarding their productivity. She would move from being dictatorial to sad and depressed, asking subordinates to bail her out of one crisis after another.

Abusive types of leadership can be found in either men or women and can be directed toward both men and women. The issues relate to the use of power, need for control, consideration of subordinates feelings and needs, and outright emotional attacks with an underlying conviction that one's own tension-release is acceptable–regardless of the cost to subordinates and/or colleagues.

A HUMANISTIC LEADERSHIP STYLE
But what of a possible combination–a blending of the most effective components of leadership by both genders into a style that challenges the violence of today's world? This style of effective leadership would stand in contrast to many of the more aggressive leadership

styles, some of which reflect the violence we see and experience in the world around us.

Further, this humanistic leadership would be nonabrasive, relational, and instrumental, focusing on the accomplishment of tasks in a caring manner that takes into consideration the feelings and needs of subordinates, as well as colleagues and superiors. The input of everyone involved would be valued, regardless of the ultimate decisions that were made. No abusive behavior would be allowed at any level in the leadership system, and sanctions would include demotion for outright and continuous abuse. This involves a whole shift in which the means is perceived as crucial in creating the end-products–both a humanistic business environment and an excellent product.

Robert, executive of a large investment firm, held weekly meetings in which subordinates' input was sought, valued, and often integrated. He had staff cooperation in predicting, rather than only reacting to, problems and potential crises. He was clear in communicating expectations, expressing and rewarding excellence, and encouraging mentoring. He established rewards for helping others and included a number of family considerations in his workplace, such as childcare provisions and a rule against interfering with family vacations when work pressures mounted. He made it clear that he valued teamwork, and that everyone's input was important in getting the job done. There were monthly seminars on human relations. The morale and productivity were both high. When an employee had a problem with spouse abuse, she was immediately sent to a counselor at the company's expense,

This norm of a violence-free, abuse-free workplace would include a trusting climate of cooperation in which leadership encouraged all employees to make each other look good in the sense of combining skills to create an excellent product. Furthermore, humanistic leadership would involve a model in which task completion was not allowed to be embraced by violence and abuse of any kind. This nonembracing of violence and the unwillingness to allow victimization in the workplace would offer a prototype for peaceful interaction in our world.

In America, the violence in our world infiltrates the workplace in such instances as an employee who is shot on the job by an abusive husband stalking his partner, and the postal employee who is fired and later returns in a rage to kill other employees. In addition, injuries are sometimes caused by desperate individuals who are fired from their jobs because of downsizing, subsequently reacting violently in our violent world. Further distress at work is caused by battered women who try to hide their bruises, yet desperately seek help from fellow employees. While a humanistic workplace may not eliminate the violence in our world, it can contribute toward building peaceful prototypes of corporate functioning, which must be matched by other models of nonviolent social and family interaction and productivity.

Attempts to recognize and respect differences in style, gender or personality are as crucial to a respectful and peaceful workplace and world climate as is working toward a relational and instrumental style of leadership. Tasks will be more effectively completed in an atmosphere where leadership recognizes and expresses concern about individuals who are discharged, physically battered, and/or depressed. Furthermore, creating norms, expectations, and training in the areas of mutually cooperative, nonabusive styles of leadership gives humanistic direction to our business world and to our larger society.

REFERENCES

Eagly, A.H., & Johnson, B.T. (1990). Gender and leadership style: A meta–analysis. *Psychological Bulletin, 108,* 233- 256.

Goh, S. C. (1991). Sex differences in perceptions of interpersonal work style, career emphasis, supervisory monitoring behavior, and job satisfaction. *Sex Roles, 24,* 701-710.

Lipman-Blumen, J. (1992). Connective leadership: Female leadership styles in the 21st-century workplace. *Sociological Perspectives, 35,* 183-203.

Meeker, B.F., & Weitzel-O'Neil, P.A. (1977). Sex roles and interpersonal behavior in task-oriented groups. *American Sociological Review, 42,* 91-104.

NiCarthy, G., Gottlieb, N., & Coffman, S. (l993). *You don't have to take it: A woman's guide to confronting emotional abuse at work.* Seattle,WA:Seal.

Russel, J.E., Rush, M.C., & Herd, A.M. (1988). An exploration of women's expectations of effective male and female leadership. *Sex Roles, 18,* 279-287.

Statham, A. (1987). The gender model revisited: Differences in the management styles of men and women. *Sex Roles, 16,* 409-427.

ADVICE TO FRONT LINE LEADERS–FROM
A TRAINING AND DEVELOPMENT SPECIALIST

By
Linda S. Feuerbacher

THE CASE OF LEON

I'll never forget Leon. He was a first line supervisor at a former employer of mine. Now, Leon was a fellow who managed the old fashioned way–he kept a close eye on his people at all times, did not trust them, and believed all they wanted was a paycheck and to complain to everybody.

I was assigned to assist Leon and his department to help them deal with all the complaints we were getting from his direct reports and others who had to interact with him. His people were in constant turmoil over the way he managed them, embarrassed them in front of their peers, barked orders at them, etc. He had been accused of racial slurs, using foul language, harassment–in short, Leon was in serious trouble as a manager, and his job was in jeopardy.

One of the things I remember most about Leon was his uncanny ability to irritate and intimidate the people he dealt with–including me. Whenever I went out to his area on the plant floor he would call me "little" girl (neither descriptor fits), allow me to discuss the week's most urgent people problem with him, and help him problem solve and role–play the solution. Then he would promptly go out and do as he pleased. I talked openly with him about his resistance, and he agreed he was giving lip service to my efforts. Worst of all he would smile and say, "You just go ahead and do whatever you need to do, little girl, and I will do what I need to do." Clearly, we had reached an impasse.

But I was not ready to give up on him. I racked my brain for new ways to approach Leon, to find ways to explain things differently. I knew the only way he would change was to understand that he needed his people's support and would get better results by treating his work group differently.

Late one afternoon I was finishing work with a group on second shift when an idea came to mind. I knew Leon usually stayed over to plan for the next day, so I went to his office and asked him to step out on the plant floor with me. Since second shift was a maintenance shift only, the plant was quiet and very dimly lit. We walked to the middle of the plant and stopped.

"Listen, Leon," I said to him. "What do you hear?"

"What are you talking about?" he replied.

"Just answer the question, Leon. What do you hear?"

"All I hear is you asking me questions!," he said, obviously annoyed.

"And what is happening in this plant at this very moment?" I asked.

"There is nothing going on, little girl. Nothing, nothing, nothing. Now, what do you *really* want. Why did you drag me out of my office?" he asked.

"I did it to show you that this is what you will get, Leon, if you don't change the way you are dealing with your people–nothing, nothing, nothing. They will not give you information, they will not bother to do anything extra for your customers, and they will not be concerned about the department's results. You may as well just turn out the lights and go home because that is what you will accomplish by continuing to manage them the way you are now."

SELECT MANAGERS FOR THEIR PEOPLE SKILLS

What happened to Leon, you ask? Eventually, Leon 'retired', or so I was told. Actually, Leon's dilemma is all too familiar; companies often promote technically competent people into leadership positions without giving them a chance to develop any people skills. Technical background is helpful, but the job of any leader is to get the work done *through their people.* Companies must select leaders the same way they select people for other positions, based on whether the candidate's skills and behaviors match the job. If there is no match, the company has two options; choose another candidate, or develop the candidate's skills to a level adequate for the job. Of course, this implies the company has a well-defined leadership development process already in place. It also implies the company is willing to wait for "good" results, something I have rarely seen happen even in the best-intentioned companies.

DO NOT ASSUME LEADERS LEAD PEOPLE.

People skills and leadership skills are totally different from the technical skills used in functional specialties. Companies tend to assume that bestowing a functional specialist with the title, compensation, and/or office space reserved for front line leaders *automatically* gives them leadership skills. I have often heard phrases like, "That is what I pay them to do..." and "They already know that, or they would not have been promoted..." Most individuals on the receiving end of a promotion need hear those phrases only once to get the impression that *admitting one's own shortcomings is akin to career suicide.*

To deal with this phenomena, companies can do several things. *First,* there should be a specific job description and measures of performance defined for front line leaders and their departments. Also, there should be a description of physical or technical output; and skills showing the ability to correct poor behavior in a positive way or deal equitably with all employees regardless of race, gender, etc., should be included. Work plans should be created to develop those skills and apply them on the job, real time. Performance should be audited and compared to the original measures for the job to continuously improve and develop people's skills. Most leaders say they have those things in place, but when we really look at what exists, many are surprised at the broadly defined people items as compared to the more specific production items. So, being specific about people skills and leadership expectations is the *first* step.

TEACH THEM HOW

The *second* step is probably most critical. After defining what leaders should do and identifying the degree to which he/she is able to do it correctly, companies must create development plans that are *customized* to each leader's needs. Yes, I said customized! Generalized classes are good for skill overviews, but trainees need specialized mentoring by someone who is skillful at the task and skillful at giving feedback to a learner. Unfortunately, many leaders do not see the critical importance in teaching others their skills. Even in so-called world class companies, this step of leadership development is seldom practiced because mentors believe they are "too busy" to devote time to doing it. Since this one step could provide the basis for continuous improvement of the leadership system, this is one of the most helpful tactics leaders can use to be sure their leadership system stays current and their managers are skilled.

GET TO THE ROOT CAUSE

Even with specific expectations written down and a mentioning process in place, it cannot be assumed leaders know how and are willing to document, track, and deal with performance problems; probably 85% of the leaders I have worked with *did not* handle performance management well. When a leader explains a process problem, he/she must ask *why* it is happening that way and listen to the explanations. Then, ask why again and listen. Ask why up to 5 times to get to the root cause of the problem. Chances are, one will find there are 4-7 contributing factors to every process problem out there, and fixing just one of those pieces will not make the problem go away. Shooting from the hip with quick fixes to recurring problems will no longer work. Leaders must keep asking "why" to actually reduce the number of problems they deal with every week, month, or year. Leaders need to be suspicious of the quick fix technique and instead go for immediate countermeasures with long term investigation/problem solving as the main focus.

This applies to people problems as well. More interest should be taken in doing performance reviews on time, often (quarterly is suggested), with some thought behind them, and follow up done afterwards to see if the countermeasures are working. It should be understood that reviews are not a judgment of a person's worth, but an actual accounting of the skills the person has to offer vs. what he/she is *actually contributing* to the organization's results. The leader's role is *not* to control people's actions or make them want to do something; it is to keep score on how well they are doing and show ways they can have an even more positive impact. Finally, for any review to be effective, *follow-up* must occur to see that the improvement continues. Most of the time it is believed that simply because the problem is mentioned it will resolve itself. This is rarely the case.

UNDERSTAND WHAT TRAINING AND DEVELOPMENT CAN DO FOR THE BUSINESS

Many professionals in the Training and Development field lament that operations people do not understand the direct impact of a Training and Development Department to the business' bottom line. To learn the true impact that training and people issues might have on an operation's results, leaders should try to figure the real cost or quality impact of typical training issues. Try to quantify how much a de-motivated person might affect the customer's product. Identify what information could be tracked to determine whether training really fits the needs of the business. Ask instructors to attend production meetings so they can understand operation's problems and work with team leaders to help solve them.

A TRAINING HORROR STORY

To help leaders understand how training can impact their operation, here is an example. A large manufacturing firm had instilled in their team members (during a training class) to stop the production line if there were any quality problems, a very noble goal but, when taken literally, can shut the operation down. I am very quality minded, but I also believe some quality problems take time to resolve, and one does not want to destroy the customer base for minor quality problems. A team member saw a group of scratched parts, decided that scratched parts were not good quality, and shut down the line. These parts were to be covered with paint and another part installed over them. No one would see the scratch unless he/she took the component apart. A leader told the team member, "Thanks for spotting that. We will talk with the vendor to see if we can eliminate those scratches." But the team member said he was taught not to use defective parts, period. After much ado, several calls to the vendor, and hours of time spent trying to figure out what to do (not to mention an assembly line stopped for over three hours), it was decided to send the team member with his leader to visit the vendor and try to eliminate the scratch on the stamped parts.

The vendor agreed to collect data and meet back with the two the following week. The scratch would remain, it seemed, unless they could use a stronger type of steel in making the part-water hardened steel. Unfortunately, this would cost much more than the original part cost. Is the picture becoming clear? Because of a quality statement made in a training class and because the student took the statement to its extreme, the impact on cost and quality was enormous. Over the course of one year, after adding leadership and staff problem solving time, downtime on the line, increased materials cost per product, travel costs, and tool and die re-work costs, this one incident cost the company a whopping $13 million dollars! All for a scratch that could not be seen on the final product and which had no potential for part failure. Plus, the additional cost was added to the customer's price.

GET INVOLVED WITH TRAINING AND DEVELOPMENT

Sounds crazy, doesn't it? Now, one might be saying, that wouldn't happen here, our training classes do not have the same impact, etc. A closer look should be taken at the impact training *does* have on the day-to-day operation, the topics instructors address, and the type of follow up information operational leaders discuss with the Training and Development department. It cannot be emphasized enough how helpful it is to develop a mutual understanding between operations and training. The more that is understood, the more helpful each can be to the other. This is the best way to enable the Training Department to customize operations training.

PREPARE FOR THE FUTURE

A recent book by Paul Kennedy titled *Preparing for the Twenty-First Century* gives readers some fascinating statistics, logical possibilities, and issues to think about and link with training and development in order to prepare them and their companies to do business in the next 5–50 years. Here are just a few of his insights / issues:

- in 35 years there will be more elderly than children in the U.S.
- to compensate for this fact, there may be a significant influx of legal (and illegal) aliens to take their place in the workforce
- regardless of who takes the place of the aging workforce, training will be key (examples: language skills, basic math skills, diversity training for leaders, increased testing during interviewing processes, increased teaching/monitoring responsibilities for staff, more OJT)
- educated technical people will be at a premium price
- people will need incentives to stay at one company, rather than "job hop"

Brainstorm any one of these issues for a specific location and listen to the concerns (and answers!) people have for the future. Chances are, many of the issues can be eased with some type of training or development strategy. In any case, waiting until the year 2000 to begin dealing with them may be too late to catch up.

REFERENCES

Kennedy, P. (1993) *Preparing for the twenty–first century.* New York: Random House.

LEADERSHIP AND EMPLOYEE EMPOWERMENT: THE FOUNDATION FOR ORGANIZATIONAL SUCCESS AND PROFIT IN THE TEWNTY-FIRST CENTURY

By
Kay Payne, Joseph P. Cangemi,
Harold Fuqua, Jr., Rhonda Muhleakamp

Power interests people involved in romantic relationships, as well as in workplace organizations. Many people spend entire lifetimes attempting to acquire power in the workplace, while others seek positions of authority (which will not be the subject of this article) in order to control people, resources, and information. Some people desire power in order to gain large sums of money to purchase expensive homes, cars, and membership in country clubs, or to travel, going first class, or visit exotic places around the world. Employees in many organizations seek decision making power, or power to gain the ear of their superiors over issues which affect their daily work lives. People who know how to use power lead more effectively than those who do not or will not use power. This article defines power, focuses on the sources and types of power, how leaders can increase their power, and how effective leaders use power without hurting the organization and its members.

POWER DEFINED

In relation to organizations, Russell (1938) defined power as the production of intended effects. Bierstedt (1950) defined it as the ability to employ force. Weber (1954) defined it as the possibility of imposing one's will upon the behavior of others. French (1956) defined it as the maximum force A can induce on B minus the maximum force which B can mobilize against A. Dahl (1957) claimed A had power over B only to the extent A could get B to do something which B would otherwise not do. Etzioni (1961) wrote power relates to an actor's ability to induce or influence other actors to carry out his or her directives or any other norms he or she supports. Tannenbaum (1962) believed effective leaders had the ability, through interpersonal influence, to cause their subordinates to attain specific personal, as well as organizational, goals. Rogers (1973) described it as the potential for using influence which suggests it may or may not be used. Hersey & Blanchard (1982) suggested that effective leadership acts as the process of influencing the activities of an individual or group in efforts toward goal achievement in a given situation. Krausz (1986) argued "Power is the ability to influence the actions of others, individuals or groups. It is understood as the leader's influence potential" (p.69). Cangemi (1992) asserted: "Power is the individual's capacity to move others, to entice others, to persuade and encourage others to attain specific goals or to engage in specific behavior; it is the capacity to influence and motivate others" (p.499). Verderber and Verderber (1992) argued "social power is a potential for changing attitudes, beliefs, and behaviors of others" (p.280). Those in power have the ability and capacity to get others to do what they want them to do. Folger, Poole, and Stutman (1993) defined power as "the capacity to act effectively" (p.69). Clarifying these definitions we might say leadership includes any attempt to influence, using either position power or social power, or both, within organizations as influence potential. Therefore, we might say power is a resource which enables a leader to induce compliance.

These definitions of power focus on the successful way leaders influence their followers to produce an effect. Cangemi (1992) believed successful leaders move and influence people through their power toward greater accomplishments for themselves and their organizations. Tannenbaum (1962) believed effective leaders have the ability, through interpersonal influence, to cause their subordinates to attain specific personal, as well as organizational, goals. Hersey & Blanchard (1982) suggested effective leadership acts as the process of influencing the activities of an individual or group in efforts toward goal achievement in a given situation. In organizations today, many sources of power become lost in legislation, negotiation, or bureaucratic policies.

Sources and Types of Power

The currency of leadership, essential to influencing others, involves a wide variety of factors. Varying authors (French & Raven, 1959; Baldridge, 1971; Kanter, 1977; Hackman & Johnson, 1991; King, 1987) describe sources, types, and uses of power essential to effective leadership. Eight primary sources of power pooled from these varying authors include: support systems, information, credibility, visibility, legitimacy, persuasiveness, charisma, and agenda setting. Support systems include both formal and informal opportunities for networking. Having connections among a wide variety of people enables a leader to access both formal and informal power. Information, the second source of power, involves not only what one knows, but how fast one finds out, which encourages power players to be good listeners. Power flows to those who have the information and know-how to accomplish organizational tasks. The third power source, credibility, resides in how much respect one attains. We rely on highly credible people who have established a history of experience and expertise. The fourth source of power, visibility, means taking on tough jobs so people take notice. Legitimacy, the fifth source of power, works in concert with visibility and involves having respected power players commend one publicly, thereby creating acceptance among any would be doubters. Legitimacy also includes the notion of authority, or formal role, held by a person. The sixth source of power, persuasiveness, determines how successfully a person uses rational or emotional appeals. One's ability to persuade depends on personality, content of a task, motivation and confidence. The seventh source of power, charisma, incorporates many other ethical qualities of leadership together. Charisma includes a leader's reputation, sincerity, trustworthiness, expertise, and dynamism. Describing this artistic proof of leadership by saying it involves a leader's aura, the emanations of his or her spirit- the amount of "psychic space" taken up, helps explain it. The last source of power, agenda setting, rests in knowing when meetings will be held and accessing the group leader to put items on the agenda at just the right time. Two of the by-products of networks and alliances involve access to decision-making arenas and the ability to influence the agendas in those arenas. People or groups who have access to agenda setting frequently represent their positions, while the interests and concerns of those not present may become distorted or ignored (Lukes, 1974; Brown, 1986).

While operating in a system, knowing how to identify power makes it easier to access the type which works best. The five most commonly known types of power include: coercive, reward, legitimate, expert, and referent (French & Raven, 1959). Coercive power bases its effectiveness on the ability to administer punishment or give negative reinforcements. With this type of power, followers need to know a leader will impose costs or sanctions, for example, reprimands, cuts in pay, transfers, demotions, or even dismissal. Leaders must follow through when using coercive power or it will lose its' impact. The second type, reward power, rests on the ability to deliver something valued by the receiver. People who can deliver money, jobs, transfers, or political support have something other people want and therefore become extremely powerful in organizations. A leader needs to carefully distinguish between rewards allocated for average and outstanding performance so that individuals do not loose their motivation and commitment to the company. Legitimate power, the third type, resides in a person's position, or formal role, rather than the actual person him or herself. This type of formal power relies on position in an authority hierarchy. A leader has legitimate, or position power, when he or she induces an employee to do something because of the position he or she holds. Legitimate power, or position power, tends to flow downward in an organization. Occasionally, people with legitimate power fail to recognize they have it, and then they may begin to notice others going around them to accomplish their goals. The fourth type, expert power, relies on a person's special knowledge and expertise in a given area. Anyone can have it if he or she formally and informally prepares sufficiently. The last type, referent power, includes admiration of a leader, which usually produces influence and acceptance by subordinates (French & Raven, 1959). Referent power acts a little like role model power. It depends on respecting, liking, and holding another individual in high esteem. When a person derives their power from their followers they have personal or referent power, which suggests their power flows upward from the followers. It usually develops over a long period of time and often depends upon the way a leader treats his or her people. Etzioni (1961) suggested leaders who hold both legitimate and referent power generate a positive situation. Machiavelli (1950) indicates legitimate power involves fear of reprisal from a leader, while referent power involves love from a leader.

Among these five types of power, creating a positive operating climate involves choosing the most appropriate compliance-gaining tactics, which tend to lead to greater "life" or job satisfaction (Plax, Kearney & Downs, 1986). McCroskey, Richmond, Plax, and Kearney (1985) claimed relying on expert, reward, and referent power appeared to produce the greatest satisfaction, while reliance on coercive and legitimate power had the opposite effect (McCroskey et al., 1985). Rahim (1989) found legitimate power useful in gaining compliance, but satisfaction from supervisees decreased. Expert and referent power bases correlated with both compliance and satisfaction. Rahim (1989, p.555) also noted effective leaders can "enhance their referent power base if they learn to be considerate of their subordinates' needs and feelings, treat them fairly, and defend their interests when acting as their representative." Effective leaders combine the various bases and sources of power, electing to use them in appropriate situations. An effective leader rarely depends on only one source or base of power.

In a study by Student (1968), employees rated the extent to which a leader utilized various power bases (French and Raven 1959). The results, in order, beginning with the strongest reason for compliance include: 1) legitimate, 2) expert, 3) reward, 4) referent and the last reason, 5) coercive power. Curiously, Student (1968) found legitimate power did not relate to the performance of the work groups. Reward and coercive power related positively to some performance measures (suggestions submitted, supply cost performance) but negatively related to others (average earnings, maintenance cost performance). Expert and referent power significantly and positively related to four and five measures of power, and thus emerged as the most effective supervisory base of power. Idiosyncratic in character, expert and referent power depended on an individual's role behavior, while legitimate and coercive power resulted from organizational roles. Employees did not experience satisfaction with leaders whose influence attempts emerged entirely on position-based power (legitimate, reward, and coercive). Bachman, Smith, and Slesinger (1966) found the same results as Student (1968) except reward and referent power traded places in importance. Again, with referent and expert power, employee satisfaction and performance correlated positively. Reward power resulted in poor performance, and marked dissatisfaction. Coercive and legitimate power did not result in higher performance and were associated with dissatisfaction. Bachman, Bowers, and Marcus (1968) found expert and legitimate the most important reasons for complying with superiors. Referent and reward power each ranked third among some organizations, and fourth in others. Coercive power ranked last, again. Expert and referent power strongly and positively correlated with satisfaction. Reward and legitimate power were not strongly related to satisfaction. Coercive power consistently related to dissatisfaction. In summary, where referent and expert power predominates, performance correlates positively with satisfaction.

Low performance and much dissatisfaction correlate with the strong use of reward power. Coercive and legitimate power aroused dissatisfaction but did not affect performance.

When studying classroom power, Jamieson and Thomas (1974) found high school students wanted legitimate, followed by coercive, expert, referent and reward power. Undergraduate college students viewed coercive power as most important, followed by legitimate, expert, reward, and referent power. Graduate students perceived expert power first, followed by legitimate, reward, coercive, and referent power. Coercive power strongly and negatively associated with satisfaction among all three groups of students.

EFFECTIVE LEADERS BECOME MORE POWERFUL

To increase one's organizational power, effective leaders recognize the importance of developing their own personal power. Kotter (1977) asserted the importance of planning, organizing, budgeting, staffing, controlling, and evaluating the people on whom the leader depends. Trying to control others solely by directing them on the basis of authority associated with one's position rarely works. Effective leaders often become dependent upon individuals over whom they have no formal authority. Also, in this modern age, few employees passively accept and obey authorities who issue a constant stream of commands simply because they play the role of boss.

To increase one's organizational power in another way, a person can exhibit an attitude of trust in other organizational members. At the same time, developing a high degree of expertise within the organization increases a subordinates trust in their leader because they learn to rely (trust) that person to steer them in the right direction. Subordinates gain respect for leaders when expertise increases and subordinates develop an attitude of trust toward the leader. Increasing one's own achievements and making them known establish a higher organizational standard which subordinates can look up to and respect. As respect increases among the subordinates through a track record of accomplishments, the leader's personal power increases in the organization (Kotter, 1977). Failure of the leader to recognize the need for the development and the importance of personal power will most likely increase subordinates' resistance to change or direction.

Situational leadership (Hersey, Blanchard & Natemeyer, 1979) claims effective leadership correlates with readiness of individuals or groups to take responsibility for directing their own behavior in a given situation. Readiness relates to task maturity. Measurement of task maturity moves along a continuum from unwilling and unable at one end to willing and able at the other end with regard to a specific job. Situational leadership proponents claim the readiness of followers dictates which style of leadership and power will have the highest probability of success. For new people on the job, who may not be especially willing and able, a leader may need to use a "telling" leadership style and a coercive style of power to motivate employees to comply. As a follower begins to move along the readiness scale to stage two, directive behavior may still be needed, but leadership increases in supportive behavior. A leader style of "selling" associated with reward power may motivate employees to comply. As the follower begins to mature further along the readiness scale to stage three, they need little direction but still may require a high level of communication and support from the leader. A participative leadership style and a referent power style may enhance productivity and satisfaction. This power base seems to instill confidence and provide encouragement, recognition, and other supportive behavior for this stage of maturity. At a high level of readiness (stage four) an employee communicates a willingness and ability to perform his or her tasks. An employee of this type responds readily to a delegating leadership style. The leader gains respect from and influences most readily a person who has both competence and confidence in their job by exhibiting expertise, knowledge, and skill. In summary, among employees with below-average readiness, the emphasis is on gaining compliance, with average readiness, the emphasis is on compliance and influence, and with above average readiness the emphasis is on influence as the most effective uses of power.

EFFECTIVE LEADERS USE POWER

Leaders who use power effectively accomplish tasks in the organization without relying on their job title. Kanter (1977) suggested powerful leaders rely more on personal power than job title, or credentials, to mobilize their resources, inspire creativity, and instill confidence among subordinates. Block (1987) said leaders become more powerful as they nurture the power of others. Jamieson and O'Mara (1991, p.163) argued that: "As a manager who empowers others, you will act as a colleague more than a boss, relying on influence, respect, and relationships to work with employees." Empowering managers seek to share power, to give it away, then hold those to whom they gave it very accountable (Stewart, 1997). They recognize and reward people for their accomplishments, contributions, and ideas. They encourage participation, solicit input, and involve people in decisions, giving credit to those who have earned it. They reward people who generate the greatest impact toward organizational goals; rewarding results rather than processes.

Powerful leaders influence followers to do what they want done. Galbraith (1983) said that a powerful leader will be judged by how effectively he or she persuaded his or her subordinates to accept solutions to problems which led to organizational goals. Filley and Grimes (1967) identified eleven reasons why a person might seek a decision from another on a variety of work-related matters in a professional organization. The reasons, in order of most frequently to least frequently mentioned, included the following: 1) responsibility and function, 2) formal authority, 3) control of resources, 4) collegiality (the person has the right to be consulted) 5) manipulation (person can get the decision made in the manner desired), 6) default or avoidance (available to deal with the problem), 7) bureaucratic rules, 8) traditional rules, 9) equity (person is fair), 10) friendship, and 11) expertise.

Winning acceptance of one's views produces an incredibly rewarding feeling of accomplishment. Competence in the political arena involves keen awareness of power, skill at using the sources and bases of power effectively, using technical skills with proficiency, using information properly, forming effective alliances within the organization, and exercising authority over others with sensitivity to their feelings (Mintzberg, 1983). What matters most in the effective use of power at the top is accessibility, networking, listening, and people skills (Stewart, 1997). Previously, at Owens-Corning, the 28th floor became stigmatized as "management." Today, recognizing the importance of how they communicate power, leadership operates in the middle of the second floor, accessible to everyone (Stewart, 1997).

Leaders who use power effectively care about people and avoid dominating them. They depend on deftness, rather than flexing their muscle. They choose respect over friendship, and want truth rather than deception. McClelland (1970) claimed that the positive or socialized face of power emphasizes a concern for group goals, finds the goals which move people, helps the group formulate them, takes the initiative in providing members of the group the means to achieve them, and gives group members a sense of support, strength, and competence needed to work hard toward achieving them. McMurry (1973) said that leaders who can persuade become capable of influencing their audiences both emotionally and rationally. They analyze their audience in terms of relevant needs, desires, and values after which they focus on a connection with their audience on common ground before moving into areas of resistance. Areas of resistance must be handled carefully, respectfully, and in a non-dogmatic way. Payne (1996) reminded leaders of the importance not only of what they say, but how they say it. People who speak with a variety of pitch, volume, and timing changes, with well organized messages, clear and well developed points, with both logical and emotional appeals, using the Standard Dialect, receive higher ratings of credibility and are perceived as more powerful, competent, and persuasive in most situations (Payne, 1996). Bolman and Deal (1991) said that individuals who possess such qualities as charisma, political skill, verbal ability, and competence to communicate their vision become powerful by virtue of these personal attributes. Yukl and Falbe (1991) suggested that persuasiveness acts as the most important skill associated with leadership's effectiveness. People not only must perceive a leader as having power, but they must perceive a leader as willing and able to use it. All behavior is based on people's perception and interpretation of truth and reality. If unwilling to use power, a leader will lose it.

The misuse of power, on the other hand, becomes an ethical issue. The unethical use of power may help a leader achieve a short-term effect, but over the long run this behavior will cause the leader to become a detriment to the organization and force the organization to move against him or her. For example, in one organization a leader changed scrap records in order to impress higher-level authorities. This unethical behavior eventually caught up to this a leader, as other unethical acts followed and the company replaced him. In another large American organization, a leader found guilty of altering the content of fruit juice paid dearly for this unethical conduct. Levinson (1978) claimed that the leader with an abrasive personality, often of high intelligence, acts as a perfectionist---pushing hard toward accomplishments, consistently producing a superior job but not working well with others, usually fails to motivate subordinates. These type leaders often fail to live up to their potential, rarely rise very high in organizations, and have trouble delegating or empowering others (Levinson, 1978). While difficult to do, if top leaders would only point out the destructive tendencies of abrasive behavior and teach their subordinate leaders that such behaviors will not be tolerated, improvement might occur.

CONCLUSION

The literature surveyed in this article explains how leaders can gain power by recognizing the sources and types of power and using it in ethical ways within the context of organizations. Leaders who work to increase their personal power, persuasiveness, and expertise will enhance their effectiveness. If leaders exercise authority over others with sensitivity, avoid dominating or threatening them, and rely on their expertise and positive aspects of their personality to influence them, they can enhance their effectiveness. Effective leaders do not engage in unethical conduct nor display the characteristics associated with an abrasive personality, which would cause them to under utilize the talents of their employees. Effective leaders increase their personal power by empowering others in the organization.

REFERENCES

Bachman, J.G., Bowers, D.G., & Marcus, P.M. (1968). Bases of supervisory power: A comparative study in five organizational settings. In A.S. Tannenbaum, Control in Organizations. New York: McGraw-Hill.

Bachman, J.G., Smith, C.G., & Slesinger, J.A. (1966). Control, performance, and satisfaction: An analysis of structural and individual effects. Journal of Personality and Social Psychology, 4, (2), 127-136.

Baldridge, J.V. (1971). Power and conflict in the university. New York: Wiley.

Beirstedt, R. (1950). An analysis of social power. American Sociological Review, 15, 730-736.

Block, P. (1987). The empowered manager: Positive political skills at work. San Francisco: Jossey-Bass.

Bolman, L., & Deal, T. (1991). Reframing organizations. San Francisco: Jossey-Bass.

Brown, L.D. (1986). Power outside organizational paradigms: Lessons from community partnerships. In S. Srivastva & Associates (Eds.), Executive power: How executives influence people and organizations. San Francisco: Jossey-Bass.

Cangemi, J. (1992). Some observations of successful leaders and their use of power and authority. Education, 112, 499-505.

Dahl, R.A. (1957). The concept of power. Behavioral Science, 2, 201-215.

Etzioni, A. (1961). A comparative analysis of complex organizations. New York: Free Press.

Etzioni, A. (1978). Comparative analysis of complex organizations. In D. Hampton, C. Summer, & R. Weber (Eds.), Organizational behavior and the practice of management. Glenview, IL: Scott, Foresman & Co.

Filley, A.C., & Grimes, A.J. (1967). The bases of power in decision processes. Industrial Relations Research Institute, University of Wisconsin, Reprint Series 104.

Folger, J., Poole, M., & Stutman, R. (1993). Working through conflict. New York: Harper Collins.

French, J.R.P. (1956). A formal theory of social power. Psychology Review, 63, 181-194.

French, J.R.P., & Raven, B. (1959). The bases of social power. In D. Cartwright & A. Zander (Eds.), Group dynamics. New York: Harper & Row.

Galbraith, J.K. (1983). Anatomy of power. Boston: Houghton Mifflin.

Hackman, M. A., & Johnson, C.E. (1991). Leadership: A communication perspective. Prospect Heights, Il.: Waveland Press.

Hersey, P., & Blanchard, K. (1982). The management of organizational behavior. Englewood Cliffs, NJ: Prentice-Hall.

Hersey, P., Blanchard, K. & Natemeyer, W.E. (1979, December). Situational leadership, perception, and the impact of power." Group and Organizational Studies, 4, (4), 418-428.

Jamieson, D., & O'Mara, J. (1991). Managing the workforce 2000. San Francisco: Jossey-Bass.

Jamieson, D., & Thomas, K. (1974). Power and conflict in the student-teacher relationship. Journal of Applied Behavioral Science, P10, 3.

Kanter, R.M. (1977). Men and women of the corporation. New York: Basic Books.

King, A. (1987). Power & communication. Prospect Heights, IL: Waveland Press.

Kotter, J.P. (1977, Jul/Aug). Power, dependence, and effective management. Harvard Business Review, 127-136.

Krausz, R. (1986). Power and leadership in organizations. Transactional Analysis Journal, 16, 85-94.

Levinson, H. (1978, May/June). The abrasive personality. Harvard Business Review, pp. 86-94.

Lukes, S. (1974). Power: A radical view. New York: Macmillan.

Machiavelli, N. (1950). Of cruelty and clemency, whether it is better to be loved or feared. The Prince and the discourses. New York: Random House. Chapter 17.

McCroskey, J.C., Richmond, V.P., Plax, T.G., & Kearney, P. (1985). Power in the classroom: Behavior alteration techniques, communication training and learning. Communication Education, 34, 214-226.

McClelland, D.C. (1970). The two faces of power. In D. Hampton, C. Summer, & R. Webber (Eds.), Organizational behavior and the practice of management. Glenview, IL: Scott Foresman.

McMurry, R.N. (1973, Nov/Dec). Power and the ambitious executive. Harvard Business Review, pp. 7-12.

Mintzberg, H. (1983). Power in and around organizations. New Jersey: Prentice-Hall.

Payne, K. (1996). Voice and diction. New York: McGraw Hill.

Plax, T.G., Kearney, P., & Downs, T.M. (1986). Communicating control in the classroom and satisfaction with teaching and students. Communication Education, 35, 379-388.

Rahim, A.M. (1989). Relationship of leader power to compliance and satisfaction with supervision: Evidence from a national sample of managers. Journal of Management, 15, 545-556.

Rogers, M.F. (1973). Instrumental and infra-resources: The bases of power. American Journal of Sociology, 79, (6), 1418-1433.

Russell, B. (1938). Power. London: Allen and Unwin.

Stewart, T.A. (1997, January 13). Get with the new power game. Fortune. 58-62.

Student, K.R. (1968). Supervisory influence and work-group performance. Journal of Applied Psychology, 4, (2), 127-136.

Tannenbaum, R. (1962). Control in organizations. Administration Science Quarterly, 7, 236-257.

Verderber, R.F., & Verderber, K.S. (1992). Inter-Act using interpersonal communication skills. Belmont: Wadsworth.

Weber, M. (1954). Max Weber on law in economy and society. Cambridge: Harvard University Press.

Yukl, G., & Falbe, C.M. (1991). Importance of different power sources in downward and lateral relations. Journal of Applied Psychology, 76, 416-423.

A CONCERN FOR LEADERS: THE GLASS CEILING —ARE WOMEN WHERE THEY SHOULD BE?

By
Stephanie Chaffins
Mary Forbes
Harold Fuqua, Jr.
Joseph P. Cangemi

The "glass ceiling" is a term coined in the early 1980's to describe the invisible barrier with which women came in contact when working up the corporate ladder. This form of discrimination has been depicted as a "barrier so subtle that it is transparent, yet so strong that it prevents women and minorities from moving up in the management hierarchy" (Morrison & Glinow, 1990). The glass ceiling has been evident in both position and pay within organizations (Frieze et al., 1990). Though it appears to still exist, the nature of the glass ceiling has changed. This article focuses on the influence of gender-based stereotypes, the illusion of equality, and the characteristics of successful women in the business world. Relevant statistics are presented which provide evidence most females are now given mere "token" positions in companies with only the appearance of power and prestige rather than being blatantly excluded from such positions, as was the case not too long ago.

BIASED PERCEPTIONS TOWARD WOMEN

Stereotypes based on gender have historically women in a nurturing, submissive role while men are seen as the dominant, more aggressive gender (Levinson, 1994). According to Bardwick & Douvan (1976), assertive behavior is considered more valuable because of its characteristics of objectivity, impartiality, and orientation toward problem solving. Stereotypical views of males suggest they are more suited to managerial positions than females because of their leadership styles (Frieze et al., 1990). Men appear to be more directive or autocratic while women opt for a more participative style (Eagly & Johnson, 1990). Further stereotypical views of the difference between men and women are observed from a psychoanalytical perspective in a recent article in the *American Psychologist* by the eminent industrial consultant Harry Levinson. According to Levinson, "The male orientation is described as penetration and thrust versus the female orientation of enveloping and surrounding. The whole psychology of management is that of aggressive attack and dominance...to be on top or on the bottom helpless, dependent and victimized" (Levinson, 1994).

Sexual discrimination often keeps women out of management positions. Cultural stereotypes suggest males are intellectually superior to women, are more emotionally stable, and are more achievement-oriented and assertive than women. Successful managers are thought to possess masculine traits. Stereotypical thinking in organizations not only influences the recruitment and selection of women to particular positions, it also affects career development and performance evaluation (Billing & Alvesson, 1989).

Societal norms and beliefs in relation to women often inhibit females from entering managerial positions in corporations. Terborg (1977) asserted the existence of a 'male managerial model,' that women should not or cannot be successful in management, which perpetuates social norms. Terborg (1977) also felt women often are discouraged or pressured by vocational counselors and family members *not* to seek nontraditional occupations, such as management positions. Goodale & Hall (1976) found high school students of both sexes who had similar aspirations for college and career choice were *not* encouraged equally by their families. Male students reported their parents displayed significantly more pressure and interest in their career goals than did the parents of female students. Women who were denied entry into medical school received *different* advice from counselors than men. Men were encouraged to reapply to more schools or to consider a doctoral program in a related field. Women, on the other hand, were warned of the hardship which would accompany a decision to pursue a medical degree and were advised to *change* their career goals to pursue a more traditional sex-role profession such as nursing (Weisman et al., 1976). In recent years, 78 percent of students enrolled in professional schools in the U.S. were men –reflecting lower admission quotas and higher admission standards for women, discouragement of part-time study for females, denial of loans and fellowships for women, and rigidity regarding scheduling and other procedures for female students (Weisman et al., 1983).

Perhaps one of the greatest reasons women do not occupy more management positions concerns the socialization of women regarding gender roles. Parents generally rear their children to conform to the roles they are expected to perform in society. Bartleson & Cangemi (1983) argued males are treated as superior to females due to the attitudes of society. They argued the concept of male superiority begins at birth and continues throughout adult life. Parents socialize males to be aggressive and females to be passive. Women, generally, are taught to feel inferior from the beginning of their lives (p. 6).

Even the fiction literature distinctly points to the difficulty a woman has in competing in the business world, as in the case of Celia in the book *Strong Medicine* by Arthur Hailey, as she spoke of her promotional opportunities in the fictional drug company Felding-Roth, "I realized I didn't have to be as good as a man in my job. I had to be better." Celia further stated, "Right now the corporate business world is like a private men's club...a woman must use whatever means...to become a member and get ahead" (Halley, 1984).

Male managers feel they perform better than female managers due to superior abilities and higher intelligence. Male leaders consider their jobs more difficult than female leaders who occupy the same positions (Pearson et al., 1985). Male-dominated professions are given higher ratings of prestige by both male and female raters (Kanekar et al., 1989). When subjects are told the number of women occupants is increasing in these occupations, ratings of prestige and desirability decrease significantly (Touhey, 1974). For women to succeed as managers *these myths have to be overcome.*

Females are considered the weaker sex, and are presumably not assertive enough to withstand the head to head competitiveness of the male-dominated board room. Females are deemed to be oriented toward people rather than tasks, which are presumably men's specialty (Lewis, 1992). Men are taught to develop the competence and skills needed to master their environment (Kamarovsky, 1950). Women are socialized to believe they are not suited for "male-oriented" positions and have difficulty overcoming cultural norms out of fear of being seen as "different." This also leads to a type of self-fulfilling prophecy. Women, in general, do not feel they are capable of performing the duties of upper level managers. Females generally accept the belief femininity and achievement are incompatible, and therefore often do not attempt to reach these high level positions out of feelings of guilt, anxiety, or uncertainty (Herkelmann et al., 1993).

Because women are the child-bearing gender, employers feel they are putting themselves at a disadvantage by hiring them. This is due to the problem of filling temporary/permanent vacancies when women take maternity leave or a leave of absence to raise children. The cultural view of women as having their place in the home increases the likelihood of problems in the workplace. Research shows equal performance by men and women is devalued if it is perceived as being performed by a woman. This holds true in both men and women's perceptions of women's performance (Goldberg, 1968; Paludi & Bauer, 1983; Paludi & Stayer, 1985). These traditional attitudes toward women have contributed substantially to gender discrimination and the glass ceiling effect.

WOMEN AS LEADERS: WHAT THE DATA REVEAL

The literature presents a different picture of the successful female. It has been cited that women possess the qualities to be the superior sex (Lair, 1980). Developmentally, men are more physically vulnerable and susceptible to stressors, both prenatally and perinatally (Jacklin, 1989; Henker, 1989). Women live longer, cope with stress better, are sick less often, and are more open and expressive (Lair, 1980). Previous studies have challenged the notion that women possess lesser skills, abilities, and motivation (Stroh et al., 1992).

Women's managerial style is considered more flexible, open, and inclusive than the traditional male style (Herkelmann et al., 1993). Female managers were rated as more interpersonally warm during their first interactions with their employees (Goktepe & Schneier, 1989; Spillman et al.,1981). Female managers provide unique qualities that men do not possess or have yet to develop. Male managers often have been discharged due to lack of sensitivity in dealing with subordinates (McCall & Lombardo, 1983). Female leaders are frequently praised for their ability to work more effectively with subordinates. Female managers communicate more openly and are more easily understood due to their clear communication style (Pearson et al., 1985). Women in leadership positions also are no more likely to have exited and reentered the work force than men (Lewis, 1992), which may be attributed to these women placing a greater priority on their careers than other women.

THE GLASS CEILING: FIRMLY ENTRENCHED

Those females who do become successful appear to share similar characteristics. On an individual basis, they have high ability, high self-esteem, and a strong academic self-concept. They also hold liberal opinions and values relating to women's roles in society. They realize their potential and are not restrained by their gender (Unger & Crawford, 1992). These women can be described as possessing *androgynous* personality characteristics. They maintain "feminine" features such as warmth and openness, but also exhibit "masculine" qualities such as rationale, assertiveness, and independence. A common variable appears to be higher education with an emphasis in mathematics. Highly educated parents and female role models appear to have had a positive effect as well. Successful females also appear to put off marriage and children, as most are single and have no or few children (Betz & Fitzgerald, 1987).

An illusion of equality has been established by government and organizations alike in an attempt to prove the glass ceiling no longer exists. The Equal Pay Act of 1963 provided that equal pay should be received for equal work, regardless of gender. However, laws can be easily sidestepped by corporations. Organizations rationalize discrimination by saying men "deserve" more pay than women because they are the traditional "breadwinners," or by giving similar jobs different titles as a basis for pay differences (Baseman & Zeithaml, 1993). Many companies justify paying females lower wages for economic reasons. The rationale is that women will terminate their employment sooner than men and are less likely to provide a return on the company's recruitment and training costs (Treiman & Terell, 1975). Women often are not offered the same training, development, and experience men of equal status receive. This decreases their chance of receiving promotions when compared to others. Therefore, women are worth less from a cost-benefit stand point (Treiman & Terell, 1975). However, research does not support the idea women terminate their employment sooner than men or cost organizations more money in training and recruitment (East, 1972; Hoffman & Nye, 1974).

Another strong indicator of the persistence of the glass ceiling is the gender gap in wages has remained constant over the past 50 years (Unger & Crawford, 1992). According to Solomon (1990), women in middle management positions make approximately $.66 for every $1.00 made by men. Women receive fewer promotions and are considered to be "stuck in jobs with little authority and relatively low pay" (Morrison & Glinow, 1990).

Though women have been increasingly employed in nontraditional occupations such as physicians, lawyers, and police officers, organizational positions held by women remain limited in both status and salary. Even though women fill one third of management positions, they are not given the same authority as men in those same positions (Morrison & Glinow, 1990). Two thirds of females in upper level federal jobs hold administrative positions, with only one third of them holding professional jobs, while one half of males hold administrative jobs and one half hold professional positions (Lewis, 1992).

Statistics are astounding relating the lack of female influence in upper-level management. Kirk and Maddox (1988) indicated females are more qualified for overseas jobs, but less than 3% hold jobs abroad. Women hold only 14% of middle management positions in the federal government, but make up 46% of government white-collar employees (Lewis, 1992).

It has become evident women are not allowed in strategic decision-making positions. When positions in *Fortune* 500 companies are compared, women hold only 2% of senior executive positions, 3.6% of board directorships, and 1.7% of corporate officerships (Morrison & Glinow, 1990). When men and women with equal education are compared, it becomes obvious they often start at similar salaries, but earn as much as 20% less ten years later (Lewis, 1992; Rix, 1990). Females who do manage to achieve vice presidential levels earn 42% less than males in these same positions (Morrison & Glinow, 1990). From the information cited above, these researchers have indicated the glass ceiling is skill firmly intact. Why has this occurred and what can be done to change it ?

THE GENDER GAP–ROOT OF THE GLASS CEILING?

Evidence to support traditional explanations of gender-based pay differences is lacking at best. Theories that females are less committed to their work, less likely to obtain further training and education, and more likely to quit their jobs have been invalidated (Unger & Crawford, 1992). The theory both males and females are biased against successful females is quite alarming. Prejudiced attitudes of both sexes are difficult to overcome.

Even when women gain access into an organization, they are considered "outsiders" by the men of the company. It is difficult, if not impossible, for a woman to be accepted into the "old-boys network," which is predominately male. Men feel more comfortable with other men and, therefore, are malevolent toward women who they usually perceive as intruders. Woman also are at a disadvantage because they lack access to female "mentors," since most senior-level executives are male. Males generally prefer other males as their proteges because such relationships usually feel more comfortable. They have difficulty taking on female proteges because they fear allegations of sexual relationships or sexual harassment, which would damage their credibility and integrity, and perhaps seriously derail their careers. For most of these executives it is simply too risky to mentor rising female executives when the situation could destroy their professional reputation, if not their careers. These phenomena increase the gender gap in the business world.

Organizations must realize the value of women in the corporate hierarchy. Women should be judged on the basis of their ability rather than their gender. Women have a more arduous task at proving their ability because their success is generally attributed to luck whereas men's achievements are credited to ability (Deaux, 1976). Women have been socialized to develop less confidence, less independence, and lower self-esteem and therefore tend to devalue their own skills and intelligence, just as others do (Herkelmann et al., 1993).

BREAKING THE GLASS CEILING

The socialization of both male and female children must be changed if the glass ceiling is ever to be permanently broken. Baumrid (1974) suggested parents need to encourage their daughters to be independent, value achievement, and avoid overprotecting them. Mothers who encourage their daughters to develop independence and assertiveness tend to produce women with the attitudes of competence and the ability and desire to succeed (Baruch, 1974). The perception of women will change as they are taught to develop more autonomous and positive skills. Females will no longer see their place in society as the passive nurturer whose place is in the home. Appropriate and encouraging childhood direction from parents will give females an equal opportunity to pursue goals they were previously discouraged from attempting.

For women to succeed in the male-dominated world of business, they must become familiar with the system, be prepared for competition, and understand and accept that sex role differences will be difficult to overcome. They must strive for excellence and refuse to give in to the pressures of a primarily male dominated business world. Women must capitalize on their strengths, recognize their weaknesses, and improve upon them. With a positive attitude and tenacity to withstand the pitfalls, more and more women will be able to achieve managerial success. Entrepreneurship has been a course of action which women have utilized in an effort to reach upper-level positions that are difficult to achieve in the traditional corporate hierarchy. Developing their own business allows women the freedom to be their own manager without the discrimination against them involved in the larger corporations.

THERE IS A CRACK–BUT THE CEILING STILL EXISTS

Sutton & Moore (1985) reported the percentage of male executives who favored women executives rose from 35 percent in 1965 to 73 percent in 1985. They also found only five percent of male executives feel a woman must be exceptional to succeed in business, compared to 90 percent in 1965. The percentage of men who feel comfortable working for women has increased from 27 percent to 47 percent in that same period (Sutton & Moore, 1985). In 1965, only 15 percent of all management and executive positions were held by women. Today that figure has risen to 40 percent with women rising to higher levels of seniority in corporations (Linden, 1964). Nonetheless, women are still lagging behind.

As the data above suggests, it is apparent the glass ceiling is still intact. Though efforts have been made to bridge the gap between the sexes, there is a long way to go before women are fully recognized in an equal capacity with men. With the strides women are making in leadership positions, the barriers which have kept them out of top-level positions in firms eventually will erode.

Future research should focus on the changing roles of women in our society, as well as the dynamics of the effects of women in the traditional organizational hierarchy, which remains dominated by men. Effectiveness of female leadership styles deserves further study to determine its positive aspects. Researchers also should focus on social and psychological implications of successful females who juggle careers and families.

REFERENCES

Anderson, L.R., & Blanchard, RN. (1982). Sex differences in taste and socio-emotional behavior. *Basic and Applied Social Psychology, 3,* 109-139.

Bardwick, J., & Douvan, E. (1976). When women work. In R. Loring & H. Otto (Eds.), *New life options.* New York: McGraw-Hill.

Bartleson, F., & Cangemi, J. (1983). A brief psychology of discrimination against women. *Journal of Instructional Psychology, 10,* 3-8.

Baruch, G.K. (1974). Maternal influence upon girls' evaluation of their competence. Unpublished manuscript.

Baumrid, D. (1974). Current patterns of paternal authority. *Developmental Psychology Monographs, 4,* (1).

Bateman, T.S., & Zeithaml, C.P. (1993). *Management function & strategy* (2nd Ed.). Homewood, IL: Irwin

Betz, N.E., & Fitzgerald, L.E. (1987). *The career psychology of women.* New York: Academic Press.

Billing, Y., & Alvesson, W. (1989). Four ways of looking at women and leadership. *Scandinavian Journal of Management, 5,* 63-80.

Deaux, K. (1976, December). Ahhh. She was just lucky. *Psychology Today,* 70-75.

Eagly, A.H., & Johnson, B.T. (1990). Gender and leadership style: A meta–analysis. *Psychological Bulletin, 108,* 233-256.

East, C. (1972). The current status of the employment of women. In M.E. Katzell & W.C. Byham (Eds.), *Women in the work force: Confrontation with change.* New York: Behavioral Publications.

England, P., & McCreary, L. (1987). Gender inequality in paid employment. In B.B. Hess & M.M. Feree (Eds.), *Analyzing gender: A handbook of social science research* (pp. 286-320). Newbury Park, CA: Sage.

Fierman, J. (1990, July). Why females still don't hit the top. *Fortune, 122,* 40-52.

Frieze, I., Olson, J., & Good, D. (1990). Perceived and actual discrimination in the salaries of male and female managers. *Journal of Applied Social Psychology, 20,* 46-67.

Goktepe, J.R., & Schneier, C.E. (1989). Role of sex and gender roles and attraction in predicting emergent leaders. *Journal of Applied Psychology, 74,* 165-167.

Goldberg, R.A. (1968). Are women prejudiced against women? *Transaction, 5,* 28-30.

Goodale, J.G., & Hall, D.T. (1976). Inheriting a career: The influence of sex, values, and parents. *Journal of Vocational Behavior, 8,* 19-30.

Hailey, A. (1984). *Strong medicine.* New York: Dell Publishing Co.

Henker, B., & Whalen, C.K. (1989). Hyperactivity and attention deficit. *American Psychologist, 44,* 216-223.

Herkelmann, K., Dennison, T., Branham, R., Bush, D.M., Pope, K.H., & Cangemi, J.P. (1993, Fall). Women in transition: Choices and conflicts. *Education, 114* (1), 127-133.

Hoffman, L.W., & Nye, F.I. (1974). *Working mothers.* San Francisco, CA.: Jossey-Bass.

Jacklin, C.M. (1989). Male & female: Issues of gender. *American Psychologist, 44,* 127- 144.

Kamarovsky, M. (1950). Functional analysis of sex-roles. *American Psychological Review, 151,* 508-516.

Kanekar, S., Kolsawalla, M.B., & Nazareth, T. (1989). Occupational prestige as a function of occupant's gender. *Journal of Applied Social Psychology, 19* (8), 681-688.

Kirk, W., & Maddox, R. (1988). International management: The new frontier for women. *Personnel, 65,* 46-49.

Lair, J. (1980). *Sex: If I didn't laugh, I'd cry.* New York: Doubleday.

Levinson, H. (1994). Why the behemoths fell. *American Psychologist, 49,* (5), 428-436.

Lewis, G.B. (1992, Winter). Men and women toward the top: Backgrounds, careers, and potential of federal middle managers. *Public Personnel Management, 21,* 473-484.

Linden, D.W. (1994, July 4). The class of 1965. *Forbes.*

McCall, M.W., & Lombardo, M.M. (1983). *Why and how successful executives get derailed.* Greensboro, N.C.: Center for Creative Leadership.

Morrison, A., & Von Glinow, M.A. (1990, February). Women and minorities in management. *American Psychologist, 45,* 200-208.

O'Leary, V.E. (1974). Some attitudinal barriers to occupational aspirations in women. *Psychological Bulletin, 81,* 809-826.

Paludi, M.A., & Bauer, W.D. (1983). Goldberg revisited: What's in an author's name? *Sex Roles, 9,* 387-390.

Paludi, M.A., & Stayer, L.A. (1985). What's in an author's name? Differential evaluations of performance as a function of author's name. *Sex Roles, 10,* 353-361.

Pearson, J.C., Turner, L.H., & Mancillas, W.T. (1985). *Gender and communication.* Dubuque, IA: William C. Brown.

Rix, S.E. (Ed.). (1990). *The American woman 1990-91: A status report.* New York: Norton.

Solomon, C. (1990, April). Careers under glass. *Personnel Journal,* 96-105.

Spillman, B., Spillman, R., & Reinking, K. (1981). Leadership emergence: Dynamic analysis of the effects of sex and androgyny. *Small Group Behavior, 12,* 139-157.

Stroh, L.K., Brett, J.M., & Reilly, A.H. (1992). All the right stuff: A comparison of female and male managers' career progression. *Journal of Applied Psychology, 77,* 251-260.

Terborg, J.R. (1977). Women in management: A research review. *Journal of Applied Psychology, 6,* 647-664.

Touhey, J.C. (1974). Effects of additional men on prestige and desirability of occupations typically performed by women. *Journal of Applied Psychology, 4* (4), 330-335.

Treiman, D.J., & Terell, K. (1975). Sex and the process of status attainment: A comparison of working women and men. *American Sociological Review, 40,* 174-200.

Unger, R., & Crawford, M. (1992). *Women and gender –A feminist psychology.* New York: McGraw-Hill, Inc.

Weisman, C.S., Morlock, L.L., Sack, D.G., & Levine, D.M. (1976). Sex differences in response to a blocked career pathway among unaccepted medical school applicants. *Sociology of Work and Occupations, 3,* 187-208.

LEADERSHIP AND THE EFFECTIVE USE 0F POWER

By
Kaye Payne
Joseph P. Cangemi
Harold E. Fuqua, Jr.

The proliferation of complex organizations and the vast world-wide competitive landscape have made it necessary for companies to find new ways to become more responsive to change. As visionary leaders bring their organizations into the twenty-first century they will need to respond quickly to change, with adaptable structures which can shift to fit new situations. We've all heard about organizations which frustrate us, exploit us, and throw us away. We also know of organizations where students learn little, products fail to work, patients remain sick, and policies make things worse rather than better. Organizations which empower their employees enable them to perform to the best of their ability because they feel personally rewarded for their efforts. Leaders who create workplace environments which empower their employees realize the importance of strong leadership, trust, culture, and communication. This article focuses on those aspects of empowerment.

Today, more than ever, individuals experience relationships with their employers which broadly influence their lives. Jamieson and O'Mara (1991) believed by empowering employees the workforce has a greater opportunity for personal choice and freedom, with the opportunity for recognition associated with their achievements and accomplishments. Also, they believed, empowered employees feel a sense of corporate ownership and personal organizational commitment.

LEADERSHIP

Traditionally, managers planned, organized, directed and controlled. But, the role of leader changes with an empowered work force.

Leaders who empower others need to create a vision and environments of support which transfer ownership and reasonable authority by funneling the decision making down to those who perform the jobs. Leaders will no longer need to dictate to employees how to handle situations or solve problems. Empowered workforces experience more autonomy and supervise themselves. The most important role of the empowering leader involves understanding what motivates people to excel. For example, people generally *want* to do a job well, to experience success advance, contribute suggestions and ideas, and desire respect and increasing responsibility.

Leaders who empower employees in today's organizations reap positive results across all areas of the workplace. When leaders empower employees it involves "passing on authority and responsibility" (Welling, Byham, & Wilson, 1991, p. 22) and giving up control (Caudron, 1995). These leaders need to learn less hands-on, more supportive leadership styles which nurture and reward good ideas and provide challenges to employees (Caudron, 1995). Reward and recognition programs offer evidence of a shifting corporate philosophy from a culture of entitlement to one of personal responsibility and performance-based rewards. Leaders who empower others do so with words of encouragement, immediate verbal feedback, and other forms of social persuasion (Conger, 1986). *They recognize employees have lives outside work and work with them to solve personal problems.* They show respect for employees, providing mentors to bring them along. They look for the right balance between direction, discipline, and individual freedom. Leaders who empower others act more as colleagues than as "bosses" and rely on influence, respect, and relationships in working with employees.

One of the most important aspects of job satisfaction involves helping employees know what they are working toward and understanding how their work affects other parts of the company. Continuous education and skills upgrading, control of the resources needed to make improvements, and measurements for feedback and reinforcement help to establish a sense of meaning in an organization. Ongoing positive reinforcement involves celebrating successes which cause employees to *want* empowerment as a style from their leaders. Eastman Chemical used elaborate plans for positively reinforcing group achievement. When a group of mechanics met an important goal, management publicly washed their cars. When employees generated $1 million in cost savings, management invited employees to come to a bank where they displayed $1 million dollars so employees could see what it looked like (Caudron, 1995).

Leadership working with empowered work group will require a broader range of training. No longer controlling and directing, leaders facilitate a much wider range of activities, many of which will be new to them. Organizations must constantly be learning, training, and encouraging throughout the empowerment process (Robinson & Rousseau,1994). To remain successful, leaders must learn fast and keep learning, be responsive to the ever changing environment or be left behind. Crucial to success, continued learning keeps leaders and employers on the cutting edge (Belasco & Stayer, 1994).

To be competitive in the future, companies must be prepared to constantly adapt to change as an important imperative. The most innovative companies will encourage their employees to look at problems thoroughly and come up with creative solutions. Leaders with empowered employees will not only need to make sure day to day processes are functioning as they should be, but will need to ensure all the new technologies are being pursued. Leaders will not have to do all the work themselves; they must encourage creativity, learning and adjustment to new ideas from the workforce.

Conger and Kanungo (1988) argued the need to empower subordinates becomes critical when subordinates feel powerless. Identifying conditions within organizations which foster a sense of powerlessness among subordinates is the first step in removing them. Leaders who empower employees share authority with their subordinates and recognize and reward them for their ideas, contributions, and achievements, giving credit for creativity (Jamieson & O'Mara, 1991). Leaders who empower their employees encourage input and involve them in decision making. Decisions in such organizations occur by consensus, encouraging leaders to give up sole authority for decision making (Darling, 1996). In these organizations, planning and development considers all ideas which, in turn, generates a synergy of creative genius. To help employees generate ideas, leaders provide empowered employees with information about the business; they give skills training, goal setting information, and ongoing feedback on how they met those goals. In other words, *they treat their employees like adults rather than rebellious children.*

NON EMPOWERING LEADERS

On the other hand, non-supportive leaders display poor inter-personal skills, which means focusing on the negative rather than the positive. They give poor direction, focus on hours of work rather than output, show lack of respect for employees, and do not empower them. For example, communist leadership styles used blatant authoritarian systems which told employees what to do, forgot creativity and ignored innovation. The communist regime lacked trust, did not reward employee initiative, and created workers who were not lazy, just uninspired (Cangemi, 1997).

Power, the capacity to influence and the essential currency of leadership,increases as leaders create conditions whereby their associates have the opportunity to develop it and utilize it themselves. Bass (1981) says distributing *authority* increases job satisfaction and performance of employees.

Hackman and Johnson (1996) described five reasons why employees prefer empowerment. *First,* people enjoy their jobs more, appear more concerned with work innovation, and take greater pride in their work when empowered. When employees feel powerless (they have no influence) they often respond by becoming defensive, cautious, critical, negative, and paranoid. *Second,* sharing authority with employees fosters cooperation, which in turn develops group accomplishment. Uncooperative group members often withhold information, refuse to participate, and may even sabotage efforts of the group. On the other hand, combining individual efforts to achieve group goals generates combined genius beyond the capability of one person. Kouze and Posner (1987) claimed enabling others, or releasing the creative power of employees, describes a truly great leader. *Third,* empowering others means a group survives rather than fails. One of the best ways to remain competitive in a global economy involves developing organizational structures which distribute decision making authority to lower level leaders. Decentralizing decision making structures releases employees to think for themselves. Consequently, employees can move quickly to meet the challenges of fast paced market conditions, as well as foster creativity and innovation. *Fourth,* empowering others stimulates employees to become mature, responsible individuals. When employees tackle new challenges, learn new skills, and find greater fulfillment, they experience job satisfaction and commitment. The individual grows, and the group gains a more committed and skilled member. *Fifth,* Hackman and Johnson (1996) believed authority should be shared with subordinates to prevent authority abuses. Authority in the hands of a few people generally tends to corrupt and usually causes them to focus on their own self-interests and take advantage of employees by oppressing them. Leaders who trust their employees enough to share authority with them become the essence of *servant leadership.*

EMPLOYEE REGARD IN OTHER COUNTRIES

A sampling of some human resource practices in other countries which demonstrate a high regard for employees might be unbelievable to American leaders. Caudron (1995) provided examples of new ways to think about providing respect for employees. For example, in Mexico, labor law requires employees receive full pay for 365 days a year. In Austria and Brazil, employees with one year of service automatically receive 30 days of paid vacation. Some jurisdictions in Canada have legislated pay equity–known in the United States as comparable worth between male and female intensive jobs. In Japan, levels of compensation are determined using the objective factors of age, length of service and educational background, rather than skill, ability and performance— and performance does not count until after an employee reaches age 45. In the United Kingdom, employees are allowed to take up to 40 weeks of maternity leave and employees are required to provide a government mandated amount of pay for 18 of those weeks. In 87% of large Swedish companies, the head of human resources is on the board of directors.

The objective in looking at what companies in other countries do for their employees in no way reflects a desire to provide a new entitlement program. Rather, the objective involves seeking new and better ways to enable employees to think about work when they are on the job. Helping reduce the obstacles which get in the way of accomplishing life problems energizes employees for work. For example, some companies provide a florist, cleaner, bank, restaurant and travel agent on company property to eliminate some of the every day hassles of life.

EMPLOYEE EMPOWERMENT AND THE TWENTY-FIRST CENTURY

The twenty-first century, like the twentieth century, will demand numerous and significant changes from companies and other organizations if they plan to survive. The twenty-first century will require the leadership in organizations to transform from:

- *domination oriented to cooperation oriented*
- *control oriented to involvement oriented*
- *coercion oriented to commitment oriented*
- *compliance oriented to vision-identified oriented*
- *command oriented to motivation oriented*
- *developing threatening and fear oriented work cultures to developing secure, satisfying and growth oriented work cultures*
- *thinking in terms of the manager vs. the managed*

In order to create these more positive work cultures, leaders of the twenty-first century will need to master the art of developing trust for subordinates–the capability of "letting go" (Evered & Selman, 1991). The easiest thing for a leader to do is to take full control of an organization and "command it." As one general responded to the following question, posed to him by one of the authors of this article, the concept of domination, control, coercion, compliance and fear becomes ever so clear: " General, what is your definition of leadership?" The general's response was "Giving orders!"

It is clear this kind of leadership style will not lead organizations to the peak of competitiveness in the twenty-first century, especially now that U.S. businesses are in competition with the rest of the world. Organizations today need leaders who bring out the best in associates, who encourage them to risk, to think, to create, to harmonize and to contribute maximally to *the organization's goals and success. Domination of any sort works against the better development and maximum growth and contribution of associates.* The result of dominating, threatening, fear oriented leadership behavior is seen quite remarkably in the movie *The Bedford Incident.* The captain of the U.S.S. Bedford, a naval ship, believes the best way to develop subordinate leaders is to constantly "put them down"–show them who's boss– demand full and total compliance with no back-lip. His leadership philosophy was: the tougher you are on subordinates the tougher and stronger they become. To see how tough most people become and what the results are under such leadership behavior, it would be advisable to rent the movie, now in video format, at one of the popular video rental locations nationwide. The same leadership behavior and similar results will be found in viewing the video *The Great Santini* and, in a more domestic version of autocratic behavior (a husband dominating and putting down his wife), see the video *Shirley Valentine*. The end result in each of these situations is similar–the recipients of these bulling behaviors either developed incredibly low level confidence and poor self esteem–or they rebelled *big time*. Is this what leaders want from associates in the twenty-first century? How will their organizations compete and survive? How will associates keep their eyes and commitment on the organization's vision and goals when their minds and hearts are on protecting themselves from further psychological damage? How do associates give their best when they are fearful–not necessarily fearful of losing their jobs, but fearful of being put down, humiliated and hurt psychologically, especially in front of their peers?

ALFRED ADLER: LIFE IS A SEARCH FOR SIGNIFICANCE

The eminent psychiatrist, Alfred Adler, has stated *all human beings hunger to feel significant; life is a continual search for significance.* The bully-type leader feels he/she has found a sense of significance in being able to dominate and abuse others. But this leader is very short-sighted. While his/her sense of significance is being bolstered (temporarily), consideration of the consequences of this type of leadership style on subordinates is rarely considered–and, more usually, not thought about or even cared about. The consequences are usually disastrous!! Such behavior often is the prelude to employees seeking association with a third party to protect them–a union, for example, or other forms of limited compliance on their part, often cleverly concealed from the "know it all" leadership.

Twenty first century leaders must understand Adler's admonition: They must create an environment where subordinates feel significant, important and appreciated and where their incredible talents and capabilities can be freed to pursue organizational goals with a strong sense of personal commitment. Evidence suggests an empowered work force is the end result of the creation of a positive work environment, where threats and fear are rare experiences for the majority of the work force. On the contrary, the typical experience of the empowered work force is one whereby employees feel encouraged to solve their own problems in cooperation with peers (teams), thereby developing a sense of strong capability, self-assurance and self-confidence, which leads to the development of Adler's "sense of significance." A sense of significance, according to humanistic psychologist (Maslow, 1970), tends to open-up and free human beings to create, to risk, to think, to invent, and "to see possibilities," where others typically see obstacles. In such an empowered work force, *leaders usually see themselves as partners and coaches with their associates,* as opposed to their "bosses." Bosses usually kill and stifle creativity, taking risk and thinking; they usually demand and get deference and compliance, to the detriment of the organization.

CASE STUDY: FROM TOTAL CONTROL TO INVOLVEMENT, COMMITMENT–AND EMPOWERMENT

Dr. J.P. Cangemi, one of the authors of this article, had an interesting experience in observing, first hand, the effects of transition from bullying, dictatorial leadership behavior to employee empowerment in the same facility with essentially the same personnel. Under autocratic leadership behavior, which was the previous leader's typical behavior in the facility mentioned here, the organization had significant absentee problems with associates---including salary employees, high turnover, terrible quality problems, behavioral problems and not much financial return upon investment. All this led to a morale problem within the facility. An example of the bullying behavior people had to live with in this facility was what this leader was heard to say to many associates, at one time or another, after they asked a question or made a comment: "Shut up and sit down" or "Mind your own f-------- business." To say the least, people related (confidentially) their strong distaste for this leader and his behavior. Eventually, top corporate leadership got wind of what was happening in this facility and made the decision to remove this leader. He was replaced with a more secure, people oriented, trusting leader whose basic philosophy was "How can we help you to succeed?" "What can we do to help you?" "We're not here to get in your way–we have confidence in you to go out and do your jobs and solve, in your work teams, your own problems." "Come to us if there is anything we can do to lend a hand--but we believe you know how to do your jobs H we, the leadership, support you and get out of your way." "We're here as a resource for you–and so are the rest of the leaders." That was how the new leader began his responsibilities over this low morale, defeated, unsure-of-itself facility.

Nine months later, the proof of the advantage in the difference in leadership style was in the results. There was almost 100% increase in profits, turnover was drastically reduced, and absenteeism was curbed. The attitudes in the facility unmistakably transformed into optimism, encouragement, "can-do" cooperation and involvement, and job satisfaction. People related they now enjoyed the experience of coming to work in this facility–in the past they hated it.

On a follow up survey, associates were asked how they were able to produce such drastically positive results in less than a year. Their collective response was:

- Associates were encouraged to take risks.
- Associates were told the leadership believed in them to make the right calls, the right decisions concerning safety, quality and productivity.
- Associates were assured there would be no punishment if there was an error--just to go ahead and do what was thought to be right. *The fear was taken away*
- Associates were told working together was an opportunity to learn from each other and were *encouraged* work together and think together.
- Associates were encouraged to ask each other in work groups, "What do we need to do to fix this problem?" "How can we make this better?" "What's wrong here?" "How do we help each other?"
- Associates at all levels were encouraged to come up with new ideas–"to *step outside* the box."
- Associates felt free "to think," to make decisions, because they knew *there would be no job loss if they made a mistake.* On the contrary, mistakes were now viewed as opportunities to learn and improve.

The results of this more dignified, positive, empowering leadership behavior were remarkable–as expressed through action research conducted with samples of all associates from this facility. This facility is now the shining light among a whole host of similar facilities in this important *Fortune 500* corporation–yet, nine months earlier it was at the bottom of the barrel.

EMPOWERMENT THROUGH TRUST

The concept of trust includes the notion of placing oneself within the care or keeping of another. It also includes the permission to stay or go, or to do something without fear or misgiving. It includes an assured reliance on the character, ability, strength, or truth of someone or something. *People place their confidence in someone they trust.* Trust involves expectations, which in turn become relevant to assessing the status of the trust (Rousseau, 1989). When organizations transform themselves and empower their employees, *fear of the unknown* surfaces among even the most stable people. During the transition, *which may last for several years,* employees need the reassurance which enables them to continue toward their goals. Employers and employees alike cannot form a complete picture of their expectations in advance. Unexpected opportunities and disappointments may produce situations which increase or decrease trust as each observes the response of the other (Rousseau & Parks, 1993).

Talk about empowerment often brings fear to both leaders and employees. Leaders must create environments which reduce fear so employees can learn (Deming, 1986). Leaders can lower the level of fear through two way communication, consistently recognizing desired levels of performance, having an open door policy, providing clear information, clarifying roles and responsibilities, encouraging creativity, providing training, stomping out rumor mills, and creating a personal/family environment of open, encouraging communication (Kivenko, 1994). Often, traditional leaders are reluctant to empower employees and are leery to share information they possess. Leaders fear a change in organizational structure. Once leaders get accustomed to a hierarchical structure, it gives them comfort and allocates authority to them. It also defines their roles as leaders. A combination of paternalistic leadership and attachment to an established structure provides a defense against anxiety which, in turn, creates fear of change for current leaders (Levinson,1992, 1994). Essentially, it gives leaders a sense of dependency on the hierarchical structure, *which leads to a fear of empowering employees.* Leaders of empowered employees need to understand that opening up the work force will not necessarily abolish their established position; leaders will still be accountable (Jacques, 1990). Their role will be to assist teams so *team members do not fear their own jobs will go away.* Workers have been dependent on their leaders to control and direct them. They are not traditionally encouraged to accept new responsibility. *The role of the leader will be to address that fear and turn it into trust.* Fear is a normal response when employees are treated with little or no appreciation for their work, when there is no interest in input from them, when their leader is always right, when almost all communication is downward, rarely upward, when there is consistent rejection of ideas, and when little respect and dignity is shown them (Cangemi, Kowalski, & Rice, 1989). *Fear of authority usually can be predicted to destroy trust in leadership.*

An organizational culture which can be characterized as trusting and supportive tends to utilize good communication practices. An aura of open communication offers opportunities for candid expression of ideas and feelings. Even when people make mistakes in a trust oriented culture, others tend to forgive them, to cover for one another, and to compensate for their errors. A miscommunication from associates may be viewed as an opportunity to learn from mistakes, rather than as an occasion for punishment. Effective communication will do much to reinforce and enhance a trusting climate (Haney, 1986).

Developing reciprocal trust during times of turbulent change requires open communication by both the organization and its members. In American companies leaders often prefer to keep information "close to the vest." However, a willingness to informally share information usually increases trust. Also, continuous learning should be enthusiastically embraced. In fact, team leaders need to be teachers, coaches, or facilitators. A team leader needs to be seen as someone who helps the people around him or her learn. Whenever subordinates are being trained, the leader should be there providing support and encouragement. Additionally, monitoring roles in companies helps new members receive the experience and wisdom from more established employees. Helping new employees integrate into the company culture, helping them find their own way, enables new employees to understand their internal customers, their suppliers, and/or where to go for certain kinds of information (Rousseau, 1990).

Trusting team members to operate their departments as small businesses, assuming both the responsibility and the pride of ownership, helps employees gain a sense of ownership and control over their jobs (Rothman, 1994). Empowered individuals own their jobs and take an active role in decision making, resulting in employee initiative, greater productivity, and job satisfaction (Welling, Byham, & Wilson, 1991). Block (1987) saw empowerment as a state of mind, not the result of job titles, policies and practices. In organizations which empower people, anyone, irrespective of rank, can volunteer ideas and make suggestions. Brainstorming, thinking "outside the box," asking questions not asked before, encouraging employees to answer questions in ways which benefit the company, all translate into higher productivity and increased trust.

CORPORATE CULTURE

A corporate culture is a pattern of basic assumptions developed by a given group that has worked well enough together to know what works best in their organization. Because it is considered valid, employees believe it should be taught to new members as the correct way to perceive, think, and feel in relation to their problems and tasks (Bolman & Deal, 1991). Empowered employees need leaders with a vision who can communicate the corporate culture. The visionary leader establishes a pattern of values within the company which members pass on to one another. The same set of values must be shared by all the organizational members in order to instill a strong corporate culture. But, similarity regarding organizational values, while necessary, is not enough. The set of organizational values must be regarded as important and desirable. Therefore, visionary leaders must communicate the shared values in such a way as to depict them as not only desirable but of primary importance. *The idea of a group value as opposed to an individual value produces a connection between members. As* group values become congruent with top management's values, those departments, or teams, become more influential because they will be seen as "like us" and, therefore, worthy of trust. As an entire organization begins to hold congruent values with visionary leaders, the whole workforce moves in the same direction, thereby increasing a cohesively strong culture.

To make empowerment successful, leaders need to make sure a strong corporate culture exists either *prior to* the empowerment or *during* the installation of empowered employee teams. The culture should provide direction from the leaders to steer the work of the teams in the desired direction. A strong culture reduces the chance of mixed signals, provides the basic values on which to base all decisions, and reinforces the basic theme of the corporate vision statement. Empowered employees, guided by training and a corporate culture, will deliver consistent products with the corporate goals in mind. A strong culture not only encourages employees toward success in their own job responsibilities, but in the corporation as well. A culture consistent with empowering employees encourages communication, ensures trust, aides in assuring the necessary resources to meet the desired goals, encourages learning, personal growth, and creativity. Leaders who empower others encourage a company culture of pride (Bennis & Nanus, 1985).

Members of organizations can learn the company culture by watching how the culture reacts to events, applies meaning to those events, and interprets what might be seen as ambiguous and uncertain. Observers can watch leaders to see what they pay attention to, measure, and control. They can observe how the leader reacts to critical incidents and organizational crises. As leaders reinforce certain role models, certain strategies for teaching, coaching, or facilitation, members can determine organizational values. How leaders allocate rewards, status and scarce resources says a great deal about what the leader wants to enculturate. His or her criteria for recruitment, selection, promotion, retirement, and excommunication help members determine cultural values. Because the messages transmitted by these mechanisms will often be implicit, conflicting messages may be received by organizational members. Additionally, important secondary messages received by organizational members come from the organizational design and structure, systems and procedures, design of physical space, stories, legends, myths, parables about important events and people, and formal statements about the organizational philosophy (Bolman & Deal, 1991). In diverse organizations, the opportunity for miscommunication of the organizational vision must be carefully monitored.

Why diverse organizational members misunderstand the corporate culture may be embedded in their native cultural traditions. These traditions may range from collectivist (communistic) to individualistic (democratic) native systems of understanding organizational culture and empowerment. Cox, Lobel, and McLeod (1993) discovered groups composed of people from collectivist cultural traditions displayed more cooperative behaviors than groups composed of people from individualistic cultural traditions. Even though all participants resided within the United States, national cultural traditions from their country of origin influenced their behavior. Earley (1993) found individualists performed better when they worked alone and found support confirming "social loafing" or sluffing off at work among cultures reflecting individualism. What then causes the United States and Great Britain, which place a higher value on individualism than do other cultures, to believe they can effectively empower employees? One answer may revolve around the concept of "power distance" defined by Hofstede (1980)

Power distance involves free will, control, and dominance over the environment (Kluckholn & Strodbeck, 1961). Implemented since the 70's, American companies strive toward more participative organizational systems which value the assumptions that people want a say in the decisions which affect them, want to determine their future, believe in personal efficacy, want control over their own circumstances and, to a degree, their environment (Fried & Ferris, 1987; Griffin, 1989; Levine, 1990). While free will is not solely a U.S. value, it does differentiate the U.S. from other cultures (Chikudate, 1991), as well as permeate American management theories. Consequently, leaders should look carefully at the applicability of those theories to other cultures which hold different values. Leadership styles which reflect local cultures can produce equal levels of productivity independent of whether leaders empower their employees or operate under centralized, autocratic control.

Structural and political views of culture often focus on structure, goals, roles, power, conflict, and the allocation of scarce resources. Cultural aspects of empowered organizations focus on the facts which humans have chosen to construct–based on the messages received from their visionary leaders. Leaders can communicate with strong empowered cultures as the basis for optimism about the possibilities of organizational change. Empowered organizations create worlds where employees can manage or resist change with greater comfort (Brown, 1978).

COMMUNICATION/COMMUNICATORS

Effective organizational communication links formal communication with informal communication. If highly effective communication operates within work teams and among leader-employee relationships but employees feel alienated from the organization, then somehow *the process of empowering employees has failed.* Regardless of the formality, the needs of the organization and the needs of the individual must dovetail to produce a healthy communication climate. A healthy communicator openly expresses his or her wants and needs, satisfaction and dissatisfaction. An unhealthy communicator gratifies his or her basic needs through self-centeredness, devoting his or her energies to satisfying security needs, acceptance from others, or achieving social status. Typically, such a person distracts the organization from fulfilling its mission. Healthy communicators make use of open communication with discretion. Because of the nature of the working environment, a healthy communicator selectively picks and chooses when to be open and when to control the amount of information released to others. Open communication involves a two-way, regenerative process. The more people experience open positive communication, the more positive their sentiments about each other become.

The relationship a person develops with his or her supervisors and peers becomes the most important aspect of organizational life. They act as sources of information and support, feedback and news. As individuals participate in empowered groups, they may play a variety of group communication task and maintenance roles. *Group task roles* include information requester, information giver, procedure facilitator, opinion requester, opinion giver, clarifier, and summarizer-evaluator. *Group maintenance roles* include those of social support, harmonizer, tension reliever, energizer, leader, follower, compromiser, and gatekeeper. *Self-centered roles,* which tend toward destruction of groups, include those of blocker, dominator, attacker, and clown. Interpersonal effectiveness can be achieved through active listening, positive descriptive language, message ownership, development of effective messages which contribute to goals and objectives, developing structure and providing feedback (Benne & Sheats, 1948).

Listening, a fundamental group skill for empowered employees, includes the processes of hearing, assigning meaning, and verifying interpretations. It begins with the attitude about one's role in the organization. A positive active listening attitude begins with a genuine concern for understanding what others intend for one to hear, and to sense meaning from another person's point of view. This attitude includes *empathy* for others and a willingness to override one's own emotions to facilitate mutual understanding. Active listeners attempt to control mental arguments, avoid jumping to conclusions, and carefully avoid stereotyping others. They stop talking long enough to hear what others have to say. They provide feedback to speakers by paraphrasing what they said to confirm meaning. They use questions for meaning clarification and *rarely interrupt* to explain their own ideas or positions. Active listeners summarize main points and evaluate facts and evidence before responding. These skills play just as important a part when communicators disagree, as well as when they agree (Wolff, Marsnik, Tacey, & Nichols, 1983).

Another important communication skill among empowered employees involves the processes of problem solving and decision making. Groups which make decisions and problem solve need an awareness of individual predispositions, strategies and tactics in a variety of circumstances, and knowledge and sensitivity for the processes. Having a structure for conducting problem-solving or decision-making tasks encourages work groups to operate more effectively through these deliberations. Conducting effective meetings enables people to exhibit productive individual behaviors and avoid behaviors destructive to effective communication. Often employees who have not received training in problem solving or decision making fail to recognize the importance of the general principles for structuring effective group discussions, such as focusing on the problem, preparing a statement of the problem, brainstorming, avoiding group-think, implementation and follow-up, to name just a few (Brilhart, 1986). Empowered organizations need to be certain individuals receive communication training in problem solving and decision making skills.

In traditional plants, most workers experience only downward communication (not upward), enabling them to know only what they need to know to get their jobs done Even the horizontal flow of information across different work cells seldom occurs. Unfortunately, when information does not flow in all directions, distrust may develop and grapevine communication may begin which often carries untrue or distorted information. Leaders in traditional settings tend to hold on to information, fostering their own power and establishing their dominant position. *With an empowered workforce leaders must change these communication styles.* They must enhance and further build their ability to effectively communicate. Not only do they have to open up and share their information, they must learn how to communicate to others with better written, verbal, and nonverbal skills.

Empowered workforce leaders must help to facilitate and increase an open communication flow. All information which employees need to do their jobs effectively must be available to them to enable them to make sound decisions. An individual without information cannot take responsibility; an individual who has information usually cannot help but take responsibility–or at least is encouraged to do so.

Traditional styles of communication slow down information flow, the information flow often becoming bogged and distorted. Varied channels of communication encourage abundant opportunities to experiment with new, easier methods of communication between people. Some effective communication techniques include: informal informational sessions with top leaders, message boards, notes posted in frequented employee areas, electronic display boards, regular employee meetings, and free standing computer terminals for accessing internet channels and e-mail. Leaders and employees in an empowered workforce must be computer literate to access corporate data bases and other information when they need it. New visionary leaders must stay on the cutting edge, enable employees to access information, coach employees and help them find all the information they need to do their jobs.

Empowered organizations often do not reflect orderly, rational, objective communication structures. Rather, they act as loosely coupled systems (March & Olson, 1976), with problems needing solutions, and/ or people selling their pet ideas (or solutions), chance opportunities for actions, and sets of resources which could be marshaled. Conflict abounds! When leaders and work teams take action, often it results not so much from planned problem solving but rather from the confluence of the right opportunities, available solutions, people who advocate for a particular solution or use of a resource (Meltzer & Nord, 1981). The internal state of the communication system often is the result of "organized chaos."

CONCLUSION

In summary, leaders who empower their employees authorize and enable them to do their jobs. Empowered employees plan their own work, receive training, receive the tools necessary to do their jobs, and use their broader authority to work. They become empowered because visionary leaders create an environment which enables them to experience support, training, shared authority, and decentralized decision making. Visionary leaders communicate highly important and desirable values. Members and leaders share these values in a commitment to high quality products, good service, and general excellence. As leaders and members operate in an empowered culture they express trust between one another through open communication. Effective communicators use an open style, understand effective procedures for conducting problem solving and decision making meetings, and effectively listen to understand and provide feedback. These aspects of empowered organizations usually facilitate employee satisfaction, improved quality and higher productivity (Rothman, 1994).

REFERENCES

Bass, B. (1981). *Stogdill's handbook of leadership.* New York: The Free Press.

Belasco, J., & Stayer, R. (1994, March/April). Why empowerment doesn't empower: The bankruptcy of current paradigms. *Business Horizons, 29-39.*

Benne, K.D., & Sheats, P. (1948). Functional roles of group members. *Journal of Social Issues, 1 (4), 41-9.*

Bennis,W., &Nanus,B. (1981). *Leaders: The strategies for taking charge.* New York: Harper & Row.

Block, P. (1987). *The empowered manager: Positive political skills at work.* San Francisco: Jossey-Bass.

Bolman, L., & Deal, T. (1991). *Reframing organizations.* San Francisco, CA: JosseyBass.

Brilhart,J.K. (1986). *Effective group discussion.* Dubuque, Iowa: Brown.

Brown, R.H.(1978). Bureaucracy as praxis: Toward a political phenomenology of formal organizations. *Administrative Science Quarterly: 23,* 365-382.

Cangemi, J., Kowalski, C., & Rice, J. (1989, Winter). The development, decline and renewal of trust in an organization: Some observations. *Organization Development Journal,* 2-9.

Cangemi, J. (1997, In Press). Developing power---A requisite for effective leadership in organizations. *Chinese Journal of Applied Psychology*

Caudron, S. (1995). Create an empowering environment. *Personnel Journal, 74,* 10.

Chikudate, N. (1991). Cross-cultural analysis of cognitive systems in organizations: A comparison between Japanese and American organizations. *Management: International Review, 31 (3),* 219-231.

Conger, J. (1986). *Empowering leadership.* Working paper. McGill University, Montreal.

Conger, J., & Kanungo, R. (1988). The empowerment process: Integrating theory and practice. *Academy of Management Review, 13, 471-482.*

Cox, T.H., Lobel, S.A., & McLeod, P.L (1993). Effects of ethnic group culture differences on cooperative and competitive behavior on a group task. *Academy of Management Journal. 34* (4), 837-847.

Darling, M. (1996, May). Empowerment. *Vital Speeches, 1-9.*

Deming,W.E. (1986). *Out of the crisis.* Cambridge,MA: MA Institute of Technology, Center for Advanced Engineering Study.

Earley, P.C. (1993). East meets West meets Midwest: Further explorations of collectivistic and individualistic work groups. *Academy of Management Journal, 36* (2), 319-348.

Evered, R.D., & Selman, J.C. (1991). Coaching and the art of management. *Organizational Dynamics,* 114-130.

Fried, Y., & Ferris, G.R. (1987). The validity of the job characteristics model: A review and meta analysis. *Personal Psychology 40,* 287-322.

Griffin, R.W. (1989). Work redesign effects on employee attitudes and behaviors: A long-term field experiment. *Academy of Management Best Paper Proceedings,* 216-217.

Hackman, M., & Johnson, C. (1996). *Leadership: A communication perspective.* Illinois: Waveland Press.

Haney, W.V. (1986). *Communication and interpersonal relations.* Homewood, IL: Richard D. Irwin, Inc.

Hofstede, G. (1980). *Cultures consequences: International differences in work related values.* Beverly Hills, CA: Sage Publications.

Jacques, E. (1990, January/February). In praise of hierarchy. *Harper Business Review. 127-133.*

Jamieson, D., & O'Mara, J. (1991). *Managing workforce 2000.* San Francisco: Jossey- Bass.

Kivenko, K. (1994). Improve performance by driving out fear. *Quality Progress, 77-79.*

Kluckholn, F. R., & Strodbeck, F. L. (1961). *Variations in value organizations.* Evanston, IL: Row-Peterson.

Kotter,J.P. (1973). The psychological contract. *California Management Review, 15,* 91 - 99.

Krouze, J.M., & Posner, B.Z. (1987). *The leadership challenge: How to get extraordinary things done in organizations.* San Francisco: Jossey-Bass.

Levine, D.l. (1990). Participation, productivity, and the firm's environment. *California Management Review 32 (4),* 86-100.

Levinson, H. (1962). *Men, management, and mental health.* Cambridge, MA: Harvard UP.

Levinson, H. (1994, May). Why the Behemoths fell. *American Psychologist,* 428-435.

March, J.G., & Olson, J.P. (1976). *Ambiguity and choice in organizations.* Oslo: Univesitets Forlaget.

Maslow, A. (1970). *Motivation and personality* (2nd ed.). New York: Harper & Row.

Meltzer, H., & Nord, W. (1981). *Making organizations humane and productive.* NY: John Wiley & Sons.

Robinson, S.L., & Rousseau, D.M. (1994). Violating the psychological contract: Not the exception but the norm. *Journal of Organizational Behavior, 15,* 249-59.

Rothman, H. (1994, February). Quality's link to productivity. *Nation's Business, 82* (2), 33 37

Rousseau, D.M. (1989). Psychological and implied contracts in organizations. *Employee Rights and Responsibilities Journal, 2,* 121 -139.

Rousseau, D.M. (1990). New hire perceptions of their own and their `employer's obligations: A study of psychological contracts. *Journal of Organizational Behavior, 11,* 389-400.

Rousseau, D.M., & Parks, J.M. (1993). The contracts of individuals and organizations. In L.L. Cummings & B.M. Staw (Eds.), *Research in organizational behavior, 15,* 1- 43. Greenwich, CT: JAI Press.

Schein, E.H. (1980). *Organizational psychology (3rd* ed.). Englewood Cliffs, NJ: Prentice Hall.

Welling, R., Byham, W., & Wilson, J. (1991). *Empowered teams.* San Francisco: Jossey- Bass.

Wolff, F. I., Marsnik, N.C., Tacey, W.S., & Nichols, R.G. (1983). *Perceptive listening.* NY: CBS College Publishing.

OBSERVATIONS OF SUCCESSFUL LEADERS AND THEIR USE OF POWER AND AUTHORITY

By
Joseph P. Cangemi

Over the last 30 years I have been privileged to work and associate with many business/industrial leaders in various parts of the world. I paid close attention to these leaders in order to weave together observations of their behavior that could be utilized to help other business/industrial leaders in the future.

One of the most interesting and consistent observations over the years of association with these leaders has been their use of *power* as opposed to their use of *authority*. To say the least, there is widespread use and meaning of both the words power and authority (Batten,1989; Cohen & Bradford, 1990; Conger & Kanungo, 1988; Kouzes & Posner, 1989; McClelland & Burnham, 1983; Mintzberg, 1983; Schein 1980; Steers, 1981; Kanter, 1983; Kotter, 1983). Based upon my direct observations, authority grants the *legitimate* right of a leader to entice, even force, others to do what is considered important to achieve. Authority gives the right to coerce, punish or reward individuals in the leader's endeavor to achieve goals. The keyword here is legitimate, and this legitimate right is conferred officially upon the leader by some organization or group, allowing him/her to behave in expedient ways to achieve oganizational goals. Another view of authority is that it can be taken or assumed, as in the case of a general who invades a city, overpowers it, then sets himself up as the legitimate head of state.

Power, however, to me, differs from authority, differs in the way it is obtained. Power is the individual's *capacity* to move others, to entice others, to persuade and encourage others to attain specific goals or to engage in specific behavior; it is the *capacity* to influence and motivate others. While authority is either taken, as in the case of the general, or awarded by an organization or group, power is not taken. *It cannot be taken. Power is awarded* to an individual by a group who then allow this individual to lead it toward goal attainment and success. As I have come to view it, power is given as a kind of reward from those who will become subordinates or followers, even though all involved initially in this process might have been equals. One other factor in power is its capacity to withstand and remain unaffected by the authority and power of others. From my observations, *power may be more desirable than authority.* I am sure this may be a controversial statement to many, so I would like to pursue this concept further. For example, what authority did Mahatma Gandhi have? Yet he succeeded, and is largely credited with instigating the freeing of India from British rule. What real authority did Martin Luther King, Jr. have? Yet he inspired a nation to acknowledge the time of racial equality was at hand and is largely credited with the advancement experienced by African Americans today. What real earthly authority did Jesus Christ *as man* have? Yet many would agree His power is perhaps amongst the greatest ever experienced on our planet. What authority did Corazon Aquino of the Philippines have when she led the revolt against the Marcos dictatorship? None of these individuals had authority—the legitimate right to act as they did. However, because of their incredible power, they succeeded in their missions. They had the *capacity* to influence and move people. I found that a leader's development and use of power is highly desirable leadership behavior. Power can *really* motivate and lead people to accomplishment, often—great accomplishment. I have observed authority, as a leadership position in the business world, usually suffers in its capacity to achieve high level success through others with any consistency. George Uhlig, a well respected leader in higher education, has written to the author "Your observation that power is more effective than authority is consistent with my own experiences... it amazes me that institutions and individuals in higher education 'turn over' on the average every three years. Clearly, I think, cases of authority wearing out and power never developing. Generally, a Dean... President, from the outside is appointed and is awarded authority. Power may never develop" (Uhlig, 1991).

DEVELOPING POWER/LOSING POWER

The most successful business (and other) leaders seem to have a sense for developing and utilizing power, even though they in fact *have* authority. Their respective organizations provided these leaders with authority. However, they generate power for themselves and find this much more effective in accomplishing organizational goals.

Based on a number of personal observations and experiences, positive/constructive power seems solidly based on *respect. Those who earn the respect of their group or organization in certain areas or in certain ways generically are given power to lead them in those areas or in those ways.* The problem with power, however, is that it is fickle and delicate. It can be retracted from the leader easier than it was bequeathed upon him/her in the beginning. For example, sometimes *a single act* destroys years and years of a leader's power, leaving the leader with only authority, which turns out to be insufficient to accomplish the leader's role mandated responsibilities. In most cases, those leaders who lost power and who only were able to hang onto authority were forced to leave the organization and seek another group with which to associate because *their power was gone.* They lost the group's respect and could only accomplish tasks through force and coercion. An example is ex-president Richard Nixon. One can argue that President Nixon retained his authority, but he no longer held the respect of the masses he once had when he entered office. The mounting disrespect toward his perceived behavior would have created enormous problems, both for himself and for the country. He lost power and was forced to leave office, yet he retained substantial authority until the day he resigned. Another intriguing presidential example of retaining authority but losing power is that of Jimmy Carter. Did he not lose the respect of numerous voters, and hence the power to lead them?

Some examples of activities observed on the part of leaders that destroyed their power are as follows:
- a deliberate lie–especially one that affected a group or group member's livelihood, family, status, career, location, etc.;
- an irresponsible act–such as driving DUI and then getting involved in some sort of hit and run incident and later being publicly exposed;
- a messy, ugly marital split-up-especially one involving an extramarital affair that destroyed relationships and became a public spectacle;
- a foolish or anti-social act that led to even brief incarcertion;
- alienating particular groups, such as the press;
- immoral behavior that brought widespread attention and criticism;
- unethical behavior, especially leading to personal gain at the expense of others or the organization;

- ruthless, brutal interpersonal behavior ;
- physically abusing others to solve problems, including one's family;
- personal habits that generally lead to disrespected

activity,such as alcoholism, gambling, drug abuse, sexual addition, etc.

As indicated previously, numerous observations suggest *it frequently only takes once*—one action of the type mentioned above, to lose the years required to generate and maintain the *respect* which developed *power*, as identified in this article. Once power diminishes, only authority remains. The rewards the authority oriented leader uses rarely seem to have sustained impact on the behavior of subordinates as does their use of punishment, threats, and force. The possibility of the leader's using threats and some sort of coercion seems to linger in the thinking of subordinates, rendering rewards from this leader less potent in their shaping and motivating of desired subordinates' behavior.

LEADING BY AUTHORITY: THE PROBLEM

A business leader can certainly lead through authority, but this kind of authority usually brings with it organizational morale problems. One of the effects of morale problems is employee turnover. I have identified two kinds of employee turnover—one is *physical* and the other is *mental*. Physical turnover identifies those employees who quit the organization and go elsewhere. Mental turnover identifies those employees who *quit and stay*. This kind of turnover does not show up on the organization's records but may cause considerable organizational damage in cost and lost productivity. These employees are demonstrating passive resistance: they are there physically, but are often absent mentally. They rarely give a good, solid day's performance, doing just enough to get them by, or worse, doing less than quality work. For example, in some of the business organizations with which I have been involved, it would not be un-usual that employees were paid for eight hours work per day, but in reality averaged a maximum of 4.5 to 5.0 hours of work per day. For the rest of their eight hour shift they might be found in the cafeteria smoking, playing cards or dominoes, or talking—even when offered attractive financial incentives to continue working and producing more until the end of their shift. *These types of employees have quit and stayed.* Leaders who relish leading by authority alone, because they seem to enjoy their legitimate right to use force, seem to develop multitudes of these types of employees over time. Among this group of employees we will find all levels of the organization represented, from those in management, close to the top, right down to the lowest–level ranking employee. Unfortunately, employees quitting and staying saddle the authority oriented leader with a serious dilemma when organizational objectives are not met: how to get them "turned back on." Although not easy, it can be done (see Carkhuff, 1984).

Many poor performing business/industrial organizations choose not to attempt to turn these employees around. It generally takes two to five years to turn an unhealthy organization around (Carkhuff, 1984; Cangemi, Rice, & Kowalski,1989). For this reason, companies often choose to move their physical facilities from one geographic location to another–including foreign locations such as the border between the United States and Mexico, where some 300 United States corporations alone are across the border from El Paso, Texas. Personal conversations with the leaders of several organizations revealed they feel it would be easier to move the machinery, etc., from one location in the United States to El Paso, Texas, or other locations, and train workers there than it would be to attempt the long process of attempting to turn around a "turned–off' work force. Although labor cost is a positive factor in a move, the difficulty in modifying employee attitudes is also a substantial factor in the decision for relocation. Yet this aspect of the problem is rarely mentioned as a reason for choosing another business location–especially one on foreign soil. It appears to be an easier chore for an organization to start over again elsewhere than to turn a work force back on once the employees decide to "quit and stay" and develop the bad habits that accompany this attitude.

FIVE KEY RELATIONSHIPS—A STRONG BASIS FOR GENERATING A LEADER'S POWER

Business leaders who have developed substantial respect for themselves seem to have fused their activities into five relationships (four within the organization and one outside the organization) that are highly integrated and involved with their personal success, the organization's success, and the generation and management of their own power. These relationships have been categorized as follows:

1. Relationship with self.
2. Relationship with others.
3. Relationship with the organization.
4. Relationship with the business.
5. Relationship with the community.

Relationship with self. Relationship with self suggests these individuals are at peace with themselves, understand themselves and have a high level of self-confidence. These individuals have turned their perceptive and intuitive capabilities onto themselves and have accomplished a significant self-study. These leaders are introspective; they know themselves quite well. They are tuned into their own strengths, weaknesses, motivation, interests, goals, etc. They make a habit of studying themselves in order to know themselves better. They seem highly aware of the consequences of their behavior and often reflect upon them before acting, usually leading them to consistent, decisive, and astute behavior. These individuals do not demonstrate arrogance in the least and exude high self-regard. Their feet never seem to leave the ground, no matter how successful they become. They are realists and seek truth. They know their limitations and work within these limits. They set high standards for themselves and work religiously to achieve them. Although they work hard (often 50-60 or more hours per week), they also make time to play and find opportunities for self-rejuvenation. Because they are in tune with themselves, they know when they need a break and how to deal with stress in a positive manner. They do not develop problematical habits such as drug and alcohol abuse. Many of the successful leaders I have observed rarely drank or used tobacco. They also built exercise into their daily or weekly routine.

These leaders are generally "up" and quite optimistic. They tend to see possibilities where others see obstacles. Being around them is often a motivating experience because their optimism is infectious, yet they are not naive in their optimism. They are believable in the way they express themselves to others; their body language is usually congruent with their words: they "walk the way they talk." They are not deceivers. They are aware of how important it is for the leader to be trusted and behave in a way that discourages the development of distrust on the part of colleagues, subordinates, and others. Their behavior in their private life is likewise consistent with their behavior in their business life. There is nothing phony about them. Their repertoire of consistent behavior to those who deal with them and observe them suggests *they should be trusted.*

These leaders have an abundance of energy and it seems to stem from the very strong drive they have toward goal attainment. They have been intelligent enough to fuse their own personal achievement objectives with organizational goals. Hence, their motivation and energy is fueled by combining personal and organizational goals harmoniously. In short, they are optimistic, encouraging, and motivating people to be around who convey this attitude to the organization. To quote Voltaire, "An organization is the lengthened shadow of its leader."

Relationship with others. These leaders have developed a knack for developing good, positive relationships with others. They are considered friendly by superiors, subordinates and colleagues alike. They know how to get along with others without giving the organization away. They retain a very solid independence when dealing with others in terms of decision-making. They welcome suggestions without being swayed by them. They respect others and others sense, feel and recognize this respect. These leaders are never condescending and know how to disagree without being disagreeable. Fits of uncontrollable temper and rage are never part of their behavior. They know how to cope with anger and demonstrate it in controllable ways. Their anger is never aimed at people; it is always directed at behavior or issues. They rarely force their ideas on others, instead finding success in recommending, suggesting, and asking others to consider their perspective. They rarely have to compel others to accomplish tasks. The respect subordinates and others have for them *gives them power* to encourage and motivate others to accomplish often lofty and difficult goals. Their relationship with their family often is their highest priority. They will not jeopardize their family for their own success. Rather, they know how to balance the relationship between work and family.

Relationship with the organization. These individuals keep abreast of developments in their organization or group. They know that subordinates want to keep their jobs, and hence make it easy for them to be honest so they do not have to fear their loss. They ask good, nonthreatening questions to tap into the perceptions of subordinates. They usually accomplish this by walking around and talking to employees; as well as through frequent meetings with individuals from various departments to get a more broad-based view of employees' feelings and perceptions. These leaders have a high degree of trust for their own intuitive, perceptive sensibilities, yet are consistently searching for valid information. They are sensitive to the needs and concerns of their people. They know they cannot lead from a desk so they explore things themselves, a parallel to the Japanese mandate *genbutsu–genba: go see for yourself.*

These leaders have a vision of what they expect the organization or group to accomplish. They are committed to this vision and have the skills to seek input from subordinates and others and then motivate them to attain it.

These leaders hire the best professionals they can find and usually give them maximum independence to perform their responsibilities. They know better than to get involved in all the details of their work, other than to demonstrate interest and allow them to "show their stuff." They establish highly effective reward systems to encourage individuals to give their best to the organization. They make it easy for subordinates to satisfy their own personal goals while at the same time achieving organizational success. In short, they cultivate a special, positive relationship with the organization over a period of time.

Relationship with business. These individuals are very knowledgeable about their business–whatever it is. They are about the competition and the strategies utilized by the competition, should they be in a profit motive organization. Their methods are always ethical. They are constantly upgrading themselves with knowledge about their own business *and* about the competition. They understand that to survive today, a business organization must embrace change and must be prepared to embrace it at a rapid pace. They take seriously the responsibility to lead change and are its vanguard in their organization.

Relationship with the community. These individuals find time to give something back to the community and society as a whole. They make time to work with others, particularly the less fortunate. They give of their talents, insights, abilities, and energy to worthwhile causes and projects. They are not selfish; on the contrary, they usually are more givers than takers. They often become mentors for younger colleagues. Leaders who develop, demonstrate and retain these five relationships will generate *power* which should ensure them continued success at the helm of their organization.

CASE: A SUCCESSFUL ORGANIZATIONAL RENEWAL THROUGH THE USE OF POWER

In the "turn around" of a very large industrial facility in which I became involved several years ago, I was able to closely observe the behavior of the new top leader, with whom I had developed an ongoing professional relationship for over five years. This organization was a shambles before the five year period began.

Authority oriented leaders had dominated the facility. The organization experienced at least 4 strikes a year and had 92 sit-downs and slowdowns in the year previous to our intervention. The organization was losing considerable sums of money and was producing a poor-quality product. In general, it could be characterized as essentially loaded with employees who had "quit and stayed." This facility employed over 2,000 individuals and was plagued by poor morale and poor work habits. The new leader of this facility was an individual who was people-oriented, employee-centered, and very much interested in a participative style of leadership behavior. He led this organization during the five years he was associated with it to successes that were not thought possible in his corporation. This large facility was turned around so completely it won great recognition from its customers and competitors alike. In the five year duration of this project only one slowdown occurred, not a single strike was experienced, production and profits were raised to record levels, employees developed more positive attitudes, and the facility was singled out many times for exemplary performance. It would have been scheduled for closure eventually under its previous conditions. Although this leader had total authority, he was not interested in using it; it was used only when it became absolutely necessary and was the last option available to him. In the five years I was associated with him, he rarely used it. He did not have to. Instead, he led through power based on his subordinates' and superiors' respect for his behavior. He was an achievement-oriented leader who was always interested in the success of his people. His sincere interest in their achievement brought him an immense amount of *respect*, and subsequently *power.*

SUMMARY

In this article an attempt has been made to describe a perspective on power and authority, derived from three decades of association with numerous business/industrial leaders. What has resulted from this experience is a view of power as a capacity won from others out or respect for certain consistently demonstrated, admired/desired qualities or abilities on the part or the leader. These allow him/her to guide the energies, the group/organization toward goal attainment and success. Power was differentiated from authority in that authority was categorized as the legitimate right to require subordinates to do what the leader directs them to do, frequently through coercion and force. While it was acknowledged that the authority-oriented leader can use rewards to accomplish organizational objectives, it was observed that rewards seemed not as effective or successful in *sustaining* desired behavior. The constant fear of possible punishment often seemed to weaken the effect of rewards.

REFERENCES

Batten, J.D. (1989). *Tough-minded leadership.* New York: AMCOM

Cangemi, J., Kowalski, C., & Rice J. (1989). The development, decline, and renewal of trust in an organization. *Organization Development Journal, 7* (4). 2-9.

Cohen, A.R., & Bradford, D. L. (1990). *Influence without authority.* New York: John Wiley & Sons.

Conger, J. A., Kanungo, R.N., & Associates. (1988). *Charismatic leadership.* San Francisco: Jossey-Bass Publishers.

Kanter, R.M. (1983). Power failure in management circuits. In C.G. Collins (Ed.), *Executive success: Making it in managment.* New York: John Wiley & Sons.

Kotter, J.P. (1983). Power, dependence, and effective management. In C.G. Collins (Ed.), *Executive success: Making it in managment.* New York: John Wiley & Sons.

Kouzes, J., & Posner, B. Z. (1989). *Leadership challenge.* San Francisco: Jossey-Bass Publishcrs.

McClelland, D.C., & Burnham, D. (1983). Power is the great movivator. In C.G.Collins (Ed.), *Executive success: Making it in management.* New York: John Wiley & Sons.

Mintzberg, H. (1983). *Power in and around organizations.* Englewood Cliffs, N.J.: Premice-Hall.

Schein, E. (1980). *Organizational psychology.* Englewood Cliffs, N.J.: Prentice-Hall.

Steers, R.M. (1981). *Introduction to organizational behavior.* Santa Monica, CA: Goodyear.

Uhlig, G. (1991). Personal correspondence received by the author.

SUCCESSFUL SENIOR LEVEL LEADERS —WHAT ARE THEY LIKE?

By

Joseph P. Cangemi   K. Habib Khan

The following is a study completed by a *Fortune* 100 company, with which the senior author has worked, of the behaviors found in successful leaders at senior levels within the company. These characteristics, found after a detailed analysis of the behavior of these senior level leaders, are offered as a brief perspective to be studied for the benefit of those who are interested in the leadership endeavor.

THOUGHT BEHAVIOR

1. Ability to abstract. Leaders do not need a lot of data. Leaders are broad in their knowledge. They intuitively know how far forward to project their vision.

2. Leaders are capable of balancing multiple problems. Too high an endurance compulsion in one area impairs their vision and judgment. The requirement here is flexibility, and this is one of the most important aspects of their behavior.

3. Toleration of ambiguity. This is probably one of the most significant abilities leaders must possess. They are not threatened by the unknown or lack of feedback. Gray areas do not disturb them. They are able to get along well without immediate feedback. They seem to be able to deal well with problems others seem unable to handle, because they cannot deal with the ambiguity.

4. Intelligence/perception. Successful senior level leaders are very perceptive, intuitive individuals. They have an abundance of what might be called "street smarts." They are able to get to the heart of any matter at hand intuitively–very quickly. They have an amazing ability to sort out the relevant from the irrelevant almost instantaneously.

MANAGEMENT OF AGGRESSION

5. Capacity to take charge. They can assume roles as senior leaders, after having been appointed by the organization, with no apologies, regardless of others in the environment who thought they should have been chosen for the position. The rejection, or envy and jealousy regarding them, will not interfere in their assuming the responsibilities attendant to their position.

6. Perseverance. Successful senior level leaders are not rigid. They certainly are not dogmatic. They seem to be able to stick with something until it is accomplished, even if the point of view on which they are embarking is unpopular. They seem to know intuitively which ideas to stick with, yet are very interested in data whenever it is available. They do not deter in the face of rejection or opposition.

7. Capacity to interact. Successful leaders have the ability to contain hostility and to deal effectively with it when they feel it. They seem to be able to field it well–by this we mean dissipate it. They have developed good verbal skills, tact, are able to communicate easily with all levels of the organization, and because of their skill at interpersonal interaction, can develop substantial support for themselves and their ideas. They have superior ability in managing their own hostility and aggression.

8. Initiative. Successful senior leaders are proactive. They lead the attack. They see opportunity where others do not and will move on it. They know *when* to move–which is part of their intuitive makeup. While others hesitate, they move forward. Their proactive initiative suggests one great quality of successful leaders.

9. Energy. It is very difficult to be successful as leaders without stamina–without physical and mental capability. Their strong mental and physical "make up" is fueled by enormous energy. Successful leaders can hang in there, both physically and mentally, while others tire and fall by the wayside.

CASE IN POINT: The president of a well-known organization was interested in interviewing a recent MBA graduate from a prestigious university. The staff of the president was very much impressed by the young fellow, and they had given the gentleman their stamp of approval. The last interview was with the president himself. In the early evening, when the interview was to be held and the young man was finally face-to-face with the president, the president decided that everyone should go out to dinner, and at that point called a couple of vice presidents and invited them, together with their wives, out to dinner with the MBA candidate. After dinner, drinks, and some socialization, the vice presidents and their wives went on home, as it was now approaching eleven p.m. At this point the president of the company invited the young man to his home for the interview. The young man at this point balked, stated he was tired, and told the president he had to go home and get some rest.

To say the least, the president found out what he was looking for. He was unwilling to accept a young man into the organization who did not understand that sometime business required a dedication way into the night. What would he do if he were dealing with a very significant customer, and the customer was settling down to negotiating at midnight? Would he tell the customer that he is too tired and it would have to occur in the morning? The president decided the young MBA was not the person to be hired by his company. The young man was not invited back for any more interviews.

MANAGEMENT OF AFFECTION

10. Capacity to invest in others. Successful leaders enjoy monitoring others, advising others, helping others to develop, and spending time on other kinds of uplifting projects. They especially enjoy spending time guiding other human beings. They are available to help others grow, develop, and move ahead in the organization.

11. Sensitivity. Senior level managers are sensitive to the feelings of others. They have empathy. They can put themselves in the place of others and feel how they feel. They have a kind of personal radar, when with an individual or in front of a group. They can sense what others are feeling, even thinking. They are guided by that intuitive radar inside them–and they usually are quite accurate.

12. Identification rather than compensation. Most successful senior level leaders are able to accept disappointment without feeling defeated and humiliated. They are interested in the pursuit of achievement; they never try to be omnipotent, that is trying to be everywhere, trying to do everybody else's job, trying to be perceived as being able to do everything themselves. These high level leaders are able to delegate. They are really not interested in authority per se, but are more interested in achievement. They get real satisfaction out of seeing others achieve, rather than developing an immense amount of authority for themselves. The "power" they accumulate will come from the respect given them by others. They are not grabbers, trying to grab more and more authority within the organization, because they know they have a substantial amount of it and do not really need to use it generally for success. They know who they are, are pleased with who they are (they have strong personal identifaction), and have a lot of self confidence. Because of this they are able to confront unpopular issues and problems. *They are never arrogant.*

13. Truly successful leaders are compassionate. The most successful leaders show compassion, without a need to be liked in return. They can give honest and accurate evaluations to subordinates, knowing full well it is impossible to make everybody happy. This will not deter them. They can be compassionate toward others, yet at the same time manage their own guilt/not permitting guilt to grow to a point that makes them defeated or impotent. They well recognize if they have a strong need to be liked by everyone they cannot take charge. Again, because of their very strong sense of self confidence, they are able to confront unpopular issues and problems.

14. *They are interested in building the organization rather than building themselves.* They have very strong interests in leaving something behind. Their greatest need is *not* to seek control over others. They are not interested in having the organization built around them. When these leaders leave they want to leave something behind; they do not want to take it all out with them.

15. Senior level successful leaders have a fierce streak of independence. They know their limits, get along with others, are interested in the inputs of others, and are good listeners. When it comes time to making the final decision however, they can be fiercely independent. Once they make the decision, based upon all the facts at hand, they usually will stick with it. They will not be coerced into making decisions they do not believe in, or which will make them popular. They would sooner quit than be forced into making decisions that are against their values and beliefs.

EGO IDEAL

    16. Flexibility. They do not need to stick to one project at a time; they can handle multiple tasks. They can also shift from one direction to another when it is essential. They are always open to new ideas, new thinking, new processes. They work on being flexible, understanding that it is very easy to become headstrong in what one wants and what one desires.

    17. Tolerance for stress. They know how to take care of their bodies and their minds so they can manage their own stress levels. They understand that a balanced life is absolutely essential for dealing with stress. They live intelligently. They manage their life. They manage time. Time and life do not manage them. They feel good about themselves and get up every day looking forward to the events awaiting them. When they feel stressed out they know how to deal with it so it does not cause them physical or mental harm.

    18. Successful leaders have a cause. They have a personal conviction/purpose. Their life has purpose; their work has purpose. They do not just get up every day and embrace the world. They have a plan, they have a purpose, and every day takes them closer to realizing this purpose. Their purpose is usually embodied in a vision, a *vision for their corporation or company, a vision for their life.* They are able to talk about this vision and even enjoy talking about it. They are able to talk philosophically. They are not so concrete they cannot develop a vision which guides them, drives them.

    19. They are community leaders. They use their power and authority to help a community. They take their responsibilities seriously and are always alert not to poison the environment or do other things that can hurt the environment or people. They give of their time, effort, and vitality to groups in the community. They have a commitment to help the community improve. They will use the resources at their disposal to help the community around them.

    20. Good sense of humor. Most successful senior leaders have a great sense of humor. They see something humorous where others see tragedy. They are able to laugh in the face of adversity. They are not deterred by the negative; they can always elicit something good out of a tough situation. They rarely see insurmontable problems; they see opportunities. And when they mess up, they admit it, laugh at it, and get on with it. They do not look for others to hang. They never blow things out of proportion.

21. There are no gaps in their ego ideal. They have a very good idea of who they are, what they are all about, how they are currently living–in all senses of the word. They work very hard to walk the talk. They are consistently working on eliminating gaps between what they say and what they do. Because their ego ideal and their current behavior is consistently and predictably congruent, they literally are at peace with themselves, are easy to get close to, and can help others around them feel comfortable, no matter what their rank is in the organization. Because of this congruence people are simply not afraid of them, enjoy being around them, and literally will come to them to express concerns and views, which they would otherwise not do if the congruence were not observable.

CONCLUSION

When one observes these characteristics found in senior level leaders of a *Fortune* 100 corporation, it gives food for thought. It offers an opportunity to compare one's current behavior with the leadership behavior portrayed through this survey. It also may help to close the gap between one's current behavior and one's ego ideal, as expressed in this study.

GROUPTHINK: A HINDRANCE TO EFFECTIVE DECISION-MAKING FOR LEADERS IN ORGANIZATIONS

By
Harold E. Fuqua, Jr.
Joseph Cangemi
Stephanie Chaffins
Casimir J. Kowalski

Irving Janis defined groupthink as a way of thinking when people are members of a cohesive in-group and, when striving for group unanimity, choose not to realistically appraise alternative courses of action. "Groupthink refers to a deterioration of mental efficiency, reality testing, and moral judgment that results from group pressure" (Janis, 1972, p. 9). McCauley (1989) referred to the phenomenon as a process whereby groups become involved in premature consensus-seeking that usually ends up with internalizations and/or compliance. In groupthink, groups actually begin to reach a premature consensus before the facts are gathered in a particular situation. Johnson and Weaver (1992) suggested in groupthink the attempt to achieve unanimity overrides realistic thought, and the pressure to conform to the group's viewpoint often results in behavior in which the group would not normally engage. Members of groups involved in groupthink are so loyal to one another their collective loyalty interferes with the sound judgment capable on the part of each member of the group. Tetlock, Peterson, McGuire, Shi-jie, and Feld (1992) stated the "pressures for uniformity and loyalty can build up within groups to the point where they seriously interfere with both cognitive efficiency and moral judgments" (p. 403). It is clear decision-making groups must strive to remain open-minded if they are to avoid such faulty decision-making processes.

SYMPTOMS OF GROUPTHINK

Symptoms of groupthink become evident when a group begins yielding to pressures. For example, Janis and Mann (1977) outlined

eight symptoms of groupthink:
- an illusion of invulnerability
- collective efforts to rationalize
- an unquestioning belief in the group's inherent morality
- stereotyped views of rivals and enemies
- direct pressure on a member who expresses arguments against any of the group's stereotypes, illusions, or commitments
- self-censorship of deviations from apparent group consensus
- a shared illusion/perception of unanimity
- the emergence of self-appointed *mindguards*

A group exhibiting these symptoms is likely to be functioning in a groupthink mode in its decision-making processes. These symptoms usually lead to serious problems for organizations, terminating in groupthink tendencies which saturate the group's members.

One of the serious flaws within groups occurs when members start to value the group more than the vital decisions they are expected to make. Members purposely ignore the facts of specific situations so they will not appear to disrupt the group by making objections to certain facts with which they have some discrepancy.

Organizations engaging in groupthink often suffer from an illusion of morality. Moorehead, Ference, and Neck (1992) found "group members often believe, without question, in the inherent morality of their position. They tend to ignore the ethical or moral consequences of their decisions" (p. 543). Sims (1992) implied group members are very capable of engaging in unethical acts when the culture of an organization overwhelms the personal belief system of its individual members. Groupthink causes members to believe in the morality of their actions no matter how unethical or unlawful the course of action may be.

GROUPTHINK IN COMMERCIAL ORGANIZATIONS

Many organizations in the commercial/industrial world succumb to groupthink. Sims (1992) stated the evidence weighs heavily on the side of frequent occurrence of groupthink in the business world. Harry Levinson, the eminent industrial/business psychologist, observed:

> When information from the outside is ignored or rejected, those in the inside can neither see nor hear what their environments are telling them. As a result, they lose their ability to compete. The design and marketing of the ill-fated Edsel automobile have been attributed to groupthink. (Levinson, 1994, p. 652)

A great deal of unethical behavior also can be attributed to groupthink. Sims (1992) found groupthink occurs in organizations when groups place a higher priority on organizational counternorms that lead to organizational benefits which, in turn, encourages organizational members to support and commit unethical acts. Groupthink occurs within organizations when the group knowingly commits unethical acts, when the group is cohesive, when the leader promotes solutions or ideas that are unethical, and when the group has no internal rules or controls to enforce ethical behavior (Sims, 1992).

The greatest contributing factor leading to the unethical decision-making is when members of the group desire the approval of fellow group members and their leader (Sims, 1992). In these situations, the group will engage in unethical behavior and reject any opinion which does not support group goals and its leader. For example, Beech-Nut engaged in unethical practices due to groupthink attitudes and pressures when the company sold millions of jars of *phony* apple juice. Due to financial problems and a false belief many other companies were also selling deceptively-labeled juice, Beech-Nut managers believed their actions were justified. They were under an illusion the deliberately falsely-labeled juice was appropriate to drink (Sims, 1992).

A primary symptom of groupthink not previously mentioned is defense-avoidance. According to Janis (1972), this occurs when the leader of the group "receives social support from advisors who concur with his judgments and share in developing rationalizations that bolster the least objectionable choice" (p. 129).

LOYALTY AND GROUPTHINK

Groupthink most generally occurs in highly cohesive groups in which individual members are close to one another. As indicated earlier, the members of the group are so loyal to each other they do not want to disrupt the harmony of the group by voicing objections to critical decisions. Janis (1972) noted, "In a sense, members consider loyalty to the group the highest form of morality" (p. 12). For example, in Romania during the Communist reign, Communist party political leaders entered into the province of engineering and construction, demanding that buildings be made of inferior steel–yet be made large, monolithic in structure, and at the same time be of high quality and cost-effective. The individuals making these demands had no idea how to construct buildings because the individuals were political appointees and not engineers. Nonetheless, they did not seek more qualified opinion to determine if such demands were feasible, and they rejected analyses of highly-qualified and experienced Romanian engineers. No opposition was voiced from the engineering groups receiving this dictate, only signals of agreement and compliance (B. Diaconescu, personal communication, May 23, 1994).

Another example from Romania of groupthink that still permeates Romanian society today and shows itself in current decision-making practices is in the form of a joke: there is the tendency, left over from the Communist regime, that people go to meetings with hands already up in the air in agreement before the meeting even starts–agreeing with the leadership–same as they did in the Communist era. Result: little progress in Romania today; the old system of groupthink remains intact. (Seventy percent of Romanian enterprises still remain in government hands and only 30% have been moved to private enterprise; $8 billion have been invested in Hungary–$4 billion since 1989, yet only $800 million have been invested in Romania since 1989.) According to Romania professionals, groupthink and group compliance is retarding Romania's progress in comparison to its Eastern European neighbors (I. Mihut, personal communication, May 25,1994).

A SENSE OF INVULNERABILITY AND GROUPTHINK

Janis (1972) viewed members of groups as developing "rationalizations supporting shared illusions about the invulnerability of their organization or nation and displayed other symptoms of 'groupthink'– collective pattern of defensive-avoidance" (p. 129). When President Truman and his advisors ignored the risks involved in the decision to send U.S. troops into North Korea to conquer all of Korea, they overlooked China's warning of intervention if the U.S. crossed the 38th parallel. President Truman, General Douglas McArthur, and the president's advisors did not take the warnings seriously. They shared an illusion of invulnerability; they were sure Chinese forces would not intervene in the war. This was a serious miscalculation that almost lost the war for the United States (Janis, 1972).

The illusion of invulnerability and groupthink occurred during the Watergate scandal when President Nixon and his advisors believed the Watergate cover-up was not serious. Gouran (1986) noted, "a detailed examination of the presidential transcripts reveals in nearly every instance of conjecture on issues related to the desirability of perpetuating the Watergate cover-up, the president and those with whom he talked reached the wrong conclusion" (p. 109). According to Gouran (1986), the communication between President Nixon and fellow conspirators served to reinforce poor judgment. Inappropriate estimates were made as to whether the Watergate committee could be manipulated, the reliability of the Watergate defendants, and if executive privilege could shield the president from the release of the Watergate tapes (Gouran, 1986). The president and his small group of advisors severely underestimated the Watergate committee and the American public.

THE CHALLENGER DISASTER

The Challenger disaster, which occurred on January 28, 1986, was another tragic example of groupthink. Seven astronauts died in the tragic accident. Moorehead et al. (1991) argued that "the presidential commission that investigated the accident pointed to a flawed decision-making process as a primary contributed cause" (p. 540). Moorehead et al. (1991) also noted there were three reasons groupthink contributed to the Challenger disaster. These were (a) the presence of a cohesive group, (b) leader preference, and (c) deliberate isolation from expert opinions.

The people who made the decision to launch the Challenger had worked together for many years. Two of the top-level managers at NASA had actively promoted their pro-launch opinions in the face of opposition. Several other managers pushed for the launch of the shuttle despite the fact the temperature was low, according to the commission's report. The top-level, decision-making group knew of the objections the engineers had made earlier in the evening; still, the group decided to go on with the launch as planned. Moorehead et al. (1991) stated, "the top-level, decision-making team was isolated from engineers who possessed the expertise regarding the functioning of the equipment" (p. 542). The illusion of invulnerability led the group to take unnecessary risks in order to see the Challenger take off on schedule. Manz and Sims (1982) determined the illusion of invulnerability caused group members to display excessive optimism and... take extreme risks when making decisions. Top-level managers at NASA decided to override the engineers' arguments, and the engineers succumbed to group pressures by reversing their original resolve to not allow the space shuttle to take off due to unsafe conditions. According to this case study, if the top-level managers had listened to the engineers, and if the engineers had not given in to the pressure to conform to the group, the disaster may have been prevented (Manz & Sims, 1982).

GROUPTHINK AND THE BAY OF PIGS, CUBA

Another example of groupthink occurred during the Bay of Pigs calamity. Janis (1972) noted the Bay of Pigs invasion was planned by some of the most brilliant men in the councils of the United States government. All the major assumptions supporting the plan were wrong. One of the false assumptions of Kennedy's advisors was the belief that Castro's army was so weak that a small Cuban brigade could establish a well-protected beach head. This contradicted the reports of the experts in the State Department. According to Janis (1972). "The CIA planners chose to ignore the experts' reports, and Kennedy's policy advisors did not pursue their questions far enough to become aware of the contradictory estimates, which would have revealed the shakiness of the CIA's assumptions" (p. 23). Janis (1972) also found secrecy and threats to personal reputations and status were key ingredients which led to groupthink and a very calamitous failure on the part of President Kennedy and his advisors, for which we are still paying today.

Evidence of groupthink occurs and pervades when group members believe they are invincible and all-powerful. Janis (1972) argued when group members acknowledge no single member among them as having anything in particular to add to the group, or has no special credibility, they are under the illusion the group as a whole is a *supergroup*, capable of overcoming and handling all obstacles which pose a threat to their desired course of action. Decisions emanating from such a group can almost inevitably lead to a disaster. Such a group usually believes they cannot be stopped. An example of this flawed judgment occurred when the United States grossly underestimated the capacity of the North Vietnamese and the Viet Cong during the Vietnam war (Janis, 1972).

In an experiment conducted by Cline (1990), 72 undergraduate students from an introductory speech communication course at a large Eastern university volunteered to participate in an investigation to determine if groupthink actually occurred in small groups. The study focused on efficient decision-making within these groups. The researchers set up two groups, a *groupthink group* and a *non-groupthink* group. This study validated previous research that suggested *when a group is under the influence of groupthink, positive relationships frequently will override critical thinking* (Cline, 1990).

THE NEED TO AVOID CONFLICT AND GROUPTHINK

Groups are more likely to engage in groupthink when they are faced with stressful situations. Griffin and Hensley (1986) argued:

> The more cohesive the group becomes under conditions of stress, the more its members rely on each other for security and acceptance. The more members of a group rely on each other for approval, the more they will seek unanimity in their decisions so as to avoid conflict with one an other. (p. 499)

The tendency to avoid conflict at all costs causes groups to become victims of groupthink because they fear if any of the members voice disapproval for a particular idea, which is clearly not appropriate for the group, the other members will put direct pressure on the disapproving member to conform to group consensus (Griffin & Hensley, 1986).

Griffin and Hensley (1986) conducted a study on groupthink at Kent State University, which involved a controversy between the trustees of the university and the student body/faculty. The controversy, which occurred in 1977, centered around a decision by the trustees to build a gymnasium on the site where students and Ohio National Guard members confronted each other just before the tragic shooting of May 4, 1970. Despite opposition from the student body and faculty, large-scale protest activities, massive arrests, and numerous third-party efforts to resolve the conflict, the trustees refused to reconsider their decision. The trustees were a close, cohesive group who refused to listen, even though the students and faculty strongly objected. The group was more interested in maintaining perceptions of solidarity and unanimity concerning their judgments rather than succumbing to the opposition (Griffin & Hensley, 1986)

AVOIDING CONFLICT: THE JAPANESE NAVAL DEFEAT AT MIDWAY ISLAND

Another symptom of groupthink which permeates small groups is the withholding of personal doubts concerning a decision made by the group. Group members usually avoid saying anything that might disturb the cohesive mindset of the group which sees its course of action as correct. Group members believe their policies are correct and will succeed no matter what others may think. Group members under this tendency are afraid to voice their doubts to other members of the group. They have reservations about a course of action, but in order to preserve the unity of the group and, out of fear of disapproval, no one in the group voices objections to a policy which may prove disastrous in the end (Janis, 1972). Take, for example, the battle of Midway Island in 1942 between Japanese and American naval forces. Admiral Yamamoto, the victorious commander of the successful raid on Pearl Harbor, with its immobilizing effect on the United Slates Pacific fleet, decided it would not be necessary to utilize the entire Japanese fleet to take Midway Island, a significant and valuable island territory needed in order to realize further Japan's Pacific goals. The immense popularity of Admiral Yamamoto, his strong character, his domination of his staff, and his biased views of Japanese naval superiority–cleverly made known to his staff, all welded together to create a situation of significant pressure on his staff. Together with the illusion at that time *they were invincible,* the group approved a battle plan with which they *were not* in agreement, but which they chose *not* to voice disapproval: splitting the fleet so part of it would go to the Aleutian Islands and take Attu and Kiska, while the other portion would lake Midway Island. The approval on the part of Yamamoto's staff, a groupthink decision made because the members did not want to disappoint their strong leader, led to perhaps the most significant naval and military setback for the Japanese in the war in the Pacific (Agawa, 1979). To put it in terms used on another occasion by Winston Churchill, Yamamoto's decision and resulting move was not the beginning of the end of the war, but *it was the end of the beginning of the war* (Churchill,1948). Because of this groupthink decision, Japan's offensive advancement in the Pacific had been checked; thereafter, Japan's posture in the Pacific essentially would he *defensive.*

MIND GUARDS/HIGH STATUS INDIVIDUALS AND GROUPTHINK

When groupthink overruns a group, a self–appointed mind guard usually evolves. Mind guards protect a leader from input that may discourage him/her, as in the case of Admiral Yamamoto. Janis (1972) noted a mind guard protects the leader from virtually anything that might damage confidence regarding the soundness of the policies to which the leader is committed. In other words, objections from members of the group questioning the validity of a decision are struck down by other members who act as mind guards.

A more recent example of groupthink occurred during the Reagan administration, involving several of Reagan's cabinet members and perhaps the President himself. Sims (1992) believed pressures for uniformity characterized the process surrounding the flawed decision of the Reagan administration to exchange arms for hostages with Iran. Money from the sale of arms was given to the Nicaraguan Contras in order to stop a communist takeover in that country. This course of action was taken by the group despite the fact that several congressional amendments limited or banned aid to the Contras.

High-status individuals often exert influence over lower-status group members. Gouran and Hirokawa (1986) noted that, in a group, high-status individuals who displayed deficiencies in thinking or reasoning infected the whole group. Everyone becomes deficient in their thinking and reasoning skills because *no one in the group questioned the high-status individuals.* Influential leaders and members in a group should use their influence to insist on critical thinking skills and objectivity of the other members of the group.

These are just a few examples of the potential problems related to groupthink. Weber-Posner (1987) viewed the potential consequences of groupthink as "poor decision-making, violent actions against out-groups, and almost total isolation of the in-group" (p. 119). Weber-Posner (1987) further noted that "Groupthink in a small group situation is extremely undesirable and it is vital to know the symptoms which can lead to this negative condition" (p. 119).

AVOIDING GROUPTHINK

Not all groups within organizations experience groupthink. Janis (1972) asserted, "Not all cohesive groups suffer from groupthink, although all may display some of its symptoms from time to time" (p. 295). Groups with members who are individually involved in critical inquiry, whose members are highly competent and who have properly defined roles, gen- erally do not fall victims to groupthink (Janis, 1972).

Certain strategies exist which can be utilized to prevent groupthink from entering the decision-making process of small groups. One way to prevent it from saturating the group is for the leader to insist on gathering and receiving all available data relevant to the subject at hand from all members of the group. Janis (1972) stated, "The leader of a policy-forming group at the onset should assign the role of critical evaluator to each member, encouraging the group to give high priority to airing objections and doubts" (p. 296). A leader does not need to be surrounded by a group of *yes persons*. Critical feedback can prevent decisions, such as the examples cited previously, from occurring.

Small groups can avoid groupthink by having the leader appoint members to/of the group who will play devil's advocate, raising questions that force an in-depth review of the group's decision-making process (Sims, 1992). Playing devil's advocate is necessary in order to identify the potential pitfalls or unethical behavior involved in a particular course of action. Concerns are critically evaluated by those assigned this role within the group. Sims suggested this role be rotated among members so no single person is identified as the critic of all decisions. This provides a fresh viewpoint from different group members (Sims, 1992).

Another way a group can prevent groupthink from dominating the decision-making process is for the leader to maintain impartial viewpoints. Janis and Mann (1977) believed:

The leader, when assigning a policy-planning mission to a group, should be impartial instead of stating his preference and expectations at the outset. This practice requires each leader to limit his briefings to unbiased statements about the scope of the problem and the limitations of available resources, without advocating specific proposals he/she would like to see adopted. (p. 399)

Perhaps if Yamamoto had done this, the decision regarding splitting the Japanese fleet might have been different, and the outcome of the Pacific War might have been different. If leaders would adopt this policy, they would not influence their subordinates in such a way they are afraid to disagree with them. Leaders' biased opinions often influence group members to agree with their policies without providing critical feedback—a potentially disastrous situation.

In **conclusion**, groupthink often pervades groups and causes biased and flawed decision-making. Many tragic disasters could have been avoided if groupthink had not prevailed within the organizations where they occurred. In every case where groupthink invades groups, a breakdown in communication among group members takes place. Leaders refuse to listen, and members refuse to voice their concerns or objections. Powerful leaders and members exert strong influence over a group in order to achieve consensus. Leaders must solicit feedback and critical evaluation from other members on all issues. With the hard work of the leader and the members, and through open communication and discussion, groupthink can be eliminated and disasters avoided (Bennis, 1993; Cangemi, Kowalski, & Claypool, 1985).

REFERENCES

Agawa, H. (1979). *The reluctant admiral.* San Francisco: Kondansha International/USA Limited.

Bennis, W. (1993). *An invented life: Reflections on leadership and change.* Reading, MA: Addison-Wesley Publishing Co.

Cangemi, J., Kowalski, C., & Claypool, J. (1995). *Participative management.* New York: Philosophical Library.

Churchill, W. (1948). *The second world war.* New York: Houghton MifflinCo.

Cline, R.J. (199(1). Detecting groupthink: Methods for observing the illusion the unanimity. *Communication Quarterly, 38,* 112-126.

Gouran, D.S. (1986). *Inferential errors, interaction, and group decision-making: Communication and group decision-making.* New York: Sage Publication, Inc.

Gouran, D.S., & Hirokawa, R.Y. (1986). *Counteractive functions of communication in effective group decision–making: Communication and group decision–making.* NewYork: Sage Publication, Inc.

Hensley, T.R., & Grimn, H.R. (1986). Victims of groupthink: The Kent State University board of trustees and the 1977 gymnasium controversy. *Journal of Conflict Resolution, 30,* 497-531.

Janis, I.L. (1972). *Victims of groupthink.* Boston: Houghton Miffin.

Janis, I.L. (1982). *Stress, attitudes, and decisions.* New York: Praeger Publishers.

Janis, I.L., & Mann, L. (1977). *Decision making: A psychological analysis of conflict, choice, and commitment.* New York: The Free Press.

Johnson, D., & Weaver, L. (1992). Groupthink and the classroom: Changing familiar patterns to encourage critical thought. *Journal of Industrial Psychology, 19,* 99-106.

Manz, C., & Sims, P. (1982). The potential for groupthink in autonomous work groups. *Human Relations, 35,* 773-784.

McCauley, C. (1989). The nature of social influence in groupthink: Compliance and internalization. *Journal of Personality and Social Psychology, 57,* 250-260.

Moorehead, G., Ference, R., & Neek, P. (1991). Group decision fias-
        coes continue. Space shuttle Challenger and a revised
        groupthink framework. *Human Relations, 44,* 539-550.
Sims, R. (1992). Linking groupthink to unethical behavior in organiza-
        tions. *Journal of Business Ethics, 11*, 651-662.
Tetlock, P., Peterson, R.S., McGuire, C., Shi-jie, & Feld, P. (1992).
        Assessing political group dynamics: A test of the groupthink
        mode. *Journal of Personality and Social Psychology, 63*, 403-
        425.
Weber-Posner, C. (1987). Update on groupthink. *Small Group Behavior,
        18,* 118-125.

HOW BUSINESS/INDUSTRIAL LEADERS AND THEIR ORGANIZATIONS HANDLE STRESS

By
Joseph P. Cangemi
K. Habib Khan

Stress in business and industrial organizations is a common experience most people employed will undergo and endure at sometime in their working lives. There are many reasons why those working in the business and industrial sector will undergo stress. Among them are:

- customer demands
- downsizing/rightsizing/re-engineering (they are the same essentially)
- hostile take over
- new ownership
- federal/state government investigations
- quality problems
- loss of market share
- community attack
- significant decrease in sales
- dwindling profits
- changes at the top
- change in management style
- work overload
- union organizing attempt/campaign
- union demands
- walkout/wildcat strike
- threatened closure
- threatened removal of facility for placement in another location, particularly offshore
- down turn in the economy
- movement of personnel from one location to another
- reduction in salary and benefits

Some additional causes of organizational stress have been noted by Singh (1991):

    a. *Lack of Group Cohesiveness:* reflects a situation of stress whereby people do not stick together on group decisions and do not get along well with each other.

    b. *Role Conflict:* represents a situation of stress where contradictory demands are made on the role of the incumbent.

    c. *Feeling of Inequity:* is expected to create stress when the incumbent feels the inadequate compensation for her/his energetic input is not justified.

    d. *Role Ambiguity:* refers to a stressful situation where the incumbent is not clear about his/her requirements of the job.

    e. *Role Overload:* is a situation creating stress whereby the incumbent feels she/he is required to do too much within the assigned time and resources.

    f. *Lack of Leadership Support:* represents a situation of stress where the role of leadership is perceived as passive in helping out the incumbent with a problem.

    g. *Constraints of Change:* represents a stressful situation where the incumbent experiences problems in coping with fast, technological changes and rigid rule regulations in the job.

    h. *Job Difficulty:* represents a stressful situation whereby the incumbent feels the job is taxing to her/his ability.

    i. *Job Requirement Capability Mismatch:* reflects a situation of stress where the incumbent feels her/his abilities significantly differ from the requirements of the job.

    j. *Inadequacy of Role Authority:* represents a situation of stress where the incumbent perceives he/she was not provided with the required amount of authority to discharge responsibilities.

The above list does not include all the causes of stress that potentially could plague an organization, particularly business and/or industrial organizations. However, most organizations survive these ordeals, though during periods of prolonged stress destabilization of employees often occurs. Usually, like a ship on a stormy sea rolling from one side to another, the ship most generally stabilizes. There may be casualties due to the inclement weather, but the ship adjusts to the conditions, stabilizes, and continues on its way. Sinking is uncommon; so too with organizations (Singh,1991).

Take, for example, the trauma created for an organization losing money, losing market share, losing revenues, and losing customer confidence. Such an organization undoubtedly will become a stressful place in which to work. The way this organization will handle the trauma probably will be in one of two ways: healthy or unhealthy. Unfortunately, far too many organizations invariably will choose the unhealthy method (Cangemi et al.,1985):

- there will be threats
- coercion will be commonplace
- people will be terminated
- managers will be reassigned at whim
- the work force will be decreased by an appreciable percent
- respect for seniority will be ignored, quite possibly even held against many of those who have rightfully earned it
  (and who have performed quality service in the past)
- younger people often will be brought in to replace older employees
- a deliberate attempt will be made to chase older employees out the door
- an authoritarian model of leadership likely will be introduced
- communication will most generally be directed downward with upward communication discouraged and discarded
- "group think" will be evident in the upper echelon of the organization, as the leaders perceive they know better than their subordinates
- a sense of doom, despair, helplessness, and distrust will permeate the organization

Some organizations, few in number to be sure, handle the trauma of these same types of problems in a healthy manner:

- they go to their employees and explain the dilemmas facing the organization
- they solicit input from their employees
- they brainstorm with employees, seeking *their* perceptions of problems
- they form teams and create opportunities for employees to develop solutions to problems

- they encourage employees to be creative–to break with tradtion
- they *listen* to the suggestions of their employees and act upon those that are reasonable
- they send employees and managers as small teams into the market place, to visit their customers, in order to come back with ideas that can help to resolve problems as well as get the voice of the customer back into the organization
- the leadership stays positive during this period of time and permeates an encouraging and optimistic attitude toward employees
- an appropriate consultant is utilized during this time to facilitate groups and encourage and work with both management and employees to provide an objective"outside" perspective to assist the organization through the challenges it faces
- leaders walk around and mingle with employees, talking with them and listening to them so they can see for themselves their leaders are interested in them and their ideas
- consistent feedback is generated to employees so they will know of the progress being made

CASE STUDY I: A HEALTHY APPROACH

Take for example, this case, which actually happened. This particular organization was terribly traumatized due to a fall off of sales—clients simply were not buying the product (the market was saturated with the product at this time). The situation, and the stress created by it, was grave. The organization's leadership had to do something. The financial loses were mounting. They had done everything to improve sales but nothing seemed to work. There was no other recourse; headcount had to be reduced substantially because expenditures had to be reduced. The organization could no longer wait. The leadership went to the employees—there were over 600 of them, and explained the situation regarding the need to reduce expenditures by reducing headcount. They had reduced expenditures prior to this in every way possible to avoid reducing headcount, but there were no options left now. Reducing headcount was the last straw and it had to be done or the organization would go bankrupt. A team was formed composed of both employees and managers to study the most effective, yet humane, way to reduce headcount. The team came up with a solution which then was agreed to by the workforce: rather than take jobs away from fellow employees, *all employees, including the leadership,* would work four days a week, thereby cutting the payroll 20 percent. Everybody shared in the pain, and the mood and atmosphere permeating the organization was upbeat and optimistic because the employees had had some voice in the solution to the problem with which they would have to live. Unfortunately, business continued to drop off further, and further reductions in expenditures were required to save the business, necessitating additional headcount reduction. The teams formed again, and again *it* was decided to reduce wages another 20 percent by now only working, *employees and management alike,* three days per week. Everybody again shared in the pain rather than put fellow employees out the door. And again the mood was upbeat and optimistic, even though everyone was earning 40 percent less income! Business continued to decline and, unfortunately, employee headcount again had to be reduced, but this time on a more permanent basis. Even then, because management took the time to explain the situation to every single employee, when the time came for permanent separation of those employees selected to leave, they left with a good attitude and a positive impression toward the company and the leadership. Some time later, after an additional drop off of revenues, the business was sold, the facility was closed, and the organization, as it was known, ceased to exist, with perhaps a handful of employees moving with the business to a new location some distance away. Some 10 years later, the hundreds of employees who worked in this facility and who were either separated early or separated later when the facility closed, even though they went through and endured much pain during the downsizing, still reflect with enthusiasm and delight the time when they were employed by this organization. There are no regrets, there is no rancor. This case represents a healthy way of dealing with the trauma and stress created by the marketplace.

      Another significant stressful event that occurs in a commercial organization is when a union attempts to organize a facility. The resulting response inside the organization on the part of management is usually war. A state of siege becomes ever present. The stress created during this period of time is usually handled by management having massive numbers of meetings with employees to determine their perceptions so more channels of communications can be opened and utilized. At this point management sensitivity to employees' needs is one of the prime methods utilized to cope with the stress generated by previously unmet employee concerns. This technique usually works – the first time, as long as management begins to address the issues. The stress usually dissipates, and the organization usually remains non-union after this first unionizing attempt.

CASE STUDY II: A SUCCESSFUL RESOLUTION

An actual case in point is the following. An industrial complex with 1,100 employees was inundated with four events creating much stress for the employees:

- there was a significant quality problem
- there was a costly scheduling problem
- there was low morale permeating the entire organization
- there was a union camped just outside the facility working hard to unionize the employees—and management was dead set against the organization becoming unionized

In an effort to resolve the problems and diminish the stress, a new plant manager was hired who in turn hired a consultant to work with him to get to the bottom of the problems, to determine *the reasons* the problems were being created. In an effort to get a quick "read" of the organization, the consultant requested an interview with all 22 of the supervisors employed by the organization. The reason the supervisors were selected as opposed to upper management or other subordinates in the organization is because supervision usually is the recipient of the behavior of those above them, who in turn usually pass it down to those working below them—to that part of the work force essential to win over if these four problems were to be resolved. The consultant started at 8:00 a.m. on a Wednesday morning with the 22 supervisors by asking one question, "What do you feel needs to be done in order to make this organization a better place in which to work, a place where your current problems would be diminished or eliminated entirely." The consultant started writing the responses of the supervisors at 8:30 a.m. Wednesday and finished at 4:00 p.m. on Friday, three days and 177 items later. The root causes of the four major problems had been revealed. The 177 items were analyzed and condensed into 12 major concerns annoying the work force. Now the new leader of the facility had data which could be used to start correcting the conditions creating the four major problems listed above. The leader responded quickly, organizing meetings, opening up communications, reassigning some managers whose negative management style and negative attitudes fueled negative employee attitudes, getting out on the floor to talk with employees every single day, and instituting management development seminars for staff and management level employees. Communication meetings with employees were held with the organization's leader on a weekly basis, composed of representative groups of 12-14 employees from all over the facility, thereby giving employees an opportunity to voice concerns *directly to the top person.* All this brought about a decrease in the stress level of employees, who then worked with management to form teams to resolve the problems. The facility overcame the four problems plaguing it in record time. Within weeks after the consultant and the new leader uncovered the 12 major problems/concerns of the supervisors, the quality began to return to the product and shipments left on time, thereby saving a considerable sum of money that had been required in order to charter planes specifically to get the product to customers as soon as possible—an expenditure of considerable dollars, and all unnecessary if the product had been shipped on time and through normal channels. Morale improved considerably and optimism once again permeated the organization. The employees decided to give management a chance to turn things around, resulting in maintaining its non-union status. By paying attention to the employees' needs and perceptions, stress within the organization was reduced and the trauma permeating the organization dissipated. The organization went on to become one of the most successful and most profitable in its entire corporation.

ALL CHANGE RESULTS IN LOSS

Any change in an organization usually creates significant stress for employees, as well as trauma throughout the organization. Organizations can handle the trauma more constructively and successfully if they would reflect on this axiom of behavior: all change is loss, whether the change is positive or negative. Harry Levinson of Harvard University has suggested there are four types of loss when an organization embarks on change (Levinson, 1973):

- Loss of love

- Loss of support

- Loss of sensory input

- Loss of the capacity to act on oneself or to act on the outside world

Loss of love occurs when one is removed from one's colleagues, people who were depended on for skills, competencies, approval, interaction, association, friendship, and regards. Leaving them behind usually is experienced with substantial emotional pain. People suffer loss of love when they are separated from highly regarded colleagues.

Loss of support is experienced when we are separated from individuals with whom we have had close personal and professional ties, when we move, when career changes are made, when we are required to develop new ties, forge new relationships, meet new people on whom to depend, learn new ways of doing things, build new skills and practices, and utilize new theories. Loss of support is felt even when a long sought after promotion/advancement is received.

Loss of sensory input occurs when one cannot obtain appropriate data needed for self-protection and orientation. For example, when an individual is faced with new situations there is a need to pick up cues, behavioral codes, regarding appropriate behavior in a given situation/location–such as a new company, or new owners. This is especially a problem when one does not know what to expect, when one does not know the new behavior codes–both formal and informal.

Loss of the capacity to act on one's own behalf occurs when one cannot do things for one self; to solve one's own problems. People do not like to feel inadequate; they prefer to develop their own solutions, to feel mastery over their own lives, over their own fate (see Levinson, 1973).

When individuals in organizations undergo trauma they generally feel:
- more vulnerable
- more frustrated
- more angry
- more depressed
- more frightened
- more defensive
- more aggressive
- more hostile (from Levinson, 1973)

Whatever is done in organizations that causes trauma (reorganization, merger, downsizing, etc.) steps must be taken to prevent employees from developing a sense of loss – a sense of hopelessness, a sense of helplessness.

SOME RECOMMENDATIONS FOR HANDLING TRAUMA/ STRESS IN ORGANIZATIONS

Some general methods to deal with and reduce organizational stress are as follows (Brody,1991):

- Management takes significant action to reduce stress
- Mental health benefits are provided
- Employer has formal employee communications program
- Employees are regularly given information on coping with stress
- Employees have current and clear job descriptions
- Management and employees talk openly with each other
- Employees are free to talk with one another
- Employer offers exercise and other stress-reduction classes
- Employees are recognized for their contributions
- Work rules are published and are the same for every one
- Child care programs are available
- Employees can work flexible hours
- Perquisites are granted fairly based on level in the organization
- Employees have access to the technology they need
- Employees and management are trained in resolving conflicts
- Employees receive training when assigned new tasks
- Employer encourages work and personal support groups
- Employees have a place and time to relax during the workday
- An employee assistance program is available
- Each employee's work space is not crowded
- Employees can put up personal items in their work areas
- Management appreciates humor in the workplace

CONCLUSIONS

Organizations can do much to deal with the effects of stress felt by employees. To assist employees with workplace stress can have significant societal benefits, such as a reduction in health care costs, as well as lower costs for goods and services. Additional benefits include job safety and welfare of employees (Ivancevich et al., 1990).

Stress in organizations is a common occurrence; it cannot be avoided. However, it is within the province of management to create conditions within the organization so that stress levels are kept to a minimum and do not result in negative attitudes, sickness, or even death of employees. With intelligence, sensitivity, and human concern, this is certainly attainable.

REFERENCES

Brody, J.(1991,July 23). Stress on the job. *Courier Journal.*

Cangemi, J., Kowalski, C., & Claypool, J. (1985). *Participative management.* New York: Philosophical Library.

Ivancevich, J., Matteson, M., Breedman, S., & Philips, J. (1990). Worksite stress management interventions. *American Psychologist, 45* (2), 252-261.

Levinson, H. (1973). *The great jackass fallacy.* Boston: Harvard Graduate School of Business Press.

Singh, S. (1991). Executives under stress: Search for some preventive measures. *Social Science International, 7* (1).

WHY TOTAL QUALITY MANAGEMENT FAILS
– PERSPECTIVE OF TOP MANAGEMENT

By
Richard L. Miller
Joseph P. Cangemi

The Total Quality Management TQM philosophy provides the frame work by which continuous improvement is possible in an organization. It is a people-oriented, measurement–driven, customer focused management philosophy using structured, disciplined operating methodology (Saylor,1992). A simple way of thinking of TQM is doing the right things right the first time, on time, and all the time.

While U.S. Industry has supported the TQM principle in theory, it has struggled to implement its practice in a cost effective manner. A.T. Kearney, an international consulting firm in Chicago, reports that in the late 1980's poor quality products were estimated at 10% to 20% of sales dollars in the average U.S. Company. This figure constituted from two to four times the average profit margin. In general, manufacturing was spending 25% of its sales dollars fixing quality problems and some service industries were spending as much as 40% of operating costs to fix similar problems ("Demystifying...," *Black Enterprise,* June 1992, p. 284).

Philip B. Crosby (1990) has looked at this expenditure for quality and states that quality is conformance to requirements, insuring that the customer receives what is promised each and every time. His basic measure of quality is zero defects. Utilizing this standard, he then employs his basic measurement, which is money—how much it costs the organization to do it wrong as opposed to doing it right the first time.

Even when a quality focus does exist in organizations, the people who shape these efforts are still restricted. One 1990 survey by the American Society of Quality Control reported that more than 36% of employees in United States organizations do not participate in quality improvement programs, even when a quality program currently exists in their facilities. In one particular study of some 1,237 employees, it was noted that one out of every four employees was dissatisfied with his/her company's quality program (Getting...," *Black Enterprise,* 1992).

Harari (1993) similarly notes that American companies often fail to utilize employees and customers. Less than 30% of employees are utilized in TQM programs with regards to their ideas/suggestions and even fewer customers seem to be involved in the development of TQM programs.

If employees and customers are not involved, then what would the shelf life of such programs be? Apparently American companies rely limitedly on the suggestions of both employees and customers. With such feeble efforts, is it any wonder that many organizations decide that TQM is not producing a sufficient benefit to warrant its continuance?

COMPARISON OF TQM V/S TRADITIONAL MANAGEMENT

The day-to-day operation of TQM is inherently different from management approaches which are characteristically associated with American industry, particularly that of manufacturing. Listed below are several points first noted by Saylor (1992) and restated by the authors:

TRADITIONAL MANAGEMENT
- Looks for quick fix to problems
- Fire-fights problems in a reactive style
- Focuses short-term to meet production at any cost
- Inspects for errors after product is produced
- Decisions based upon opinions of a few key people
- Motivated by profit
- Throws resources at a task

TOTAL QUALITY MANAGEMENT
- Adopts new management philosophy
- Structured, disciplined operations which analyze for prevention
- Stresses long-term, continuous improvement
- Prevents errors and emphasizes quality of design
- Decisions on data-driven facts drawn from many people
- Uses people/resources to improve
- Motivated by customer satisfaction

TQM GUIDING PRINCIPLES

The principles of TQM presume full commitment from all levels of management in both words and actions to a process in which quality is an integral part of production. The company is seen as a dynamic, customer-driven organization which is constantly responding to changing customer needs and technology advancement. Continuous improvement is a daily process in which all levels from the floor to the CEO have responsibility and ownership. The central directive in this organization is to involve people...all people...in this improvement process. Employees jointly develop and own a vision of the organization, participate in the necessary training to accomplish this vision and are empowered with sufficient authority to produce the quality standard represented in the vision. As success is achieved, employees are regularly recognized and rewarded for their efforts. The organization is involved daily in bench marking and measuring the input and output of the working environment. Customers are constantly surveyed to determine their satisfaction with products which are received and this customer concept is extended back into the organization to include internal customers (e.g., those individuals who receive the work of others in an assembly process in a manufacturing facility).

RESPONDING TO CHANGING MARKET CONDITIONS
Quality is not sufficient in itself to guarantee the success of a company. Occasionally, management focuses totally on the quality of the product and forgets about consumer interests, needs, and changing market conditions. For example, one of the past winners of the Malcolm Baldridge Award, an AT&T facility, recently announced a closure date, at which time 1,000 people will lose their jobs. How can it be that an award-winning facility closes a short period of time after winning the Malcolm Baldridge Award? AT&T says it is because management lost sight of customer needs, changing market technology, changing market conditions, and the changing marketplace. As a result, AT&T is saddled with a facility making excellent quality, but with products no one is buying ("AT&T Layoffs," *USA Today,* 1993).

Harari (1993) notes a similar circumstance when stating that some managers tend to become internally focused, and lose site of what is occurring in the external world. The preoccupation with TQM by top management serves to diminish managers' attention to the external factors affecting the organization and its products, such as shifting preferences of customers, as well as changing marketplace conditions and technological improvements. Internally focused managers may, in the eyes of the customer, produce products that are outdated, misguided, or unacceptable. Harari states that one manager related to a colleague of his that "Before we invested in TQM, the rap on our company was that we turn out poorly made products that customers don't want. Now, after TQM, things have changed. Now we turn out well–made products that customers don't want."

WHY TQM FAILS: LACK OF TOTAL OWNERSHIP

Managers cannot delegate quality. They seem to fail to understand that quality must be ingrained in everyone who receives a paycheck from the organization. It must be central to everyone's job description and job role. They fail to understand that quality must be an obsession for everyone within the organization. A common perception in upper management is that quality is the domain of the quality department. As a result, many members of top management presume that the quality department is totally responsible for the quality in the product. Therefore, this absolves them of being personally accountable for any significant effort to increase quality. Many managers simply fail to recognize that quality really must be the foundation of their company's strategy and strategic planning, as well as its daily operations.

CREATING TQM WITH THE USE OF A CONSULTANT

Contributing to the difficulties of implementing a significant quality program is the proliferation of consultants who regularly offer their services to organizations interested in developing TQM programs. Ernst & Young indicated that 945 different quality management tactics were being utilized in the TQM marketplace (Harari,1993). Which technique is correct? On occasion, consultants in the field actually add to the problems of TQM programs rather than resolve them. TQM consulting is apparently very lucrative for consultants, but the value of these consultancies to the organization needs to be evaluated carefully and the appropriate person selected to fit the facility's needs.

Further, as an outsider, the consultant must bring both knowledge of TQM and understanding of the organization together to build an atmosphere of trust in a facility. The capacity to shape a general knowledge of TQM to fit a specific organization requires establishing open communication with all levels of the organization (Miller, R. & Cangemi, J., 1988).

LACK OF INCENTIVE FOR INVOLVEMENT

A common failure of companies which attempt to implement TQM is their unwillingness to provide incentive for employee involvement in the TQM process. Lawrence Schein (1991), program director for quality research for The Conference Board, reports that within 200

of the Fortune 500 manufacturing and service companies, 86% give quality achievement awards to individuals and teams. From that group 75%
provide recognition and/or rewards on a unit or plant basis. Non–cash
awards are provided to personnel in 45% of the manufacturing facilities
while service organizations are more inclined to combine cash with
noncash awards.

Both manufacturing and service organizations prefer noncash
for team efforts toward quality achievement. Only 6% of manufactures
give cash only awards (Schein, 1991).

LEADERSHIP FAILURE

Failure of upper- and middle-management to commit to the total
quality process is a major barrier to TQM. Schein reports that obstacle
was the most commonly cited failure to implementing a new, compre-
hensive program (Schein, 1991). Additional evidence of the involvement of top management in the failure of TQM is noted in the May 18,
1992 edition of *Fortune Magazine* (Tetzeli, 1992) in which is reported
"A quality program works only when the chief executive visibly backs
it. "A quality effort that does not have such leadership is a recipe for
disaster." According to the *Fortune* article, the reasons for TQM failure
on the part of top management include the following points:

- Failure of the CEO to work with employees to develop a vision as
  to what the company should be and where it is going.
- Failure to focus the quality effort on customer service.
- Too much emphasis on cost cutting and not enough effort on
  providing quality customer service.
- Failure to lead the company in questioning everything...every
  procedure, every idea, every way of doing business in the past.
- Failure to create small teams, whereby employees develop the
  confidence to solve problems related to their jobs and to the
  product they are making.
- Failure to encourage employee suggestions and then to allow
  employees to follow up on their suggestions and make
  necessary changes as they see fit.
- Failure to reward employees for improving the way the
  organization serves its customers.
- Overlooking the communications process within the
  company so that employees are kept informed of the
  success or failure of the quality programs in which they are
  involved.

- Failure to show a continued and passionate interest in the entire quality process.

This failure to commit is frequently seen in the half-hearted endorsement top leadership gives the new program. Harari states that the TQM process, on the part of top management, often lacks the passion and the excitement that is sorely needed to insure the success of such programs. In an analogy, exciting music is more than playing appropriate notes. It's the passion and the excitement with which a Rubenstein played the piano, as opposed to merely touching the notes, that made all the difference in the quality of his music.

William Muzak, manager of a Bridgestone/Firestone textile facility in Canada, indicates similar reasons why management has much to do with the failure of TQM programs. He states the following:

- Management often views programs like TQM as a quick fix, something that will take care of their immediate problems, rather than as seeing such a program as a long term investment. As a result, TQM goes by the wayside, such as other programs the corporation has undertaken in the past.

- Managers and organizations often fail to "walk the talk." For example, top management may appear to personally support TQM programs in theory, but frequently delegates the responsibility for implementing the program to others lower down the organizational chain of command. These key top people then become limited in their own involvement with the program. Consequently, upper management offers little of its time or personal endorsement toward TQM's success..

- Management often fails to understand that TQM can only take place in an environment where mistakes can take place, and where problems are solved rather than blame placed.

- Management often fails to work with people who remain in the organization after down-sizing, insuring them of job continuation in the future. For example, management must give assurances to employees that, through TQM programs, and other productivity improvements, that no employee is going to lose his or her job due to these improvements. Management often fails to let people know that they will not be replaced simply because they found a better way of doing the work. When management fails to ensure people that their futures are reasonably secure, then they do not have any motivation to do things that will take them out of their own jobs, that will cost them their own jobs. For this reason, many TQM programs fail, as employees see them as vehicles to putting themselves out of business. (William Muzak, Personal communication, May 15, 1993).

NOT MEASURING THE EFFECTS OF TQM

A TQM program requires measurable expectations of work and product. Menon (1992) outlines the continuous improvement steps that are routinely followed in TQM:

1. Identify the problem
2. Quantify the problem
3. Identify the root causes
4. Take actions to rectify the problem
5. Quantify the effects of the action to determine whether the problem has been solved. Set up systems to keep the problems from recurring (Menon, page 12.).

As demonstrated above, routine TQM process requires quantification of the workplace. However, often management fails to adequately measure the TQM process and therefore cannot produce tangible evidence of improvement (Sutton, 1992). Benchmarks must be established and quality standards tracked against those base lines to determine the success or failure of the program efforts (Waasdorp, 1991).

POORLY DEVELOPED VISION/UNWILLINGNESS TO FOLLOW THAT VISION

Companies (and plants) attempt to improve quality without a clearly developed plan or strategy. Organizations need a long term outline of current conditions, future goals and specific strategies for reaching those goals developed by a wide array of personnel. This final product should be put in writing (Berry, 1993).

While visions and strategies should be regarded as dynamically responding to market and technology changes, these quality strategies in American companies, as ordained by top management, seem to change with the weather. A study by Ernst & Young found that not one consistent quality strategy has become habitual within any U.S. Industry. No company did the same thing 90% of the time!

In developing a vision, the organization must understand that the quality program supports the company's efforts to generate a cost effective, customer–desired product. It is possible to over commit to a TQM program in a legitimate attempt to improve quality. Harari (1993) describes the process as one in which TQM programs demand sequential, orderly, and quite predictable processes to succeed. As a result, one sees the development of predictable, orderly, bureaucratic systems generated to support the TQM process. The result is increased forms to fill out, new committees and councils, additional meetings, etc., and an increasing number of staff personnel to handle the entire TQM process. Harari calls this the need to "police" the entire TQM process. Unfortunately, many TQM managers see the TQM process as a numbers crunching, paper–flowing process that usually develops a life of its own within the organization, subordinating other routines and processes of importance to the organization's success. A good example of how bureaucracies can develop around TQM programs is the case of Florida Power and Light Company. The quality department utilized 85 full-time individuals to monitor over 1900 quality teams. The gains in quality were absolutely minimal; employee stress and depression because of the process were much more significant than the gains in quality. Florida Power and Light has disbanded its bureaucracy. Its TQM structure and the quality department are now headed by six individuals.

POOR ABILITY TO COMMUNICATE WITH THE WORK FORCE

Another reason TQM programs fail is that management fails to give appropriate information to employees. For example, top management fails to help employees to be able to answer such questions as: Where are our competitors? What are our own company's strengths and weaknesses? What are the strengths and weaknesses of our competitors? What is the information concerning the sales and profits of our company? Who are our most significant customers? What do our customers expect from us? How satisfied are they with what we are giving them? In some cases, employees have come to distrust the information which flows from management. Frequently underlying this distrust has been a lack of willingness on management's part to involve employees in the decision-making process. A lack of fairness has been perceived as existing in the organization and many employees fear reactions from management if they, the employees, attempt to identify problem areas to the organization (Cangemi, J., Rice, J. & Kowalski, C., 1989). As TQM is presented to the work force, management feels resistance as workers look for hidden agendas and fail to accept the new procedures as genuinely seeking and valuing their input.

PRIOR HISTORY OF WORK FORCE PRODUCES RESISTANCE

Another reason why TQM often fails is that, due to the bureaucracies formed within an organization, the breakup of such bureaucracies and predictable systems is discouraged by top management.

In reality, organizations tend to find a comfort zone, and the destruction of this status quo is fought with great rigor. As a result, TQM programs must fit within this bureaucracy, management's comfort zone, and the status quo. Miller and Harker (1986) referred to this prior history's influence as dealing with the cognitecture of an organization. The cognitecture represents an organization's past history, beliefs, structure and procedures for doing business. Consequently, a manufacturing facility with a twenty year history of producing a product in a specified way experiences substantial resistance as people from the top to bottom ask "Why should we change? We have always been profitable working the old way."

However, for quality to improve, emphasis must be placed on new strategies, new techniques, new and novel ideas, what the customer thinks and what the market demands. TQM also demands a bottom-up approach to quality that emphasizes patience and distrusts obvious answers which may obscure the deeper problems underlying quality (Catel, P. & Matthews, J., 1992). This is very difficult to accomplish if top management does not lead the group in the destruction of the status quo so that there is vitality in the organization, interest in what is best for the customer, and the constant encouragement of finding new ways to improve the product throughout the entire organization. In short, the bureaucratic, comfortable, organizational structure destroys entrepreneurship, and that destruction is also the destruction of success-ful TQM programs. It has been stated that success in the business world beyond the 1990's will depend upon management's ability to instigate and nurture organizational chaos. In the future, according to Peter Drucker, organizations must be organized for innovation. Drucker defines organization as "creative destruction." For example, Microsoft insists on destroying its current products only to replace them with new products customers will find exciting and useful (Harari, 1993).

UNION OPPOSITION

When a company-wide TQM program is implemented, changes must occur in that organization. Business simply is not conducted in the same manner as it had been in the past. Streamlining through down-sizing and combining of areas frequently occurs as employees become extensively cross-trained and team-oriented. If the employees in the facility undertaking the TQM program are represented by a union, the bargaining committee may be resistant to the new concepts. This resistance is frequently produced because of fear that the changes will undermine the protection the union has built up for its work force. The possibility of reclassification exposes some of its employees to mandatory bidding for alternate jobs as they lose their eligibility for the new classification. The union also expresses concern that seniority will be compromised. One workable approach for overcoming the union's concerns is to include the committee in the planning process prior to the implementation of TQM. Allow them to see how job protection is possible through retraining.

SHORT TERM PROFITABILITY OVERRIDES LONG—TERM PLAN

Top management frequently fails to compensate management of the organization for quality improvements. In other words, TQM processes are developed and passed on to lower level management as required responsibilities of their roles. Less than 20% of the automobile, banking, health care and computer industries, according to Ernst & Young, focus on quality performance measures such as customer satisfaction and quality defect rates as a way of determining senior management compensation (Harari, 1993). Profitability seems to be the only interest of too many organizations, not compensating top management for improvement in these aforementioned measures related to quality.

UNDERDEVELOPED RELATIONSHIP WITH SUPPLIERS

Top management fails to realize that a positive, integrated relationship with suppliers is absolutely essential to the success of TQM programs. Concepts like trust, ethics, mutual support and honesty are important parameters within which a company and its suppliers must begin to operate. Developing a substantially different relationship with suppliers today is absolutely essential to the success of a company, and this relationship should become a part of the TQM process. Because many managers fail to understand that concepts such as these are important to the success of TQM programs, the success of such programs will certainly be in jeopardy. Obviously, management must modify the perception that TQM is the province of management and teams alone within the organization. Without a good relationship with suppliers, customers, and employees, total quality is an impossibility. This means that suppliers are not jerked around, abused, threatened, cajoled and deliberately put out of business. How can a supplier be interested in what's best for any company if that particular company hammers them and threatens their security?

LACK OF WORKER EMPOWERMENT

Two primary issues arise to oppose TQM efforts. One is lack of recognition of the employees within an organization as resources and customers. As internal customers of the organization's product, they are aware of the deficiencies of the product and the process. At Federal Express an annual attitude survey is conducted to ask employees their candid opinion of how the company is doing (Martin,1991). MCI surveys its employees every 18 months (Knapp,1991). In both of the preceding companies, the key to the survey process is the company's response to the employee input....responsible company action to address the major concerns of the employees, which is the second major issue of empowerment.

The annual survey process and management's subsequent response to the results is a positive step toward empowerment. However, to fully implement a TQM program, employees must be involved on a daily basis in evaluating the quality efforts of their company and given authority to act when quality standards are not being met. Organizations must avoid the common error of relying too heavily on management staff for improvement of service quality in line performance. While this group can provide research, training and strategic insight into the   necessary components of a successful TQM program, an organization must include the line personnel in the quality improvement process.

SUPPORT FOR THE TEAM CONCEPT

The fully functioning TQM program relies heavily upon team work. Some of these teams, such as Kaizen programs, have a very short life-span as they accomplish their purpose and disband. Others such as cross-functional project teams may exist longer. But the true TQM employee empowerment is embodied in self–directed work teams. These teams are theoretically given the authority to shut down equipment if they feel safety or quality standards are not being met. The capacity to fully implement such a team driven program has met with substantial resistance throughout the U.S. even though management agrees with the concept of the empowered team. At Milliken & Company, which manufactures carpets and is a former Malcolm Baldridge winner, they report on the barriers they have encountered. Management and associates (employees) learned that they did not really know how to communicate and, particularly, how to listen to one another. Further, since the company had previously used individual incentive programs, it met substantial resistance in focusing its associates on quality and removing an incentive program which paid for production and not quality. As it moved to teams, employees cried about the loss of wages and upper, middle and lower management (in that order) had to learn the importance of the empowerment process to the future of Milliken. Training proved to be key to that conversion. In 1990, that company averaged over 90 hours of formal training per associate (Hardie, 1991).

SUMMARY

As one would expect, industry throughout North America widely embraces the philosophy of TQM but struggles to implement the mechanics of the program (Fuchsberg,1993; Niven,1993). Gloria Kazarian of Human Performance Engineering (G. Kazarian, personal communication, May 25, 1993) provides the reader with several additional points to consider for the successful installation of TQM. The authors of this article also feel these points are pertinent to the TQM process and focus on several key issues discussed earlier in this article:

1. Top Down Commitment................... As discussed earlier, top management must be a continuous, visible advocate of TQM. Kazarian suggests that it is better to be a staunch observer to the passing bandwagon of TQM than to jump aboard indiscriminately and stir up unsettling dust which then obscures the progress of the program.

2. Empowered Management Leadership Structure...... The emphasis here is on training efforts which develop the required leadership competencies for TQM. The management framework must then (a) unfreeze the factors in traditional management that stand as barriers to TQM, (b) learn new behaviors which augment the TQM process, and (c) install incentives to reward TQM related behaviors.

3. Creating Trusting Environments..... The organization must set the platform for open communication, shared information, risk–taking without reprisal, and employee involvement and development. These trusting environments reduce the need for hidden agendas and defensive, guarded behaviors.

4. Eat the TQM Elephant One Bite at a Time......... The table must be set before this meal is undertaken. Implementing TQM involves an extreme paradigm shift involving the political, structural, and cultural facets that form the foundation of traditional management. When the   necessary groundwork has been prepared, the meal is undertaken, one bite at a time. The customer, both internal and external, is constantly asked to rate their satisfaction level with the meal (product).

REFERENCES

AT&T Layoffs, (1992, Monday,May 17,Section R, page lb). *USA Today.*

Berry, L.L. (1991). *Improving customer service.* In B.H. Peters & J.L. Peters (Eds.), *Maintaining the total quality advantaqe* (pp. 35-37). New York, NY: The Conference Board.

Cangemi, J., Rice, J., & Kowalski, C. (1989). The development, decline and renewal of trust in an organization: Some observations. *Organization Development Journal, 7* (4), pp. 2-9.

Catel, P., & Matthews, J. (1992, Sept.7). The cost of quality. *Newsweek,* pp. 48-49.

Crosby, P. B. (1990). *Quality is free.* NY: Penguin.

Demystifying what quality means. (1992, June). *Black Enterprise,* pp. 284-286.

Fuchsberg, G. (1992, October 12). Total quality is termed only partial success. *The Wall Street Journal,* pp. B1, B2.

Getting management and employees in sync. (1992, June). *Black Enterprise,* pp. 286-290.

Harari, O. (1993, January). Ten reasons why TQM doesn't work. *Management Review, 82* (1), pp. 33-38.

Hardie, N. (1992). Milliken & Company. In K. Troy (Ed.), *Baldridge winners on world-class quality* (pp. 29-31). New York, NY: The Conference Board.

Knapp, G. (1991). Nurturing and motivating employees. In F. Caropreso (Ed.), *Managing globally: Key Perspectives* (pp. 10-12). New York, NY: The Conference Board.

Menon, H.G. (1992). *TQM In new product manufacturinq.* New York, NY: McGraw-Hill, Inc.

Martin, T. (1991). To succeed worldwide, ask your employees how. In F. Caropreso (Ed.), *Managing globally: Key perspectives* (pp. 13-14). New York, NY: The Conference Board.

Miller, R., & Cangemi, J. (1988). Developing trust in international companies. *Organization Development Journal, 6* (2), pp.26-28.

Miller, R., & Harker, D. (1986). Idea banking and idea development groups: Maturing an organization's cognitecture through participative management. *Organization Development Journal, 4* (4), pp. 31-34.

Niven, D. (1993, May/June). When times get tough, what happens to
        TQM? *Harvard Business Review,* pp. 20-22.
Saylor, J.H. (1992). *TQM field manual.* New York, NY: McGraw-Hill,
        Inc.
Schein, E. (1991). Communicating quality in the service sector.
        In B.H. Peters & J.L. Peters (Eds.), *Maintaining the total
        quality advantage* (pp. 40-42). New York, NY: The Confer–
        ence Board.
Sutton, J. (1992, July). Real change requires more than 'feel good'
        management. *Industrial Engineering, 24* (7), p 18.
Tetzeli, R. (1992, May 18). Making quality more than a fad.
        Fortune, 125 (10), pp. 12-13.
Waasdorp, P.L. (1991). Benchmarking for customer satisfaction.
        In B.H. Peters & J.L. Peters (Eds.), *Maintaining the total
        quality advantage* (pp. 17-18). New York, NY: The Confer–
        ence Board.

CONTRIBUTORS

Jasmine Baali Adkins earned a Master's degree in clinical psychology from Western Kentucky University in 1993.

Stephanie Chaffins, M.A., is Training Specialist, Great American Knitting Mills, Inc., Burlington, North Carolina.

R. Wilburn Clouse, Ph.D., Associate Professor of Educational Leadership, George Peabody College of Vanderbilt University, Nashville, Tennessee, is a renowned international consultant.

Stephanie Crabtree, M.A., is a therapist with Life Skills in Bowling Green, Kentucky.

Linda Feuerbacher, M.B.A., is Manager, Organizational Design and Development, Bridgestone/Firestone Fibers and Textiles Company, Kings Mountain, North Carolina.

Edward Fuqua, M.A., is an ordained minister headquartered in Greenbrier, Tennessee and an educational researcher.

Susan E. Heinbuch, Ph.D., is Visiting Fellow, Yale University Program on Non-Profit Organizations and a prolific writer in the areas of management, leadership and outsourcing; she also writes under the name of Susan Phelps, Ph.D., New York University.

Thomas Hollopeter, M.S., is Manager, Human Resources and Quality, Cobb-Vantress, a division of Tyson Foods, Siloam Springs, Arkansas, and a past plant manager with both Dayton Tire and Rubber Company and Firestone Tire and Rubber Company and a former *Fortune* 500 consultant.

Harold Lazarus, Ph.D., Mel Weitz Distinguished Professor of Business in the Department of Management at Hofstra University, has over 30 years experience in education and international management consulting.

Robert Linton, M.B.A., Redman Industries, one of the largest producers of manufactured homes in America headquartered in Dallas, Texas, also is past president of Anchor Swan, a Division of Dayco, the largest hose manufacturer in the world.

Marti Tam Loring, L.C.W.S., Ph.D., is Director of the Center for Mental Health and Human Development in Atlanta, Georgia, and a faculty member of Shorter College in Rome, Georgia.

Leadership Behavior

Sven B. Lundsted, Ph.D., is Professor of Public Policy and Management, College of Social and Behavioral Sciences, The Ohio State University, Columbus, Ohio, and Affiliate Scientist, Battelle Pacific Northwest Laboratory.

Richard L. Miller, Ph.D., Professor of Psychology, Western Kentucky University, who consults nationally and internationally, is a past Fullbright Scholar to China.

Ronda Muhlenkamp, M.B.A.,is Plant Accountant and Director of Human Resources, Nishikawa Standard Rubber Company, a division of Standard Products Company, in Fort Wayne, Indiana.

Mary Forbes Nalepa, Ed.S., is a school psychologist working for the Howard County and Frederick County public schools in Maryland.

Kay Payne, Ed.D., is Associate Professor, Department of Communications, Western Kentucky University, Bowling Green, Kentucky, and a profolic writer and researcher.

James Shanahan, M.B.A., C.P.A, is a member of the international accounting firm Price Waterhouse LLP, with several years experience providing accounting and tax service to middle market clients.

Charles Udell, M.B.A., President, Automotive Warehouse Distributors Association (AWDA) University, Kansas City, Missouri, is a recognized leader in the Automotive aftermarket in the United States.